Biosociology of Dominance and Deference

Biosociology of Dominance and Deference

Allan Mazur

ROWMAN & LITTLEFIELD PUBLISHERS, INC.
Lanham • Boulder • New York • Toronto • Oxford

ROWMAN & LITTLEFIELD PUBLISHERS, INC.

Published in the United States of America
by Rowman & Littlefield Publishers, Inc.
A wholly owned subsidiary of The Rowman & Littlefield Publishing Group, Inc.
4501 Forbes Boulevard, Suite 200, Lanham, Maryland 20706
www.rowmanlittlefield.com

P.O. Box 317, Oxford OX2 9RU, UK

British Library Cataloguing in Publication Information Available

Library of Congress Cataloging-in-Publication Data
Mazur, Allan.
　Biosociology of dominance and deference / by Allan Mazur.
　　p.　cm.
　Includes bibliographical references.
　ISBN 0-7425-3692-0 (cloth : alk. paper) — ISBN 0-7425-3693-9 (pbk. : alk. paper)
　1. Dominance (Psychology) 2. Social hierarchy in animals. 3. Psychology,
Comparative. I. Title.
BF632.5.M39 2005
158.2—dc22

2005009160

Printed in the United States of America

⊗™ The paper used in this publication meets the minimum requirements of
American National Standard for Information Sciences—Permanence of Paper
for Printed Library Materials, ANSI/NISO Z39.48-1992.

Polly, Julie, Rachel

Contents

Acknowledgments

I thank the following scholars for critically reading part or all of the text or for providing important advice: John Allman, Alan Booth, Lee Clarke, John Fleagle, Daniel Lieberman, Rachel Mazur, Ulrich Mueller, William Ritchie, Lixing Sun, Glenn Weisfeld, and Larry Wolf. This does not imply that any of them agree with all statements made here. For less recent but still relevant collaboration or influence, I thank Eugene Rosa, Marshall Segall, Caroline Keating, Joseph Berger, Hamit Fisek, Leon Robertson, John Baldwin, and Neville Dyson-Hudson. I am most deeply grateful to Uli Mueller and Alan Booth, my long-term colleagues in biosocial research, and to the late James S. Coleman, who brought me into sociology.

1

Fish . . .

My wife Polly would wake in the middle of the night to the cries of our new baby. Leaving me asleep, she sat to nurse in a rocker in our living room, the only light coming from our aquarium, the only sound the bubbling of its aerator. Three angelfish floated nearly motionless, seemingly asleep like everyone except my wife and baby. Polly says these were the most placid moments of her life.

The angelfish (*Pterophyllum scalare*) may have regarded the scene differently. Members of a dominance hierarchy, all but the top angel were vigilant to aggressive probes from a higher-ranked fish. These were not violent attacks but sufficiently assertive to induce brief flights, as if reiterating each dominant-deferent relationship. One cost of low rank to an angelfish is to be ever reminded of it.

Also in the tank were several neon tetras (*Hyphessobrycon innesi*), little fish, each with a long iridescent horizontal stripe. They formed a school, feeding together, swimming roughly in parallel, and turning in tandem. A neon hierarchy is hard to discern; we rarely see one chasing another. Their lives are not stress free, as they tend to be eaten by the angelfish, but at least they live peacefully among themselves.

There was only one betta (*Betta splendens*) in the aquarium, a male, because two males would not tolerate each other in this small space, earning them the label "Siamese fighting fish." Females are not so aggressive but also not so pretty. Fish fanciers breed males for long fins, colored in deep reds, blues, and purples. These males look splendid, especially during their dominance displays to another male (or to a mirror), when blood engorges their fins, gill covers stand out, and colors become vivid. The male's sexual and dominance displays are similar, with related functions. He must impress other males so they cede access to desirable females, and at nearly the same time he must attract females to mate.

Given a large pond with hiding places, male bettas may avoid one another, although at times they seek each other out, challenging for dominance, sometimes fighting destructively until one runs away. If a male establishes himself in a territory, he builds a nest of bubbles on the surface of the water, then tempts a female under the nest, wrapping his body around her to squeeze out eggs while excreting his own milt. Taking the eggs in his mouth, he places them in the bubbles, remaining below to guard the eggs and retrieve any that fall out, until they hatch.

Dominance hierarchies of group-living animals probably evolved from the impulse to defend a territory. If normally solitary animals are forced together by circumstances such as a scarce food supply, then actions that usually keep them spatially separated have the effect of ranking them "vertically" by power and privilege. Three or four male bettas placed in a small aquarium engage in paired dominance contests, the competitors approaching one another with gills flared, sometimes swimming side by side. If neither retreats after several seconds, one darts in with a bite to the fins, provoking either flight or counterattack. Sometimes combatants lock mouths, becoming immobile as they sink slowly to the bottom of the tank until one suddenly breaks the hold. These fights, often prolonged and severely damaging, end when one fish signals submission by fleeing. The winner may emphasize his victory with brief chases or bites, usually causing instant flight. The result of pair-wise contests is a dominance hierarchy with one top (alpha) fish, a second in rank, and so on. Occasionally there is a rematch and reversal. Low-ranked fish, wounded and persistently harassed, perhaps hugging a corner of the aquarium, have a poor chance for survival.

Probably fish fanciers could produce male bettas with diminished aggressiveness by the usual method of selective breeding, that is, choosing parents with the desired trait (low aggression) and continuing the process for several generations (e.g., Trut 1999). Placing such bettas together in an aquarium would likely produce a gentler and perhaps viable hierarchy like the one we see among angelfish, but I have not been seen such fish in the stores.

The evolution of solitary territoriality into social hierarchy required more than a diminution of aggressiveness, for that alone would not induce unconfined animals to live together—to be social. There is no reason to think gentler bettas would stay openly in proximity if they had the option to separate. A few animal behaviorists postulate the existence of an "affiliation instinct" to explain why angelfish aggregate in a group, and why neons school. An affiliation impulse, one that waxes and wanes with the seasons, conveniently explains the behavior of birds that in springtime defend individual territories for mating and raising young, then in fall flock together for migration or feeding. Ornithologists can hardly avoid some belief in a centripetal force motivating the reassembly of flocks each year.

Such instinctual forms of explanation work well enough for birds and fish but not for humans, whose primitive impulses are culturally elaborated and self-consciously modified. Without doubting that there is *some* commonality in the dominance hierarchies of fish and humans, it would be sociologically absurd to see them as simply two reflections of the same underlying behavior, explained by the same instincts or by the same acquisition of inclusive fitness. Biology is destiny for fish, but not for humans. Yet biology is not irrelevant to human behavior.

In this book, there is a continual tension between simple neurophysiological mechanisms and the complexity of human society, between the impact of genes on behavior and the influence of culturally variable socialization. We seek a middle road, avoiding the strong genetic and selectionist assumptions of classic ethology and sociobiology, while rejecting as well the biologically immaculate view of contemporary sociology.

A good start, palatable to most modern viewpoints, is to emphasize that humans are primates, apelike in some of our actions but distinguishable from apes at least in our use of language and our dependence on language-based cultures. As a result, large-scale human societies, which did not exist before ten thousand years ago, have developed sophisticated stratification systems, which in some ways are distinctive within every cultural area of the world. This makes human society unlike anything in the animal world.

Therefore, before venturing into biology, it is worth a trip into pure sociology, touring the major types of human status hierarchies. To properly place human action into its primate context, we must distinguish between hierarchical behavior that is homologous in humans and apes, and hierarchical systems that have no parallel in nonhumans, or even in the long-gone world of ancient hominids.

2

. . . And People

Modern people exhibit three major kinds of status hierarchy. First are the *dominance hierarchies* that form in face-to-face groups of social animals, including humans and other primates, and even among fish. Second are *official hierarchies* of formal organizations, which exist only in large human societies. Third are the *socioeconomic hierarchies* (or social class systems) of agrarian and industrial societies, where people in one large stratum—most not knowing one another—regard themselves (and are regarded by others) as superior (or inferior) to other large strata of people. These three kinds of hierarchies are often confused. We must understand their distinctive features because they work differently.

DOMINANCE HIERARCHIES

For a graphic if fictitious example of a dominance hierarchy, consider *Butch Cassidy and the Sundance Kid*, a film about two scoundrels of the Old West, portrayed as heroes by Paul Newman and Robert Redford. In an early scene, Butch and Sundance return to camp, finding that Harvey Logan has taken over as leader of their gang. Butch and Logan face off as "Flatnose" and other gang members watch:

BUTCH: I run things here, Harvey.

LOGAN (*a large, powerful man*): You used to—me now.

BUTCH (*appealing to the gang*): What's the matter with you guys?

FLATNOSE: You always said anyone could challenge you, Butch.

BUTCH: That's cause I figured no one would do it.

LOGAN: You figured wrong, Butch.

BUTCH: You guys can't want Logan!

LOGAN: Guns or knives, Butch?

BUTCH: Neither.

LOGAN: Pick!

BUTCH: I don't want to shoot with you, Harvey.

LOGAN: Anything you say, Butch.

(*Logan draws an enormous knife. Butch looks resigned.*)

BUTCH: Not yet, not till we get the rules straightened out.

LOGAN: Rules! In a knife fight?

(*As Logan is distracted by the implausibility of rules, Butch approaches.*)

LOGAN (*continuing*): No rules—aawww!

(*Butch has abruptly kicked Logan in the crotch; Logan falls in agony to his knees.*)

BUTCH: Well, if there ain't going to be any rules, let's get the fight started. Somebody count "One, two, three, go."

SUNDANCE: One, two, three, go!

(*On "go," Butch dispatches the incapacitated Logan, breaking his jaw.*)

FLATNOSE (*in congratulatory tone*): I was really rootin' for you, Butch.

BUTCH: Well thank you, Flatnose.

The crucial feature of this and any dominance hierarchy is that its members know one another as individuals. If they choose to compete for status, they do so on personal terms. The gang members have a long history together. Logan, knowing he is the strongest man, challenges Butch to physical combat. Butch responds with a sucker kick, demonstrating forcefully his superior intellect, his ability to control Logan, and his solid alliance with Sundance. With Butch's stature confirmed, the rebellious gang members, including Logan, fall into line.

Most of us are less violent than Butch and Logan. Professors challenge their colleagues not with fists but with intellectual brilliance, scintillating wit, and rapier-like sarcasm. These status displays can be so subtle as to escape the attention of students, even put them to sleep. Occasionally scholarly debates are nasty, drenching the academic arena in metaphorical blood. More often, thankfully, human dominance contests are gentle, even subliminal.

Dominance hierarchies occur only in face-to-face (or "primary") groups where members recognize and interact with one another as individuals. Such groups range in size from two (a dyad) to one hundred or so members. In larger groups, some individuals are strangers; some never directly interact. Nonhuman primates typically live in face-to-face groups, as presumably did humans during our millennia as hunters and gatherers. Primate social behavior evolved in the context of face-to-face groups, and the mechanisms of dominance and deference depend importantly on interaction between actors who recognize one another.

I define the dominance (or status) hierarchy of a face-to-face group to be a fairly persistent, unequal ranking of members in terms of power, influence, and access to valued prerogatives. This definition applies as well to fish and nonhuman primates as to people. High-ranking individuals do pretty much what they want and influence others in the group. Subordinate individuals have little influence, are constrained in their choices, and are limited to resources that are allowed them by—or escape the attention of—those more dominant.

Dominance hierarchies, once established, persist over time because individuals recognize and usually accept their places. Members of the group know who is dominant, who is subordinate, and where they themselves fit in. This is not simply a matter of the powerful imposing their will on the weak, for even in instances when power dissipates—as when an aging "alpha" macaque loses his canines—it may be a long time before any serious challenge from obviously stronger subordinates. Established hierarchies are accepted as normal (and in human terms as "proper" and "legitimate") by force of tradition. Rankings are not immutable, and an established group sees shifts when youngsters mature, or adults pass their prime, or there are changes in membership.

Status ranks cannot be directly observed. They must be inferred from other observations. Indicators of relative rank among primates are diverse, including who aggresses against or physically displaces whom; who has priority to food, water, space, and sexual partners; who withdraws when another animal approaches; who is at the center of activity and who is at the periphery; who makes dominant gestures (e.g., lunges, bites, stares), and who makes submissive or deferent gestures (e.g., avoiding eye contact, presenting for mounting) to whom. These measures correlate highly but not perfectly (Bernstein 1981).

We observe human groups somewhat as we would any other primate group to see who leads, who follows, who has the most prerogatives and who the least. We look for "signs"—behavioral displays or symbols—associated with high or low status (chapter 6). One of the most reliable signs, in groups of three or more humans, is the amount of talking each person does. Leaders often use their prerogative to dominate the conversation, while the most deferent members are relatively silent—with occasionally conspicuous exceptions.

When people work together to accomplish a well-defined task, either in a natural setting like at work or school, or in pursuit of a contrived laboratory goal, we observe who offers the most (and best) suggestions, whose suggestions are followed and whose ignored, who is most successful in leading the group to a solution. Among humans, whether in a task group or a purely social gathering, we can simply ask, "Who are the leaders and followers in your group, who are the most and least influential members?" Typically, these reported status rankings accord well with behavioral observations. Sometimes human respondents demur, saying everyone in their group is equal; this occurs especially in egalitarian settings. Still, behavioral observations typically show there really is a status hierarchy, though it may operate subtly.

Do dominance hierarchies *always* form in face-to-face groups? Temporary aggregations that form and disperse quickly may never develop status rankings, but often status differences can be observed within minutes. Established primary groups virtually always have discernible dominance hierarchies, though they may not be perfectly linear and transitive.

Dyads are a special case. Sometimes members of an established pair cannot be ranked, not because they are equal in status, but because they trade off the high and low ranks so no one persistently dominates. My best male friend and I are, I think, an equal-status dyad. We became well acquainted long ago when he was a doctoral student and I his major professor. With families of the same age, we socialized. After graduation he left the area and had a distinguished career in public administration. We and our wives still meet three or four times a year, sometimes at one of our homes, sometimes at places of recreation. (The male dyad is only one relationship in this group of four, but I simplify.) As we matured and his income surpassed mine, it was senseless holding onto my stature as erstwhile thesis adviser. Instead, the circumstances came to define which of us had priority. In our home visits the host dominates, the guest is deferent. When we sail, on his boat, he is the skipper. When we ski in Vermont, I—as the most avid skier—lead the way down the hill. On neutral ground we are unassertive. Still, mild challenges do erupt, sometimes in games, more often in late-night conversation or casual e-mail when one of us makes a dubious claim the other questions, leading to a stubborn impasse. We regard this as recreational argument, never taken very seriously, carefully managing our status relationship to avoid any usurpation that would threaten our friendship, which is far more important than relative rank.

Full equality in a three-person group (Tom, Dick, and Harry) would require balancing three dyads simultaneously (Tom and Dick, Tom and Harry, Dick and Harry). Some degree of rank inequality is more likely. This might be a fully transitive ranking (Tom > Dick > Harry); or Tom might dominate the undifferentiated dyad of Dick and Harry; or a dyad might dominate the third member. Even nontransitive "triangles" (Tom > Dick, Dick > Harry, but Harry > Tom), though uncommon, probably occur more often than fully egalitarian triads.

A four-person group has six dyadic relationships; a five-person group has ten; a six-person group has fifteen. In general, an n-person group has $n(n - 1)/2$ dyads. The number of dyadic relationships increases faster than group size, making it increasingly difficult to escape the emergence of a dominance hierarchy.

OFFICIAL HIERARCHIES

Important modern organizations—governments, corporations, voluntary associations—are far larger than primary groups. We often think of them as huge, impersonal, formal structures, rather than as networks of personal relationships. The official hierarchy, as defined in an organization chart, is typically pyramidal in shape with one or a few leaders at the top controlling numerous underlings they do not know as individuals.

Directives from the top of an official hierarchy are usually distributed in writing. Occasionally a spoken order flows "down the line," eventually reaching listeners who have never met the first speaker. In either case, directives have the status of formal authority for people beholden to or under control of the organization. Organizations that administer the law can punish deviants with monetary fines or imprisonment. Most organizations apply less extreme sanctions, but all presume that decisions made at the top must be carried out by those below. Otherwise operations would be chaotic; there could be no coordination or effective task implementation. A smoothly running bureaucracy, according to the classical sociologist Max Weber (1864–1920), is the best means for rational and efficient coordination of specialized tasks and technologies (Gerth and Mills 1948). Formal organizations, properly managed, can accomplish goals unimaginable for a face-to-face group: governing Rome, invading Normandy, building the interstate highway system, flying to the moon.

Modern students of bureaucracy, while accepting Weber's claims that formal organization is essential to accomplish big goals, point more often to the inefficiencies, even perversities, of organizational authority. Sociologist Lee Clarke (1999), for example, criticizes as "fantasy documents" the incredible emergency plans that government and industry have prepared for certain unlikely but potentially disastrous mishaps. Clarke's examples include the U.S. Post Office's contingency plan for delivering mail after a nuclear attack on the United States, or the unworkable cleanup plan formulated by the Alyeska consortium of petroleum companies, which owns and operates the

Alaska pipeline, in case of an oil tanker spill off the coast of Alaska. How can such fantasy plans, not to mention the mundane errors and red tape of daily life, be the products of rational, efficient organizations?

Our depersonalized view of large formal organizations is an oversimplification that renders organizationally based behavior more puzzling than it needs to be. If we zoom in on an organization chart, looking at only a few of the linked boxes, we find the number of participants sufficiently small and closely situated that they *do* know one another as individuals, working together, sometimes socializing. To a first approximation we can think of every large formal organization as comprising numerous small networks of personal associates. Each of these face-to-face groups is an entity unto itself, its members having some interests different from those espoused at the top of the organization.

Personal relationships in the local group are usually compatible with organizationally specified statuses, but not always. Sometimes a person of low formal rank rejects the authority of someone with higher formal rank—commonplace in a high school classroom. Therefore it is useful to distinguish *formal* status, as displayed on an organization chart, from *informal* status, as reflected in local group processes or individual personalities. Departments with sharp discrepancies between formal and informal hierarchies are in real trouble, their goals unlikely to be achieved efficiently, if at all. It is a profound comment on the orderliness of human society that such discrepancies are exceptions. Even in highly stressful situations like natural disasters, adults in positions of formal authority usually carry out rather than abandon their designated duties, and anxious publics follow their orders (Dynes and Tierney 1994).

Important roles and high positions within formal organizations are defined in terms of titles: king or prime minister (of a government), professor or dean (in a university), doctor (in the medical profession), general (in the army), countess (in the aristocracy), director (of an agency). These positions may be achieved through merit or ascribed by birth. Either way, formal roles are remarkably effective in designating status ranks. Knowing a person's title, but nothing else about him or her as an individual, is often enough to specify how we should (and do) treat that person or how he or she will treat us.

The *principle of local autonomy* says that primary groups within the larger organization act somewhat independently of formal authority. Perhaps this should be called the Milo Minderbender principle, after that consummate operator in Joseph Heller's antiwar novel of World War II, *Catch-22*. Milo manipulates, subverts, ignores, and violates Air Force regulations to enrich himself and his minions. He supplies his barracks with gourmet food, corners the Egyptian cotton market, even contracts with the Germans and Americans to simultaneously bomb and defend the same bridge. Milo is local autonomy personified.

The Milo principle of local autonomy might explain the creation of fantasy plans and other organizational pathologies. Perhaps a stalwart postmaster general, imbued with the fabled reliability of mail delivery (through sleet or snow or hail), wanted to uphold that tradition even under the direst conditions, and so directed the U.S. Post Office's planning department to prepare a contingency plan for mail delivery after a nuclear attack. The planning group may have had no idea how to accomplish this fantastic goal. No matter. Its *local* motivation was not to overcome a nuclear war but to produce a plan giving the appearance of doing so. The result was a fantasy document if judged by its likelihood of achieving the postmaster's ultimate goal, but it realistically fulfilled the planners' local goal. Nearly the same may be said for Alyeska's plan to almost fully clean up a very large oil spill postulated to occur off the Alaskan coast. A virtually perfect cleanup *was* the ultimate goal of state regulators, who imposed that requirement on oil corporations wanting to work in Alaska. Oil corporation executives, trying to satisfy the regulators, passed on to lower-level planners the task of preparing a contingency plan. The local goal of these planners was to produce a document acceptable to the executives. Apparently the cleanup plan they produced satisfied everyone; at least no one strenuously rejected it. Who knew that the *Exxon Valdez* would show the scheme to be an illusion?

A more ominous example of local autonomy comes from the Cuban Missile Crisis of 1962 when the United States and the Soviet Union moved as close as they ever would toward nuclear war. At the height of the crisis, an American U-2 spy plane, flying over Cuba to take reconnaissance photos, was shot down by a surface-to-air missile (SAM), killing the pilot. President John Kennedy and his advisers, regarding this as an escalation of the conflict by Soviet leader Nikita Khrushchev, considered attacking all SAM sites early the next morning but finally held back. This was fortunate because Soviet sources now available show Khrushchev was trying to *prevent* an escalation, the shoot-down occurring *despite* his attempt to limit the use of force in Cuba.

The U-2 was brought down by a SAM battery under the command of Captain N. Antonyets, who had been forbidden to fire without authorization from the commander of Soviet forces in Cuba, a man named General Pliyev. Captain Antonyets, alerted that a U-2 had been sighted in Cuban airspace, called General Pliyev's headquarters for instructions, but the general was not present. His deputy told Captain Antonyets to wait until he phoned the general, who had left strict instructions that he alone could authorize the use of force. Unable to reach the general, with time growing short before the U-2 left Cuban airspace, and thinking the flight might be precursor to an American attack, the deputy gave Captain Antonyets the order to fire. So local commanders nearly ignited a war over Cuba, despite American and Soviet leaders' strong intentions to avoid a confrontation. When General Pliyev learned that his deputy had countermanded his order, he requested a report for the

Ministry of Defense, but there was no formal reprimand (Brugioni 1990; Fursenko and Naftali 1997).

Extreme actions in wartime demonstrate most vividly the power of a local group and its leader. Consider the infantrymen of World War I who were often commanded to charge into barbed wire and heavy machine gun fire. Usually the commanding general was miles away, his formal authority diluted by his distance from the trenches. Why, then, did men repeatedly join these suicidal attacks?

It is the sergeant or lieutenant in closest proximity who is the leader of an infantryman's face-to-face dominance hierarchy and is thereby the most potent giver of orders. Psychologist Stanley Milgram (1974) illustrated the power of a minor authority figure in a famous series of experiments. Here a director, clad in a white lab coat, asks an adult subject to administer electric shocks to another person. The person "receiving" shocks is an experimental accomplice not actually being shocked. Following a script, the accomplice asks the subject to stop sending shocks, saying they are aggravating his heart condition. Typically, the subject stops. The director then tells the subject he *must* continue administering shocks, that the experiment requires it *even though the recipient of the shocks wants to quit*. Remarkably, half of all subjects follow the orders of the director, continuing to shock the unwilling recipient.

The importance of proximity is demonstrated by another of Milgram's experiments in which the white-coated director is obeyed more often when he is in the same room with the subject than when he is in the next room, giving orders over the telephone. In an organization, the *local authority* who is nearby, who sees the people below him on a daily basis, who is close enough to communicate with them face to face, has more power over them than a distant officer of higher rank.

Pressure on a soldier to obey comes not only from his leader but also from peers. Among both German and American soldiers in World War II, the major motive for engaging in combat was neither patriotism nor ideology but reluctance to let down their buddies (Stouffer et al. 1949; Shils and Janowitz 1948). These local forces converge on infantrymen in the trench when they are ordered to attack. The sergeant who has led his squad through prior dangers now urges them to follow as he leads the charge. Buddies on either side join in, yelling to bolster their spirits. Other units are advancing along the line. A lieutenant with revolver in hand screams at laggards, threatening to court-martial or shoot anyone who stays behind. Hardly anyone does.

The concept of local authority—that nearby officers have more power over the people immediately under them than do higher-ranked but more distant superiors—explains the strange phenomenon of a coup d'état, where the head of a government's organizational pyramid is replaced against his or her will by agreement of those at the second level, and the rest of the organization accepts the replacement, continuing to follow orders as before.

Today, successful coups occur most often in third-world monarchies and dictatorships where the government and military hierarchies are intertwined. Typically a coalition of generals or colonels plans the takeover as a surprise move, arresting the head of state and those of high rank who still support him. They designate a new head of state, usually one among themselves, and announce to the nation that a new government is in place. Unless the former head of state or his loyalists can repulse the plotters, the new hierarchy functions much as before only with new leadership.

There are times when the existing head of state is *legally* removed from office, perhaps by losing an election, and yet refuses to step down. As long as this person can keep the support of officers immediately under him, he may be able to retain his office and power.

These seem unlikely outcomes, for we would expect the people to rise up in protest and soldiers in the ranks to refuse orders from an illegal authority. Yet successful coups often occur. When the military command structure is the major institution in the nation, so there are no challenges from comparably powerful hierarchies based on religion, political bureaucracy, business, or the mass media, then all that the top military commander must do to take over or retain power is ensure that he has support from officers he knows personally at the level immediately below him. They in turn have control of the next level down, for the local authority of these subcommanders is usually stronger than the distant authority of the legal head of state, and so on down the line. The chain of command remains intact, those at the lower ranks following their orders, as usual.

Since the head of state can exercise his own local authority, it is difficult for the officers at the second level to organize their mutiny. Plotters who try to garner allies risk approaching a possible loyalist who will reveal the plot. Often they play their hand without reaching consensus among second-rank commanders. Perhaps the chief of the air force has joined the plot, but the chief of the army refuses and escapes the plotters. Each chief orders his branch to support his own side, causing the nation's air force to attack its army. Aviators and soldiers, now shooting each other, are pawns in the game being played at the top of the pyramid.

The power of local authority explains why soldiers sometimes commit brutal acts that otherwise seem incomprehensible, as when a company of American infantrymen murdered more than four hundred defenseless civilians in the Vietnamese village of My Lai (Walzer 1977). Instructions of the company's captain, who had stayed behind, were ambiguous according to later testimony, saying to leave nothing behind and to take no prisoners, but also ordering killing only of "enemies." Lieutenant William Calley, who led the unit into the village and commanded his men to kill nonresisting villagers, including old men, women, and children, later claimed he was following the captain's orders. A few of Calley's men refused to fire, some ran away, and one junior officer tried to stop the massacre by placing himself between the Vietnamese and the Americans, but most did as they were told.

SOCIOECONOMIC HIERARCHIES (SOCIAL CLASSES)

Modern humans and chimpanzees have a common primate ancestor, perhaps alive as recently as five million years ago. We may infer from the behavior of living primates that this ancestor was highly social, living in face-to-face groups sufficiently small in size that members knew and responded to one another as individuals, and they communicated through gestures and vocalizations. Interaction within each group was structured by a fairly stable dominance hierarchy based on age and sex classes, kinship, and individual differences, with high-ranked members enjoying more power, influence, and valued prerogatives than low-ranked members. Neither material capital nor cultural tradition were very cumulative, so different groups of our common ancestors, living thousands of years and miles apart, looked pretty much alike.

Modern *Homo sapiens* appeared about fifty thousand years ago. These people, like their *hominid* predecessors, lived in small bands as hunters, scavengers, and gatherers, finding subsistence where chance provided it. They were probably nomadic, moving to follow food sources. During seasons when food and water were especially abundant, bands may have gathered together into larger tribes for trading, for socializing and finding mates, and for ritual purposes, as is common among hunting and gathering societies alive today.

Then, rather suddenly, people began to produce most of their own food by planting crops and raising animals. This unprecedented change in lifestyle can be dated at ten thousand years ago, simultaneous with—and perhaps caused by—the end of the last Ice Age, marked by a warming climate and the recession of glaciers in the Northern Hemisphere. Some people remained nomadic, but others aggregated into settled communities, raising food in nearby fields and pastures. Within another five thousand years, in diverse regions of the world, there appeared large palaces, monuments, and ceremonial buildings, indicating the ability of societies to produce wealth and coordinate labor. As these societies grew too large for each person to know everyone else, they became differentiated into separate social classes, one better off than another. Usually land was in the hands of a king and a small hereditary aristocracy (often warriors), while a far larger peasantry farmed the land or tended herds, keeping only enough of their produce for subsistence. Formal religions arose, their doctrines typically justifying and fortifying the prevailing class arrangements.

In modern industrial societies the boundaries between classes have become blurred. Although we still use terms as if there were clearly drawn social strata ("upper class," "middle class," "working class," "underclass"), these labels are vague, and we cannot be sure who has arrived at one level or fallen from another. A better descriptor is *socioeconomic status* (SES), referring to a messy continuum based on numerous differences including financial resources (accumulated wealth or yearly income), education (highest degree, type of degree, prestige of college), occupation (the husband's occupation often remains relevant for fixing the status of women), quality of one's residential neighborhood (also size and cost of one's house), parental background, refinement of speech, fame, race, religion (say, Episcopalians compared to Southern Baptists), accomplishments of one's grown children ("my son, the doctor"), whom one associates with, where one vacations, level of conspicuous consumption, and so on (Fussell 1983). People who are high (or low) on one indicator of SES tend to be high (or low) on the others. We all know exceptions: There are uneducated people who make a lot of money, and high-salaried entertainers who never accumulate wealth. Professors' incomes are not commensurate with their education or occupational prestige (but they do have long summer vacations).

More important than the blurring of modern class boundaries is their permeability. Social class used to be almost entirely inherited; you were born an aristocrat or a peasant, as were your parents, as were your children. In industrial democracy, those who begin life at the bottom are free to reach the top, in theory. And in practice, the American dream of rags to riches has come true, more or less, for lots of people. The means for upward mobility are well known: education, hard work, making a quality product, opportune marriage, having friends in the right places, graft, and good luck. It still helps to be born rich and in a prominent family, but roughly half of the richest Americans have ordinary origins.

Some theorists claim that large-scale stratification is an emergent property of small-scale stratification, that a society's class system is nothing more than a face-to-face dominance hierarchy writ large. If true, then by artificially provisioning a chimpanzee colony so it grows large in membership within a limited space, some elementary form of social class differentiation should evolve from the chimp dominance hierarchy. Carrying out this experiment in imagination, we can envision the outcome being a microcosmic Planet of the Apes with simian social classes. In reality, such experiments are impractical to carry out on chimps but have been done on rats, which show no sign of class stratification (Calhoun 1962).

Other theorists, including myself, doubt chimpanzees are capable of participating in any system of status stratification other than their usual face-to-face dominance hierarchies. The requisite for large-scale social classes, present in humans but missing in apes (except in rudimentary form), is the ability to accumulate cultural or material assets and pass them on to our offspring. A human family that gains some advantage—wealth, power, a title—over its neighbors will lose that edge in the next generation unless it can assign the advantage as a legacy to its descendants. Only when a newborn is heir to the advantage accumulated by its parents does it start life with a predictable head start, allowing one lineage to hold sway over others from generation to generation.

Conquest is another mechanism for the creation of social classes, as when William the Conqueror invaded England in 1066, implanting his victorious Normans as the ruling class over the resident Saxons, or when Europeans enslaved or otherwise disenfranchised the indigenous peoples of the Americas. The perpetuation of these inequalities into following centuries required that Norman and Saxon children—and white and Indian children—inherit disproportionate shares of wealth and be imbued with a clear vision of the relative stature of one to the other. Given enough time for the classes to become used to their relative ranks, they tend to accept their respective roles as proper, even as ordained by God. Occasionally military or police force is required to reinforce the privileges of the haves against the have-nots, but usually not. Like the value of the dollar, which depends on the public's acceptance of it as a legitimate medium of exchange, not on gold reserves in Fort Knox, the legitimacy of a socioeconomic hierarchy is more often sustained by a socialized consensus of its participants than by the force of arms.

Just as every formal organization is overlain with face-to-face groups, so too is every social class. The once popular notion of modern America as a "lonely crowd," a "mass society" of faceless social atoms, of undifferentiated "men in gray flannel suits," is far off the mark. Virtually everyone lives and works in groups: families, peer groups, work groups, civic and religious groups, and play groups. Even homeless people subsist in networks comprising social workers, police officers, and of course other street people. From the bottom of the society to the top, no one operates alone.

High-class people socialize together; low-class people hang out together. As long as everyone in your intimate group comes from the same (or a similar) social class, it necessarily follows that class does not predict ranking in your face-to-face dominance hierarchy. (The leader and the most subordinate member of an upper-class clique both come from the upper class.) Adlai Stevenson was an American patrician: wealthy, erudite, a former governor of Illinois, twice the Democratic candidate for president, ambassador to the United Nations during the Cuban Missile Crisis. Yet President Kennedy's closest advisors during the Cuban Missile Crisis put Stevenson at the bottom of their dominance hierarchy, ignoring his recommendations and deriding him as a weakling (Hersh 1997). On the other hand, Butch Cassidy and Billy the Kid, bona fide members of the scum of the earth, were prestigious leaders in their own low-life gangs and regarded as heroes by large audiences of admirers.

But what happens when a small group contains members who differ in social class, perhaps on a jury or a work team? One of the few truly interesting results from the early days of sociological research is that in a class-mixed group, one's socioeconomic status in the larger society (by virtue of occupation, wealth, education, or race) predicts one's rank in face-to-face dominance hierarchy (Strodtbeck, James, and Hawkins 1957; Berger, Cohen, and Zelditch 1972). A physician and a plumber, meeting outside their professional roles, are likely to rank themselves so that the plumber defers to the physician, even when medical skills are unrelated to the situation. Only when the special skills of plumbing become relevant, as when the toilet is flooding, is the plumber given precedence.

CONCLUSIONS

We have looked at three kinds of status hierarchy, most importantly the dominance hierarchies of primary (face-to-face) groups. Primary groups are necessarily small in size, typically under one hundred, enabling each member to recognize and interact with all others as individuals. Nonhuman primate societies are primary groups, as apparently were human societies before the adoption of agriculture. Everyone operates in one or more primary groups, holding a position in one or more face-to-face dominance hierarchies.

Official hierarchies are far newer in human history, existing only in agrarian or industrial societies. They allow a few people at the top of a formal organization to exercise official authority over groups of strangers as large as the U.S. federal government (over three million employees, excluding the armed services). Every formal organization is overlain with primary groups, each operating somewhat autonomously. The behavior of a large organization is a compromise between the directives of its top leaders and the local goals of its constituent primary groups. Local autonomy explains some inappropriate, even perverse, behaviors of "impersonal bureaucracy" and therefore seems dysfunctional from the perspectives of top management or clients. But it is essential if a large organization is to effectively maintain a wide span of control. Top executives or generals have little direct control over far-flung workers or troops at the bottom. It falls on local authorities, leaders of the constituent primary groups, to control those at the next level down.

Socioeconomic hierarchies (social classes) are the largest, most "macro" stratification systems, encompassing whole nations. Except in theoretically classless societies, which always lapse in practice, each child inherits class membership from its parents. In traditional agrarian societies this ranking is virtually immutable. The class boundaries of today's industrial democracies have relatively but not completely permeable boundaries, ensuring both the perpetuation of inequality and the opportunity for individuals to better (or worsen) their positions.

The remainder of this book is about the biology of face-to-face dominance hierarchies, which predate and permeate all larger human social structures. Dominance and deference are evolutionarily primitive; their human forms are special adaptations of the hierarchical pattern found generally among social vertebrates and particularly among primates. It is therefore appropriate that we enter biology through its overarching paradigm, the evolution of life.

3

Evolution

The nineteenth-century gentlemen who collected fossils from cliff sides and quarries learned that particular assemblages of plants and animals are found in certain rock deposits. They realized higher rock layers in a stratified cliff side had been laid down as sediments atop those below and were therefore younger. They recognized that organisms found in lower (older) strata were different from those alive today, and that the history of life as shown in the fossil record differed from the Genesis story of the Bible.

Still there was plenty of room for ambiguity, as the geological record is anything but straightforward. Similar rocks from different locales sometimes hold different fossils; dissimilar rocks sometimes contain similar fossils. Rock layers do not always look the same from one region to another. It took a while to recognize that wholly different rocks could be contemporaneous, that plants and fish in the Old Red Sandstone of Wales, deposited from lakes and mountain basins, were alive at the same time as sea-living trilobites and brachiopods embedded in the limestone of Devon. Closure required understanding that changes in the fossils, not in the rocks themselves, are the true measure of time (Rudwick 1985). No matter how different rock layers look, if they contain identical fossils they must be the same age.

From these beginnings, paleontologists had by the early twentieth century sketched a picture of the development of life that, in basic outline, remains correct today. The fossil record, interpreted in the light of Darwinism, provides an evolutionary paradigm that guides all modern biology, including biosociology. We require an understanding of evolution to see where we came from, so that we may appreciate where we are.

19

LIFE'S RECORD

As fossil collections grew and chronologies became consistent, it appeared that there were breaks in life's record. Assemblages more or less consistent for vertical meters of rock abruptly changed, partly or wholly replaced by new organisms. The nineteenth-century paleontologists were much concerned with naming successive "periods" in the record—the Cambrian, Permian, Jurassic, Cretaceous, and so on—describing their characteristic fossils, and showing that their succession was worldwide in scope.

Boundaries of some periods were recognized as extinction events, most famously the ending of the Cretaceous with the final demise of the dinosaurs. Known as the K-T boundary (K for the Greek spelling of Cretaceous, T for Tertiary, the following period), this transition is extraordinarily sharp, appearing in the rocks near Gubbio, Italy, as a centimeter-thick layer of clay. At Gubbio and elsewhere, the transition layer is unusually rich in iridium, an element rare in the Earth's surface but abundant in asteroids. An impact crater of the proper size and age has been identified on the Yucatan Peninsula of Mexico, near the modern resort city of Cancun.

Some of life's periods are marked by the appearance of new creatures, most remarkably the very first one, the Cambrian, when a profusion of complex life forms appears directly above rocks apparently without fossils (Conway 1998). Here are the trilobites, rounded oblong arthropods living on earth for nearly one-third of a billion years before disappearing. I hunt their fossils on lazy summer days in the Devonian shale of the Finger Lakes in Upstate New York. Hard-shelled animals like trilobites fossilize well and are easy to find, so the abrupt arrival of complex life may be partly an illusion because earlier soft-bodied creatures escaped preservation or were too small to find if they did leave traces. Indeed, modern paleontologists have found simple organisms in pre-Cambrian rock. Still, this period is so amazing for its sudden onset and variety of animals it is called the "Cambrian explosion." Cambrian fossils comprise nearly every basic body plan (phylum) existing today including our own, the chordate.

There are too many periods for most of us to care about. They are nicely clumped into three great eras giving a simpler overview of life's history. The Paleozoic (ancient life) era begins in the sea with the Cambrian explosion of invertebrates, then fish, then the greening of the land with ferns and primitive trees, then its occupancy by air-breathing invertebrates, amphibians, and reptiles. The era ends with the Permian extinction—the greatest extinction ever—eliminating over 90 percent of existing sea species, trilobites among those lost. The Mesozoic (middle life) era is the age of dinosaurs; it also includes the first mammals, birds, and flowering plants; it ends with the asteroid hitting Yucatan. The Cenozoic (recent life) era is the following age of mammals, which continues today.

Never in their dreams would the Victorians have imagined that events in the fossil record could be given absolute dates. It is a wonder of science that geological clocks, based on the decay of radioactive elements, tell us the earth is 4.5 billion years old. The Cambrian explosion, when complex invertebrates first appear, occurred 550 million years ago (mya). The great Permian extinction, finishing off the trilobites and ending the Paleozoic era, was 250 mya. The asteroid causing the K-T extinction of the last dinosaurs struck the Yucatan Peninsula 65 mya.

The evolution of major kinds of living animals is shown in Figure 3.1. By 400 mya bony fish, the first major group of vertebrates, had evolved from invertebrates. Before 350 mya the first tetrapods (four-limbed vertebrates, usually living on land) evolved from fish, perhaps from air-breathing lungfish or coelacanths whose lobed fins work like protolimbs. Subsequent tetrapods, mammals, and birds, as well as amphibians and reptiles, generally have the same skeletal plan. For example, the forelimb (our arm, a bird's wing) has one upper bone closest to the body, two bones below the elbow, several smaller bones in the wrist, and then longer finger bones. Forelimbs have disappeared in snakes but were present in their ancestors. Whales and birds have no external fingers, but "finger bones" are easily seen in their skeletons. All tetrapod skeletons, however modified, resemble the same ancestral structure.

The original land animals were amphibians (tetrapods that lay eggs in water), returning to the water to reproduce, their young hatching as aquatic larvae. Some of their descendants had by 300 mya developed "amniote" eggs with tough watertight coverings and large yolks for nourishing the embryo. Immersion in water was no longer necessary for reproduction. These amniotes, the protoreptiles, could live (and love) fully on land.

Systematists attribute great importance to the number of holes—one or two—in the cheek of an amniote skull. Though seemingly without functional significance, the number of holes marks an important evolutionary branch point. Early amniotes with two cheek holes—called "diapsids"—are ancestral to today's reptiles, while amniotes with one cheek hole—called "synapsids"—are ancestral to mammals. (Fish and amphibian cheeks have no holes.)

Reptiles, among the few species surviving the great Permian extinction, diversified into niches vacated by those less fortunate. Most spectacular were the dinosaurs, dominating the land from about 200 to 65 mya when the Yucatan asteroid struck. I have in my own modest collection two coprolites—fossilized dinosaur feces—abundant in the American West because of the long tenure and huge throughput of these voracious creatures.

There is strong evidence that birds (warm-blooded diapsids with feathers) evolved from dinosaurs. Numerous fossils dating from 150 mya, including the famous *Archaeopteryx*, show feathers on creatures otherwise resembling

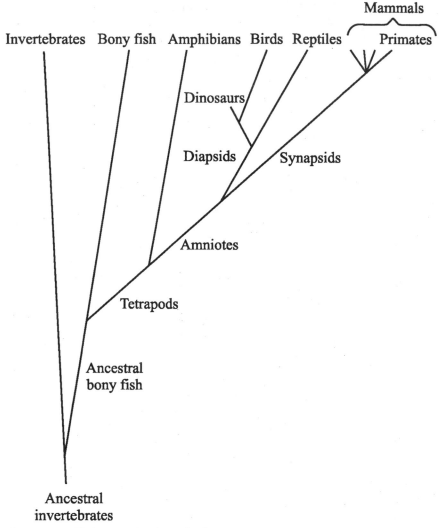

Figure 3.1.   **Phylogeny of major animal groups**

small meat-eating dinosaurs (Ackerman 1998). Paleontologists enjoy saying that dinosaurs are not extinct but live on as birds.

The first mammals (warm-blooded synapsids with hair and milk glands) predate birds, appearing about 220 mya. Small and inconspicuous at first, mammals would become the beneficiaries of the K-T extinction, diversifying to fill niches vacated by the dinosaurs. Our own order of mammals, the primates, appears by 55 mya.

TRACING PHYLOGENIES

The ability to give absolute dates to fossil species obviously helps in tracing the evolution of living animals from extinct ancestors. Still the task of reconstructing a phylogeny is like solving a jigsaw puzzle with nearly all its pieces missing. Traditionally, there have been two keys to inferring that one species derived from another. First, the two species must have lived in overlapping times and places. If fossils are greatly separated by period or geography, without recognizable links, it is impossible to connect them in a line of descent. Second, the two species must look similar but not identical. If their bones are too different, there is no reason to regard one as the ancestor of the other; if they look virtually the same, there is no reason to regard them as separate species. A sequence of fossil species that change gradually in appearance, properly linked in time and place, has long been the most secure foundation upon which to reconstruct an evolutionary line of descent.

Classification of species predates our understanding of evolution. Human languages may have always had labels for important types of animals, and nearly all cultures use broader categories like *fish, birds, reptiles,* and *mammals* to encompass similar creatures. The well-known scheme of Carolus Linnaeus (1707–1778) is an elaboration of this notion, grouping species on the basis of similarity. Linnaeus thought the orderly arrangement of the living world reflected God's plan of creation, which could be adequately described using seven levels of nested categories: kingdom, phylum, class, order, family, genus, and species (remembered as "Kings play chess on fancy glass tables"). He placed similar-looking species, say lions and tigers, in the same genus (*Panthera*), calling lions *Panthera leo,* and tigers *Panthera tigris.* At a higher level of abstraction, Linnaeus placed these big cats and domestic cats in the family Felidae (cats). Going up another step, he placed Felidae along with dogs, bears, and similar flesh eaters into the order Carnivora (carnivores). Then these were included with all animals that suckle their young in the class Mammalia (mammals), and these were lumped with other animals having a notochord—an elemental spinal column—into the phylum Chordata (chordates). Finally, all animals (organisms consuming food to obtain energy) were placed into the kingdom Animalia, separating them from the kingdom of plants (which obtain energy from the sun via photosynthesis).

In all classification schemes, the species is the fundamental unit because it conforms most closely to our notion of a "kind" of animal. Species are based on observations of animal bodies—or remnants of bodies—whereas higher categories (genus, family, etc.) are abstractions derived from comparisons among species. Despite its fundamental importance, a species is difficult to define (Hey 2001). Similar appearance is not always adequate. Dogs of different breeds, although dissimilar in looks and size, are members of a single species according to another defining criterion: that mating produces fertile offspring.

The criterion of breeding fertile offspring cannot be tested on extinct species, so paleontologists revert to visual appearance, sorting fossils into one species or another depending on evaluations of similarity. In the past, degrees of similarity were judged qualitatively; today paleontologists evaluate them statistically, combining numerous measurements on the fossils. But quantitative methods remain laced with subjectivity, and controversy abounds. There are vehement differences between "lumpers" who assign most fossils to a relatively few taxa, and "splitters" who invent a new species every time they uncover another tooth.

There is also the problem of birds, bats, and cows. Birds and bats have wings; bats and cows produce milk. Which two are most similar? Linnaeus knew God's plan contains such puzzles and solved them pretty well, here noting the wings of birds and bats are constructed differently, one using feathers, the other a skin membrane; also the "finger bones" are differently arranged within bat and bird wings. On the other side, the milk mechanism of bats and cows is nearly the same. Linnaeus therefore placed bats and cows together as mammals, a grouping from which birds are excluded.

If Linnaeus had understood evolution, he would have reached the same conclusion but for better reason. Today we say the wings of bats and birds are *analogous*, that is, they serve the same function of flying, but they are not *homologous*, or inherited from a common ancestor. Bats and birds are very distantly related, their most recently shared ancestor a flightless amniote living perhaps 300 mya. From that progenitor, flightless diapsids evolved into meat-eating dinosaurs whose descendants, around 150 mya, developed feathered wings, thus becoming the first birds. Along a different line of descent from the same ancient amniote, flightless synapsids evolved into mammals, of which one form (insectivores) had some descendants that took to the air using wings with skin membranes, and these were the first bats. The wings of bats and birds, having different hereditary origins, are an example of "parallel evolution," analogous—but not homologous—adaptations giving their possessors the advantage of flight. This wing example is easy to trace. Often it is difficult to decide if a characteristic shared by two species is analogous or homologous.

Darwin had little difficulty using Linnaeus's scheme of nested categories because it resembles a family tree: Lions and tigers belong to the same genus because they have a recent common ancestor; lions, tigers, and domestic cats are in the same family because all three have a common ancestor somewhat further back. But certain features of the Linnaean scheme have become troublesome. While God might have arranged life on seven levels, evolution did not. To describe the nearly continuous gradations in phylogenies, systematists began inserting additional levels: subphyla (e.g., vertebrates), subclasses (e.g., egg-laying mammals), suborders (e.g., marine carnivores), superfamilies, subspecies, and so on. The cladistic school of systematics rejects this kludging, eschewing all Linnaean levels above genus and species. Traditionalists retain the oft-modified levels but rarely give them deep meaning.

Cladists further object to the Linnaean scheme because it classifies animals into groupings that may not reflect lines of descent. Striving for consistency, cladists argue that any animal descended from, say, dinosaurs is itself a dinosaur. Since birds evolved from dinosaurs, birds should be regarded as dinosaurs, not placed in a separate class (Aves), as Linnaeus did. But this viewpoint has problems of its own. By the same logic, amphibians, reptiles, birds, and mammals (including humans) should all be classified as fish! Imagine what creationists would say about that.

Tracing of phylogenies has been revolutionized by molecular technology. Inferences about descent, traditionally made from fossils of extinct species, are today often based on the DNA of living species. Ideally one would like DNA from extinct animals, but it deteriorates quickly and is rarely available for study, so we depend on comparisons among contemporary species.

All living organisms—plants, animals, bacteria, fungi—are built of cells. All cells contain DNA, which is composed of nucleotides and usually is twisted into double helixes. There are four kinds of nucleotides (adenine, thymine, guanine, and cytosine), which can be strung out along the DNA in any order. A "gene" is an identifiable section of DNA. The particular ordering of nucleotides on that section—on that gene—codes a particular bit of information. Usually the coding on a gene "tells" apparatus in the cell how to assemble simple amino acids into a complex protein like hemoglobin or collagen. Many kinds of proteins are assembled to serve as the most important structural and functional elements of the body.

Members of the same species have DNA with nearly but not exactly the same coding. Tiny variations (alleles) in the genes, along with environmental variations, produce individuals that differ from one another, though all share the common characteristics of their species. Genomes of different species obviously differ more; some genes important to one species are absent from the DNA of another. Yet it is remarkable that species as far removed as humans and fruit flies hold many genes in common, coding many of the same proteins. (This is the most compelling evidence that humans and fruit flies have a common ancestor.) The genomes of humans and chimpanzees are more than 98 percent identical (Ruvolo 1997).

Inferring phylogeny from DNA requires the familiar principle of similarity: the more alike the DNA of two species, the closer their relationship, or alternatively, the more recently they had a common ancestor. Determining the coding sequence of a DNA sample is a routine laboratory task. As an example, we might compare DNA from lions, tigers, domestic cats, and dogs. (Dogs, distantly related to the felines, serve as a reference point.) We would find DNA sequences from lions and tigers most similar, hence lions and tigers have the most recent common ancestor. DNA of the domestic cat would be less similar to the lion and tiger than the big cats are to each other, but it would be closer to these cats than to the dog. Hence the domestic cat shares a more recent ancestor with the lion and tiger than any of the cats share with the dog.

Molecular methods can be used to estimate the date when the extinct ancestor of today's cats was alive. To understand how this is done, we must appreciate the complexity of proteins. Hemoglobin, for example, is composed of two identical chains, each containing 141 amino acids, and two other identical chains, each with 146 amino acids. Together these four chains form a nearly spherical structure, a shape that encloses an oxygen molecule to carry it through the bloodstream. All the information needed by a cell to assemble hemoglobin is encoded on a gene common to all vertebrates. If we zoomed in on this section of DNA, we would find a sequence of nucleotides corresponding to the constituent amino acids of the hemoglobin molecule. It turns out, however, that the coding on the DNA need not be perfect to work. A fair number of "errors" can be tolerated without ruining the resultant hemoglobin (although certain errors produce the defective hemoglobin of sickle-cell anemia or are not viable at all).

Perhaps due to solar or cosmic radiation, mutations occasionally occur to the DNA in a sperm or egg cell, altering its coding. If the mutation causes a tolerable error on the gene for hemoglobin, it is passed on to succeeding generations. Given sufficient time, a fair number of tolerable errors accumulate on the hemoglobin gene. If we compare the hemoglobin genes of lions and tigers, we find slight differences, the result of mutations that have accumulated in each line since they split from their common ancestor. If we knew the rate at which mutations accumulate, we could estimate the number of years since that split.

The mutation rate can be estimated if it is assumed to be constant over time—a strong assumption. By comparing DNA sequences from living species as distantly related as mammals, birds, and insects, one can count the number of mutations that occurred since they split from common ancestors. The lengths of time since these major taxa diverged, in millions of years, are known from the fossil record. This gives sufficient information to estimate the mutation rate. With that in hand, one can calculate the number of years since lions and tigers diverged. Using similar methods, it has been estimated that humans and chimpanzees diverged from a common ancestor as recently as five to eight million years ago, and that all humans alive today are descended from a few people—metaphorically, Adam and Eve—who lived between fifty thousand and one hundred thousand years ago.

This sounds impressive, but all such estimates must be taken with a grain of salt because molecular methodology requires dubious assumptions such as the presumed constant mutation rate. Phylogenies obtained from DNA do not always agree with those based on fossils, raising the question, which, if either, is correct? DNA comparisons have the advantage of dealing directly with the stuff of heredity. Still, molecular differences between living species may be deceptively large if they experienced very different selection pressures, or deceptively small if they experienced parallel evolution. Fossils have the advantage of being located in time and place, telling us when and where an extinct animal lived, important information not observable in DNA. Until molecular and fossil methods are reconciled, phylogenies must be regarded skeptically.

4

Soft Parts and Behavior

Soft parts of animals rarely fossilize, and except for occasionally preserved footprints or nests, there is little direct evidence about the behavior of extinct species. Knowing the DNA of an extinct animal would in principle give us a blueprint of its body and behavior but in actuality would tell little about the creature's looks or actions. How, then, can we reconstruct soft parts and behaviors of species from the distant past? There is an easy solution in a few cases because some ancient species are still with us, more or less.

Walking the Delaware shore, I occasionally find a dead or barely living horseshoe crab (*Limulus*), the classic "living fossil," scarcely different from specimens dated 300 mya. Today's scorpions also look nearly the same as ancient fossils. In 1938 a fisherman off the coast of South Africa caught a strange fish (eventually named *Latimeria chalumnae*) later identified as a lobe-finned coelacanth, thought to have gone extinct 65 mya.

Living fossils are similar but not identical to ancient fossils and therefore not truly ancestors of other living species. Indeed, orthodox Darwinians insist no species alive today evolved from another living species. A common error of this kind is to say humans evolved from chimpanzees, or, from the chimp's point of view, that chimpanzees evolved from humans. Neither claim is correct. The lineage of today's chimpanzee is exactly as old as our human lineage. The correct statement is that humans and chimps have a common ancestor, now extinct.

If one is willing to deviate a bit from orthodoxy, and nearly everyone is, then living fossils become valuable for reconstructing life's history. Since hard parts of the modern horseshoe crab look similar to ancestral fossils, it seems likely that their soft parts looked similar too. On these grounds, hardly anyone objects to using the living animal as a model for its extinct ancestor, tracing its nervous system, digestion, reproduction, and so on. Furthermore, living horseshoe crabs can be watched, their habits studied for indications of ancestral behavior. They eat a wide variety of foods, catching worms and mollusks and chopping them into small bits with the bases of their legs, also scavenging bottom debris. They tolerate large fluctuations in salinity and are often the last species driven from an estuary by human pollution. Leaving the water to lay their eggs in nests on the beach, they can survive for days in the air and sunshine. Altogether they are hardy generalists, able to live in diverse conditions, and probably their ancestors were too, which may explain why they survived with little modification (Eldredge 1991).

Is it safe to assume, just because they look alike, that today's horseshoe crabs behave like their ancestors? More generally, do any two closely related species that look similar probably act similarly? From our experience with living species, this is a reasonable assumption, but before going further it is worthwhile considering some caveats.

First, animal behavior is often flexible and modifiable by environmental circumstances. Canada geese (*Branta canadensis*) change their migration routes if the location of winter food changes. Hedge sparrows (*Prunella modularis*) studied in a single botanical garden participated in diverse mating combinations—a male and female, a male with two females, two males with one female, or two males with two or more females—depending on the size of territories, which in turn depends on the local quality of feeding and density of vegetation (Davies 1992). Beavers either build stick lodges or burrow their lodges into dirt riverbanks, depending on the availability of suitable sites and materials (Wilsson 1971). These are examples of normal environmentally contingent actions by individuals of a particular species, which collectively compose the behavioral repertoire of that species. Any claim about the behavioral similarity of living and fossil species presumes approximately similar environments.

Second, physically similar species often act differently in ways that reinforce their reproductive isolation, especially if their geographical regions overlap. Distinctive breeding songs, for example, can be important in identifying the forty-nine species of sparrows in the United States, many looking so much alike that experienced birders lump them together as LBJs ("little brown jobs"). This was pleasantly impressed upon me during sunrise walks with my daughter through the fields of Saratoga Battlefield National Park in Upstate New York where she was studying grassland birds. She recognized the subtle visual difference between a rare Henslow's sparrow (*Ammodramus henslowii*) and a common grasshopper sparrow (*Ammodramus savannarum*), which I could not, but I could easily distinguish their songs. She also recognized subtle differences in behavior: Henslow's sparrows are especially secretive, more often running low down through the grass; grasshopper sparrows perch higher up on weed stalks. Nonetheless, these bashful little sparrows are more similar in their behavior than either is to other grassland songbirds like the Eastern meadowlark (*Sturnella magna*) or bobolink (*Dolichonyx oryzivorus*).

The classic example among primates of similar-looking species acting differently is the Hamadryas baboon (*Papio hamadryas*). There are four other baboon species, all living in groups containing multiple adult males as well as females. The Hamadryas is unique in having the harem as its basic social unit. Each adult male that is capable keeps for himself several breeding females (and their offspring), which he controls through forceful measures including biting (Kummer 1968). Otherwise, Hamadryas baboons behave pretty much like other baboons (Nowak 1995).

If physically similar species occupy different geographical regions, behavioral differences are unnecessary to maintain reproductive isolation and may disappear or never develop. A good example is the beaver, which has two living species, one primarily in North America (*Castor canadensis*), the other in Eurasia (*Castor fiber*). Nearly identical in external features, they differ in chromosome number, in average size, in bones of the nasal opening, and in the character of anal gland secretions. Behaviorally they are virtually the same, constructing similar lodges, dams, and channels, though possibly the Eurasian beaver builds less frequently and impressively for lack of construction materials at many European sites (Muller Schwarze and Sun 2003). The gibbon (*Hylobates*), or lesser ape, is another instructive example, having eleven similar-looking species, with the siamang (*Hylobates syndactylus*) often distinguished from the others because of its larger size and webbing between its second and third toes. Living in different geographic areas, all gibbons have a common behavioral pattern including graceful brachiation through the trees, occasional bipedal walking, and monogamous families that are highly territorial (Nowak 1995).

These examples show that physically similar species may behave identically but do not inevitably do so in all ways or in all environments. As a rule of thumb, we may assume closely related species that look alike have comparable behavior patterns, if we do not push it too far. Some paleontologists do go further, arguing that similar-appearing *parts* of otherwise dissimilar animals serve the same behavioral functions, for example, "horns and horn-like organs (crests, frills, etc.) are found in numerous unrelated groups—from beetles and bovids to chameleons and cassowaries—and the primary function in virtually all instances (of living animals) involves sex; attracting mates and/or competing with rivals for reproductive success. . . . Therefore, the current generation of paleontologists is probably quite accurate in ascribing social functions to horns and related features present in dinosaurs" (Sampson 1997, 387). We need not go so far to presume today's horseshoe crabs in toto have soft anatomies and behaviors more or less like their fossil ancestors.

Most mammals evolved rapidly, leaving few species alive today that closely resemble ancient forms. Therefore we must go farther out on a limb, modeling the behavior of long-gone animals after that of somewhat dissimilar living relatives. We claim, for example, that since all living mammals nurse their young, all have strong mother-infant bonds, and all their juveniles play, then probably these behaviors were present in the most recent common ancestor of living mammals (even if that ancestor did not look much like any extant form).

This assumption—in essence that behavior and soft parts are conservative within lineages—while not directly testable, is nonetheless common in theorizing about extinct animals. It has been formalized by paleontologists in a methodology called the "Extant Phylogenetic Bracket," where an extinct species is tentatively assigned behaviors and soft parts found in its living descendants, unless there is contrary evidence (Witmer 1995; Bryant and Russell 1992). The assumption occurs implicitly in most discussions of long-gone lifestyles, and we will use it here.

COMPARATIVE ANATOMY

Comparative anatomy remains a part of every undergraduate course on evolution, notably in lab dissections of mudpuppies, frogs, and pigs. However, its theoretical underpinnings have lost some of their early credibility. This is partly due to the famous but now discredited "biogenetic law" of nineteenth-century anatomist Ernst Haeckel, that "ontogeny [development of an individual] recapitulates phylogeny." Comparing the development of embryos of various living species, Haeckel claimed each embryo resembles in turn its evolutionary ancestors. The human embryo, for example, looks first like a fish, then an amphibian, and so on. There is a grain of truth here—human embryos do have gill slits at one point—but Haeckel exaggerated these stages with the unintended result that many scientists became skeptical of the contribution of comparative anatomy to our understanding of evolution.

Another target of skepticism was the belief of Haeckel and other evolutionists of his time that species evolve in a progressive manner, with new forms carrying forward the design of earlier forms. Haeckel sought naturalistic reasons for this apparently directionality (or *orthogenesis*) in the fossil record, but others gave it teleological or spiritual meaning, seeing the preordained working-out of God's plan for the development of humankind. Today natural scientists agree that teleology and predestination have no role in evolution through natural selection. Each species adapts to its own ecological niche in its own way, constrained by its own evolutionary history.

Some theorists carry the argument further, insisting one cannot say humans are a "higher" species than, say, worms. Perhaps to entomologists, ornithologists, and ichthyologists this extension is entirely convincing. Personally, I cannot regard ant colonies on a par with human societies, nor can I believe there is no "progression"—in retrospect—from fish through monkeys to human beings. My perspective is frankly anthropocentric—I *am* a sociologist— so I seek in evolutionary history those changes whereby creatures moved in a particular direction, from amphibian life toward humanity (without attributing any religious or mystical significance to that development). Not all evolution was in this direction, but I am not interested here in other paths. If trout were my focal animal, I would arrange this discussion differently.

To understand our evolutionary development since the Cambrian explosion, from invertebrates to fish to amphibians to reptilians to mammals to humans, it makes sense to compare modern representatives of this sequence. The comparative anatomy of living species has always complemented interpretation of extinct fossils and is the grandparent of today's DNA comparisons. It bears repeating that modern species do not form a true evolutionary sequence; they are "cousins," related through common ancestors now extinct. Obviously, one must be wary of inferences from a constructed quasi-evolutionary sequence, but there is no good reason to reject them altogether.

In the following section I consider the evolution of the brain, that soft part of the body most intimately connected to human behavior. The method is comparative anatomy, using living species to imagine brain development from its origins to what we now have in our heads. This approach inevitably suggests, however faintly, that the evolutionary process is somehow directional, goal oriented, teleological, continuous, free of dead ends, and the like. I intend no such meaning, nor that past trends can be projected into the future. My intent, rather, is to look backward from the present, to trace how we evolved to the point where we are now.

EVOLUTION OF THE BRAIN

The central nervous system consists of the brain and spinal cord. It communicates with the rest of the body through electrical signals passed along peripheral nerves, and also via chemical hormones manufactured and injected into the bloodstream by endocrine glands (the thyroid, adrenals, testes, ovaries, etc.). Nerve and hormone signals are coordinated through two small structures, the *hypothalamus* and *pituitary*, located at the base of all vertebrate brains.

Given the close relationship of chimpanzees and humans, we expect their brains to share important features, but it may be surprising that both have homologues of the amphibian brain too. Brain evolution is conservative; once a structure appears in the central nervous system, it often remains there as one species evolves into another. Newer structures may be added and old ones modified considerably, but they rarely disappear.

Amphioxus (*Branchiostoma*), a chordate without a backbone, looking something like a small eel, spends most of its life buried in the sandy bottom of marine bays, filter feeding on microorganisms in the water. The species is primitive and must have appeared long ago. It has a fibrous rod (a *notochord*) running the length of its body, the defining feature of a chordate. (Vertebrates, a subphylum of chordates, have embryonic notochords that develop into backbones.) Above the notochord runs a neural cord with a rudimentary brain at its front, the precursor of a vertebrate's central nervous system. As in all nervous systems, electric signals are transmitted from one neuron (nerve cell) to another. There are gaps (synapses) between neurons. The signal crosses these gaps when chemical neurotransmitters, released from one neuron, flow across the synapse and lock into receptors on the other neuron. Serotonin, a neurotransmitter produced in some amphioxus neurons, is found in all nervous systems that have evolved from primitive chordates, functioning to stabilize the organism's neural circuits. Serotonin-producing neurons occupy virtually the same location in every vertebrate brain that they do in amphioxus (Allman 1999). In humans these neurons are numerous and project to all parts of the brain and spinal cord, having a profound effect on our mood. High serotonin levels are associated in humans with a sense of well-being and freedom from anxiety. Prozac and other antidepressive drugs work by increasing the concentration of serotonin in the gaps between neurons.

When some chordate evolved into a fish, fishlike behaviors were enabled by new structures added to the spinal cord and brain, including olfactory bulbs, optic lobes, a cerebellum, hypothalamus and pituitary, and small cerebral hemispheres. As fish evolved into amphibians, then amphibians evolved into reptile-like amniotes, and then amniotes into birds and mammals, new forms of behavior were associated with new or modified brain parts. Rather than replacing old structures, new elements were figuratively stacked on top, forming an agglomerate brain. We may imagine the development from fish to human looking something like the series of brains pictured in Figure 4.1 (Truax and Carpenter 1964, 120). Ignoring considerable variation within taxa, these are representative brains from modern fish, amphibians, reptiles, mammals, and humans.

When mammals evolved from reptile-like amniotes, the cerebral hemispheres expanded considerably, becoming the most prominent features of the mammalian brain. The surface (cortex) of these hemispheres is covered by gray matter a few millimeters thick called the *cerebral cortex*. This can be divided into *neocortex*, which is the most recently evolved gray matter composing most of the cortex of higher mammals, and *allocortex*, the most primitive cortex. (Neocortex has a unique structure with six neuron layers laminated onto the surface of the brain; allocortex has a simpler structure, usually

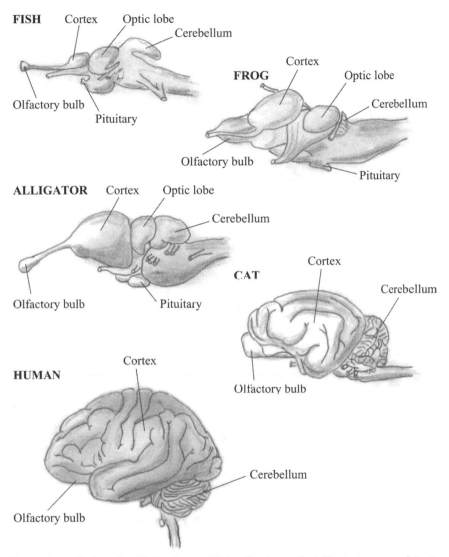

Figure 4.1. Brains of a fish (cod), amphibian (frog), reptile (alligator), mammal (cat), and human; not to scale (adapted from Truax and Carpenter 1964, 120).

with three layers of neurons.) The little cerebral cortex found in reptiles is all allocortex.

Neocortex occurs in all mammals and only in mammals. It is involved in perception, volition, memory and movement, reasoning and, in humans, language. The *corpus callosum*, found only in placental mammals, is a white band of nerve fibers connecting the neocortex of the two hemispheres and

allowing information to pass between them. (The hemispheres are also connected through the *anterior commissure*, which is present in reptiles and
birds as well as mammals.)

The neocortex is especially large (relative to both body and brain mass) in
primates. During embryonic development of apes and humans, the cerebral
hemispheres fold as they grow, cramming a lot of neocortex into the skull,
producing the convoluted walnut-like appearance of our brains. This volu-
minous neocortex—only about a third of it shows on the surface—engulfs
our allocortex, which lies buried near the middle of the brain's hemispheres,
partly encircling the corpus callosum and brainstem.

This submerged allocortex receives nerve input from several other elements within or below the hemispheres. These submerged structures are often designated the "limbic system." The term is much criticized, first because
different authors disagree on the structures to be included, and second because "system" infers a functional unity that has never been demonstrated.
Nonetheless neurologists commonly speak of the limbic system, or limbic
structures, to refer to those parts of the mammalian brain implicated in the
emotions.

Limbic structures are present in at least rudimentary form in the reptilian
brain; however, they are more developed in mammals (MacLean 1990). A
major limbic element is the *amygdala*, which increases in size and development from the lower to the higher mammals and is particularly well developed in humans. A central task of the amygdala is the establishment of links
between stimuli and their emotional value, for example, whether something
or somebody is good or bad. Bilateral destruction of the amygdala in monkeys causes reduced expressions of emotion, difficulties in social interaction
leading to isolation, and loss of aggressive and defensive reactions. In contrast to normal monkeys, those with destroyed amygdalae show no signs of
fear, as when confronted with a snake. In humans, the amygdala has been
stimulated in conjunction with brain surgery under local anesthesia. A wide
spectrum of autonomic and emotional reactions has been produced, but
most pronounced is a feeling of anxiety (Brodal 1998, 560–65).

BRAINS AND BEHAVIOR

We presume a correlation between the structure of an animal's central nervous system and its behavior; the two must have evolved in concert. The
reptilian brain necessarily fits the basic pattern of reptilian behavior, which
is asocial, cold-blooded and therefore lethargic in cool temperatures, and
stereotypic (MacLean 1990). From a human perspective, reptilian behavior
seems very simple. In some species an adult male's mates occupy his territory for long periods, but interaction between the sexes is usually brief and

limited to reproductive behavior. Caretaking of young after hatching or birth is usually absent—although alligators are relatively attentive mothers. Reptiles engage in dominance contests for desirable sites, mates, or food, using stereotyped displays of challenge or submission. Males often defend core sites from intruding neighbors, effectively spacing themselves across the ground. If circumstances such as a concentration of food induce lizards to remain in close proximity, males form a dominance hierarchy wherein the alpha male can trespass others males' sites, but they avoid his (Zug 1993). The reptile's central nervous system necessarily enables all of these behaviors as well as handling the basic drives of hunger, thirst, sex, sleep, and pain avoidance, but it lacks the capacity for much more.

Birds evolved from reptiles (via dinosaurs) but are warm-blooded and therefore more energetic. Brains of warm-blooded vertebrates tend to be larger than brains of cold-blooded vertebrates of the same body weight, accommodating new mechanisms for maintaining a constant body temperature. Birds are far more social than reptiles, usually acting cooperatively to raise their young. The typical avian behavioral pattern, with exceptions, is for the male to stake out a territory in the spring, defending it from nearby males with stereotypic auditory (songs, calls) and visual displays of dominance. These displays also attract a female to the territory, who builds a nest of a certain architecture, perhaps aided by the male. Copulation is followed by egg laying, hatching, and then prolonged feeding of the young until they fledge, much of this a cooperative undertaking between the parents. The young may stay with one or both parents after leaving the nest. Families often join flocks in the fall for migration to an area with a better winter food supply.

Similarities between reptilian and avian ways of life, including the common male propensity for territorial spacing through dominance displays, may be embedded in brain structures shared by birds and reptiles, and these probably were present in their most recent common ancestor. (Some invertebrates display analogous territorial and dominance behaviors, but lacking anything like a vertebrate brain, their actions must be governed by other mechanisms with differently evolved roots.) Differences between bird and reptile behavior, such as presence or absence of parental cooperation in rearing young, must reside proximately in structures differentiating birds from reptiles. With some exceptions, birds are generally more dependent on sight than smell, the reverse of reptiles. This is mirrored in the relative size of their olfactory and optic structures. The cerebellum, which controls coordinated movement, is far larger and more developed in birds. Brains of some birds contain microscopic grains of iron oxide, magnetite, which may aid navigation by sensing the direction of magnetic north. The *hyperstriatum*, a structure unique to the avian brain, is implicated in the imprinting of chicks to their mothers (Horn, Nicol, and Brown 2001).

The mammalian nervous system has a unique set of reflexes inducing a newborn to seek its mother's nipple with its mouth and, once the nipple is grasped, to suckle. Production of mother's milk is controlled by the hormone oxytocin, which is made in the hypothalamus. Oxytocin also stimulates maternal care in mammals. These distinctly mammalian behaviors, also including juvenile play, must involve the neocortex, which is the only brain structure unique to mammals, and the limbic system, which is considerably modified in mammals.

In classic experiments of the nineteenth century, the entire neocortex was surgically removed from animals, depriving them of "will, intelligence, memory, perception," yet they would live for months (cited in Allman 1999, 30). At about the same time it was noted that certain language abilities are degraded in patients with particular injuries to the neocortex. Lesions near the front of the left hemisphere produce loss of speaking ability. Lesions to the left *temporal* lobe (i.e., the lobe of the left hemisphere nearest the temple) produce impaired language comprehension. These specialized language areas (named for their discoverers, Broca and Wernicke) have since been verified, although today we know about 5 percent of people locate these functions on the right rather than left side of the brain.

In most people the right hemisphere controls *prosody*, the emotional or affective content given a string of spoken words by the speaker's melody, pauses, intonations, stresses, and accents. A sentence such as "I went to the store" takes different meaning and coloration depending on the tone, timing, and inflections of the utterance. Lesions to the right hemisphere have produced difficulties in producing or comprehending prosody in patients who can still speak and understand the words. Some people with left-hemisphere lesions who have lost speech can still sing lyrics, apparently enabled by the right hemisphere's capacity for prosody (Filley 1995).

EMOTION

To a first approximation, conscious thoughts and actions depend primarily on the neocortex. The limbic structures are more concerned with emotions, motivation, and affective behavior (Brodal 1998). Hormones are especially active in the emotions, producing bodily responses that are the hallmark of emotional response, for example, the flush of anger, embarrassment, or sexual excitement; the pallor, sweat, and trembling of fear.

Mammals (and some other animals) show "emotions" with recognizable human counterparts, notably rage (analogous to human anger), fear, and pleasure or contentment (roughly analogous to happiness). A small number of basic human emotions—happiness, sadness, anger, fear, and disgust—are associated with characteristic facial expressions recognizable across cultures

(Ekman and Friesen 1971). Any human youngster, without coaching, can produce appropriate faces for each of these emotions (Figure 4.2).

Not all emotions have associated facial expressions. The essence of an emotion is that we feel it viscerally, it has neurohormonal aspects, and it produces some distinct affect that motivates or inhibits our behavior (Weisfeld 1997). At least in humans and probably more broadly, maternal care is motivated by vicariously feeling comfort or discomfort expressed by the infant. The tendency to nurture one's vulnerable children makes good evolutionary sense, for otherwise parents would leave few survivors in succeeding generations. There is an emotional mechanism at work here, acting through the sympathetic attachment of mother and child, a bond that intensifies the more they interact. If an infant is content, then usually its mother is content; if the infant suffers, then its mother suffers vicariously. (Infants reflect their mother's moods too.) That is why parents take special pains to ensure the well-being of their offspring.

Figure 4.2.   My daughters making play faces to show happiness, sadness, anger, fear, and disgust

Mammals (and some other animals) vicariously attach not only to off-spring but to close associates and to members of their group, reflecting one another's fear, contentment, or agitation. Humans, especially, attach vicariously to anyone with whom we interact positively. Perhaps this is a generalization of our evolved tendency to favor our children, a spillover to all people we like, or to those we perceive to be like us. We share their joy and feel their pain, whether or not they are genetically related. Humans also attach *negatively* to people whom we dislike, or perceive as different from ourselves, or to whom we are hostile; then we are unhappy if they succeed, glad if they fail.

Coalitions based on vicarious attachment are common among social mammals. If conflict breaks out between two animals in the same group, each one's closest associates provide support. If hostilities break out between two troops or two packs, each animal reliably supports its own side. In human terms, this explains why my friend and I will set aside our own argument to coalesce against a neighbor who threatens one of us, and why we and the neighbor will set aside that dispute to join forces against foreigners. (See the appendix on stress-induced coalitions.)

IS THE BRAIN INTEGRATED?

Any conceptualization of the brain as an accretion of new structures atop ancient ones necessarily raises a question of how well these elements work together. Does the human brain operate as a fully integrated entity, or does it perform different functions in specialized modules that are not completely coordinated, pitting our emotions against our cognitions?

That separate parts of the brain are capable of independent—even conflicting—thoughts and actions is illustrated in patients undergoing split-brain surgery for the control of epilepsy. In this operation the corpus collosum is severed, thereby preventing the spread of abnormal nerve discharges from one hemisphere to the other, but at the same time halting normal communication between the hemispheres. Contrived laboratory tasks demonstrate independent operation of the two disconnected sides of the brain. For example, a patient can speak the name of an object held in the right hand, because the sensations of touch by the right hand go to the left hemisphere, where the speaking function is located; but the patient cannot say the name of an object held in the left hand, since those sensations go to the right hemisphere, now severed from the speaking function on the left.

These patients manage well in everyday life because sights and sounds from the environment usually reach both hemispheres at the same time, but occasionally peculiar behaviors result from the disconnection. Neuroscientist Joseph LeDoux tells of seeing a patient several days after surgery who was pulling his pants down with this right hand and up with his left, as if the opposite sides of his brain had different aims and the normal means of reconciliation had been broken (2002, 305). Anyone who has resolved to diet and then gorged on cookies and ice cream, or tried to quite smoking and failed, or has had sex in a manner that—or with a person who—an hour earlier seemed a foolish choice, knows the appetites and emotions generated in one part of the brain may sharply contradict the good sense residing elsewhere. The joke that God gave man two gifts, a penis and a brain, but forbade him the use of both at the same time, carries enough truth to make the point but shows as well that it can be overstated.

When split-brain research appeared in the 1960s, it triggered a wave of extreme claims, never well supported, that each hemisphere specializes in certain kinds of mental processing—the left devoted to analytic, linguistic, rational, scientific, linear thought; the right to intuitive, nonlinguistic, mystical, artistic, and holistic thought. With opposing halves vying like yin and yang, our personality was said to be determined by the dominant hemisphere.

This view is exaggerated, and it is worthwhile emphasizing the obvious but often overlooked point that split brains are anomalies. While they demonstrate the possibility of independent actions in different parts of our heads, they do not indicate that this is normal operation. The pendulum of commentary is today swinging back, emphasizing that the emotional and cognitive parts of the brain, while in some ways separate, are on the whole highly connected and intensively interdependent. Brain scans made during diverse mental tasks typically show both hemispheres participating, if not equally. Anatomically, there are dense connections among and between limbic elements and the neocortex. Emotional and cognition content are intertwined, as when depression comes with pessimistic thoughts, elation with optimistic plans (Dolan 2002). Information content in the form of bad news can make us feel down; good news cheers us up.

The deep integration of cognitions and emotions is illustrated by any escalating conflict between ethnic, religious, or nationalistic groups. Nearly every involved person's intellectual view of the conflict—how it started, whose fault it is, what solutions are just and unjust—is predictable from his emotional identification with one side or the other, whether Israeli against Palestinian, Pakistani against Indian, or Russian against Chechen. This alignment is so predictable that sociologists speak of the *Rashomon* effect (after a classic Japanese movie) when two people give inconsistent verbal accounts of the same conflict, and each account suits the teller's interests and the position he or she wants to defend (Mazur 1998). It explains why the same suicide bomber or airplane hijacker is perceived as a terrorist by his enemies and as a freedom fighter by his allies. Freudians call this *rationalization:* the devising of a self-satisfying and ostensibly cogent explanation for our beliefs and actions, when in fact their causes lie elsewhere.

The mind's attitudes, beliefs, and logical deductions are consistent with its feelings; there is an alignment of the neocortex and the limbic system. The deepest intellectual arguments of philosophy and science rarely contradict the thinker's gut emotions or sympathetic identities.

While human actions of dominance and deference are based at least partly on the same motivations as in other primates, we nonetheless rationalize them in purely human terms, constructing linguistic justifications for advantageous rank as being "legitimate," or "well deserved," or "divinely mandated." With historical hindsight, we get a better perspective on aristocracy and slavery, for example, than was available to contemporaries who preached that these social arrangements were natural, inevitable, and ordained by God. There is no better historical example than the United States in the early nineteenth century, which, despite its slavery, was an intensely liberal democracy, dedicated to individual freedom of thought and action. That these freedoms were limited to *whites* and *men* meant that America was backwardly racist and, like Europe, sexist. While these seem contradictory positions today, Americans at the time could defend the institutions of democracy and slavery in the same breath.

CONCLUSIONS

Living animals provide uncertain models for extinct ancestors, but we have no better option for visualizing features of species long gone. With proper attention to potential pitfalls, comparative anatomy helps us imagine the evolution of soft parts and behavior. By arranging living species on the basis of physical characteristics into a quasi-evolutionary series, we approximate the true evolutionary path from a distant ancestor to a living descendant. Behaviors that emerge in a smooth fashion along the quasi-evolutionary series may have followed a similar historical path. As in all evolutionary reconstructions, it is important to exclude anomalous characteristics that likely represent unique adaptations.

Species-specific behaviors must have physical underpinnings, either in the central nervous system or in some peripheral hormonal mechanism. Confirmation that a particular behavior is an evolved trait would require that the physical mechanism underlying that behavior be identified. In humans, as in other animals, there is a linkage between brain structure and behavior. No longer can we explain human thoughts and actions as if they were independent of our bodies. The mind-body distinction that has been salient in Western philosophy for the past three centuries cannot be sustained. Rationality and language do not occur on a detached mental platform, completely separated from visceral emotions. We think and we feel in tandem.

Traditional sociology has given little attention to primitive emotional processes in explaining the status hierarchies of small groups. Its theories speak in Cartesian terms of language, cognition, and symbolism. As a graduate student in sociology, I was taught that a leader emerges in a small group because "he is internally rewarded by the 'knowledge that he is right,'" that both "the leader and the members identify with a symbol system," and "the leader is identified by the members as the 'true spokesman and interpreter' of the symbol system" (Bales 1953, 139). Another popular theorist of the period, noting that girls prefer association with near-peers, explained that near-peers "are apt to hold similar values, and so they are apt to reward and like one another." (Homans 1961, 322). But monkeys also associate mostly with near-peers, and for monkeys an explanation in terms of "similar values" is meaningless. Other influential theorists thought a group's status ranking derived from chains of logical deduction by its members, as if such rankings are found only among rationally acting human beings (Berger, Cohen, and Zelditch 1972). It did not occur to most sociologists of that time that human behavior followed a broader primate pattern.

Evolution dictates that we understand the actions of *Homo sapiens* as primate behavior, unique in some ways but in other ways typical of all primates and especially of apes. So let us now focus on these cousins of ours.

5

Primates

In his great work, *Systema Naturae* (1758), Linnaeus listed the major categories of mammals, for example, the Carnivora, the Rodentia, and the Cetacea (whales and dolphins). It was obvious to naturalists of the time that the category containing humans must be classed above the rest, so Linnaeus called that order the Primates, from Latin for "first in rank."

Linnaeus named our species *Homo sapiens*—"wise man." Despite our position atop the pinnacle of wisdom, humans are genetically so similar to the African apes (chimpanzees, bonobos, and gorillas) that we must have diverged from common ancestors less than ten million years ago. For cross-species comparisons to seriously aid our understanding of human affairs, we must focus on the primates.

WHAT IS A PRIMATE?

There is no simple definition of our order because primate bodies are less specialized than the bodies of other mammals and therefore lack the unique features that make other orders easier to describe. Primatologist R. D. Martin proposes a definition running nearly two pages (1990, 639–40), far too complex for nonspecialists.

The most important thing that primates have in common is that they are or were tree-dwellers, with features useful for that habitat. Five digits at the end of each limb, including opposable thumbs and usually opposable big toes, are ideal for grasping branches. The digits end in nerve-filled pads, at least some of them backed by flat nails rather than claws, making them effective sense organs. Primates have sharp eyes, in preference to keen noses, and the eyes are set inside protective bony orbits. Rather than looking sideways, like a dog, primate eyes look forward, producing overlapping fields of view that the brain combines into depth perception, useful in moving through the three dimensions of the forest canopy.

Brains are larger in primates than in other mammals of similar size, and more elaborate in design. Usually pregnancies produce one offspring at a time, the mother carrying it for months before giving birth. Babies grow slowly and are highly dependent on maternal care—features closely connected to the development of complex social organization. The main task of primate mothers is to protect their vulnerable young and socialize them into primate society. This requires an unusually large investment of time, energy, and emotion, but it has the advantage of enabling each new generation to learn from the prior generation.

Martin points out that living species fall into six "natural groupings," reflected in one way or another in all primate taxonomies:

1. Lemurs (Madagascar; 18 genera, 35 species)
2. Lorises (Africa, South and Southeast Asia; 5 genera, 11 species)
3. Tarsiers (Southeast Asia; one genus, 4 species)
4. New World monkeys (South and Central America; 16 genera, 64 species)
5. Old World monkeys (Africa, South and Southeast Asia; 16 genera, 73 species)
6. Apes and humans (Africa, South and Southeast Asia, not counting recent human migrations; 5 genera, 12 species)[1]

The first three natural groups—lemurs, lorises, and tarsiers—are traditionally called "prosimians" as distinct from the simians (i.e., monkeys, apes, and humans).[2] As the name indicates, extant prosimians retain features common in ancestral primates and therefore regarded as primitive. These include large bony orbits around the eyes, a small brain case, a long snout, and relatively large olfactory and auditory regions of the skull (Nowak 1999; Fleagle 1999). Extant prosimians are wholly or largely arboreal, and about three-quarters of these species are nocturnal, resting during the day. The eyes of nocturnal species—therefore of most prosimians—are large compared to diurnal primates.

Many features of the jaw, teeth, and skull distinguish simians from prosimians; for example, the two frontal bones of the simian skullcap are fused along the midline suture, and a virtually complete postorbital plate separates the eye-encircling orbit from the jaw muscles. The brain case (relative to body size) is larger in simians than in prosimians.

Among the simians, New World monkeys (Ceboidea) are distinguishable from Old World monkeys (Cercopithecoidea). Those of the American tropics have flat noses and large, well-separated nostrils (called "platyrrhine" noses). Old World monkeys have narrower, close-set nostrils that point downward ("catarrhine" noses). All Old World monkeys, but no New World species, have hardened cutaneous sitting pads on their rumps. While all monkeys have tails, only New World monkeys (but not all of them) have tails that are prehensile, serving as a fifth limb in the trees.

New World monkeys are arboreal, living in the tropical forest, and nearly all are diurnal. Old World monkeys are entirely diurnal but occupy varied habitats, some living in trees while others, like baboons, spend most or all of their time on the ground. A few Old World species occupy regions that are surprisingly nontropical. One macaque (*Macaca fuscata*) lives in a region of Japan with snowy winters, and it sometimes bathes in thermal springs during subfreezing weather.

Taxonomists regard all apes and humans, both living and extinct, as a natural grouping, united by morphological characteristics including a barrel-shaped chest, absence of a tail, relatively large size, and relatively big brain. Apes have a broader version of the catarrhine nose characteristic of Old World monkeys. They differ from monkeys in dentition, larger size, broader palates, and proportionately larger brains.

The "lesser" apes, that is, gibbons and siamangs (Hylobatinae), must be distinguished from the great apes (Ponginae). Gibbons and siamangs do not exceed eleven kilograms, while great apes weigh many times more. Unlike great apes and humans, the lesser apes show little sexual dimorphism and are monogamous and territorial. Mated pairs of gibbons and siamangs do not allow mature conspecifics to remain in proximity. Essentially arboreal, these slender little apes have extremely long arms relative to body size and are the only living primates that truly brachiate, swinging from arm to arm through the trees with wondrous grace.

The "great apes" comprise two species of chimpanzee (the common chimp, *Pan troglodytes*, and the smaller bonobo, *Pan paniscus*), one or two species of gorilla (*Gorilla gorilla*, and perhaps *Gorilla beringei*), and one species of orangutan (*Pongo pygmaeus*). Chimps, bonobos, and gorillas live in Africa, the probable place of human emergence. Orangutans are outliers among the great apes, living in Borneo and Sumatra and genetically more distant from the African apes than the African apes are to each other or to humans. Mature male orangs are inexplicably asocial, wandering the forest in solitude except to engage in copulation. It is difficult to reconcile our close phylogenetic relationship to the orangutan with its unsimianlike reclusion. Gorillas, bonobos, and chimpanzees are comparably social to humans, and chimpanzees are frequently favored as a model for protohumans (de Waal 2001).

The defining features of each primate group are important to taxonomists, but for the average viewer, most monkeys, whether from the Old or New World, are visually recognizable as monkeys. The great apes, larger and more humanlike, have a considerably different appearance. Prosimians often seem more like squirrels or raccoons than monkeys, and many zoo-goers do not recognize them as primates. On virtually all dimensions, the prosimians are least like us, the apes are most like us, and monkeys hold an intermediate position.

PHYLOGENY

The oldest clearly primate fossils are prosimian in character and date from the early Cenozoic era, about fifty-five million years ago. The fossil record of early mammals is poor, and certainly primates considerably predate the earliest remains currently known. Molecular data suggest that primates diverged from other placental mammals in the mid-Cretaceous, some ninety million years ago (Tavare et al. 2002).

There are also geographical reasons to suspect an early origin for primates. Extant lemurs are found only on Madagascar, which was once connected to Africa and India but has been a large island for some ninety million years (Goodman and Benstead 2003). If the world had no primates ninety million years ago, then lemurs must have reached Madagascar later, perhaps by accidentally "rafting" across open sea. One must weigh this hypothesis against the possibility that primates populated Madagascar before its isolation was complete.

A similar problem is presented by the bifurcation of monkeys between the Old World and the New. One might guess that this important division resulted from the spreading of the Atlantic Ocean, splitting South American monkeys from their cousins in Africa. But the opening of the Atlantic is dated at one hundred million years ago, well before the putative origin of monkeys. One may turn again to the rafting hypothesis, although this would require a considerable voyage across the widening Atlantic. Another possibility is that monkeys migrated from Asia across the Bering Strait on a now-submerged land bridge. If so, a rafting hypothesis is still required because these ancestral primates would have had to cross the wide sea that separated North and South America until fairly recently when this water was bridged by Panama. There are prosimian fossils in North America but no monkey fossils to support a hypothetical northern migration.

Apart from dates of origin, there is considerable agreement about the broad outline of primate phylogeny, diagrammed in Figure 5.1 (Martin 1990; Fleagle 1999). The earliest recognizable primates were prosimians, not exactly like extant prosimians but in many ways similar to today's lemurs and lorises.

One line of ancestral prosimians evolved into ancestral monkeys (simians). The earliest identifiably simian fossils are about thirty million years old.

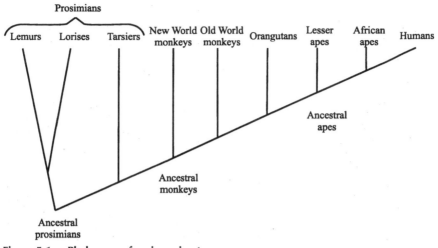

Figure 5.1.   Phylogeny of major primate groups

Older simian examples will likely turn up as more effort is devoted to filling in the fossil record, which is especially deficient in the Southern Hemisphere. At undetermined dates, New World monkeys split from this line and became isolated in tropical America, while Old World monkeys radiated across Africa and Asia.

Fossils indicate the existence of apes, derived from some kind of Old World monkey, by twenty million years ago. Relatively quickly, the ancestors of gibbons and siamangs split off the "main line" to great apes and humans. Somewhat later, the first orangutans diverged from the progenitors of today's African apes and humans.

HOMINID EVOLUTION

Genetic comparisons suggest that the common ancestors of today's chimpanzees, bonobos, gorillas, and humans lived in Africa five to eight million years ago. The descendants of these common ancestors are called "hominids" if they seem more closely related to humans than apes.

Known hominids are divided into australopithecines and *Homo*. Several species of both kinds have been identified, sometimes from meager fossils. Some of these species are controversial, in part because paleoanthropologists who have invested years in the search exaggerate the uniqueness of their finds and their importance to human history. Even when there is agreement that species have been validly described, the phylogenetic relationships among them are uncertain.

Most opinion today regards the hominid tree as having several branches, some of them dead ends (e.g., Tattersall 1995, 234). Apparently in times past, two or more hominid species were alive and in proximity, perhaps hunting one another. With no certain way to know which were ancestral to *Homo sapiens*, it may be futile to seek the exact species-to-species chain connecting us to extinct apes. A more achievable goal is to describe the grades of hominid that existed at different times, taking this as the approximate path of human descent.

The australopithecines (Australopithecinae, or southern apes) are the earliest known hominids, with numerous fossils from multiple species discovered in southern and eastern Africa and dated between five and two million years ago. They had apelike faces and projecting jaws, and their brains were similar in size to a modern ape. Their canines and molars were halfway between ape and human forms, but the important feature that classifies australopithecines as hominid was their upright stance. These were fully bipedal walkers on the road leading from ape to human. Thus, bipedalism appeared *before* greatly enlarged brains.

Paleoanthropologists place fossil skulls in the genus *Homo* if they have humanlike teeth and, more importantly, braincases comparable in size to our own. The earliest finds of this kind are dated 1.5 to 2 million years ago, the best-known specimens identified as *Homo habilis* and *Homo ergaster*. Upright walkers, they apparently used the simple stone tools sometimes found nearby. These implements are of the Oldowan style, chipped to give a single rough cutting edge but nearly indistinguishable from natural stones to the untrained eye.

Homo erectus came next and is especially important for its long tenure, wide range, and cultural advance. Fossils have been found at numerous sites across the Old World with dates from 1.5 million years to less than 200 thousand years ago. *Homo erectus* had a heavy brow ridge jutting over a chinless face, with a prominent nose and downward-facing nostrils. Its solidly constructed skull is thicker-walled, more rugged, longer, and lower than earlier hominids. This large-brained creature likely used fire, and it skillfully crafted stone tools in the advanced Achulean style, including a characteristic double-faced hand axe. *Homo erectus* was earth's dominant hominid for a million years, and probably the only living hominid for most of its reign.

By 200 thousand years ago there were people whom we call archaic *Homo sapiens* in Africa, though their fossils are not quite like modern humans. At the same time the famous Neanderthal people, usually regarded as a separate species (*Homo neanderthalensis*), were living in Europe. Neanderthals survived until 30 thousand years ago but then disappeared without descendants (Jordan 1999). Tools and other artifacts found with *Homo neanderthalensis* and archaic *Homo sapiens* are far more advanced than those of *Homo erectus*.

By 50 thousand years ago there were people whose fossil skulls fit within the normal variability found among present-day people. Artifacts from the next several millennia indicate a "creative explosion" of new cultures, including the awesome cave paintings of Europe (Pfeiffer 1982), leaving no doubt that fully modern humans had arrived.

While we get hints about Stone Age lifestyles from tools, surviving hearths, and middens of animal bones and other discards, the tangible remnants of behavior are rare. The bipedal walk of extinct hominids is inferred from the shape and connections of fossil leg bones. This was spectacularly confirmed by the discovery of footprints preserved at Laetoli, Tanzania, in volcanic ash laid down 3.7 million years ago. Apparently a light rain turned the newly fallen ash into something like wet cement. Before it dried, various creatures wandered over it, leaving tracks. Among them were two parallel sets of hominid (likely australopithecine) footprints, extending for twenty-five meters. When the volcano erupted again, new ash covered and protected the prints until recent erosion revealed them. Obviously we cannot depend on such extraordinary finds. We must look at living primates to reconstruct the evolution of behavior.

A QUASI-EVOLUTIONARY SERIES OF LIVING PRIMATES

In many respects the living members of the primate order seem to form a natural ladder, from primitive to more advanced, or specialized, types. This remarkable array provides us with living species that preserve many features that characterized primates of earlier epochs. This diversity of form can give us some idea of the pathways of primate evolution. (Fleagle 1999, 81)

We cannot go so far as to line up today's species in an unambiguous developmental path, because every surviving lineage adapted uniquely to its peculiar ecological history. But while natural selection produces modifications that improve genetic fitness, it is otherwise conservative, a tendency called "phylogenetic inertia" (DiFiore and Rendall 1994; Blomberg and Garland 2002). Amidst the diverse adaptations of extant taxa, there are central tendencies reflecting the preserved heritage of common ancestors. By tracing these modal features from prosimians, through New and Old World monkeys, to African apes, to humans, we discern the approximate evolution of human qualities.

The degree to which this primate series shows the true course of human evolution depends on the amount of change in each lineage since it diverged from the "main line" of human descent. If prosimians evolved slowly, then living prosimians are good representatives of their ancestors. The picture is complicated because lineages change at different rates. (Indeed, individual characteristics evolve at different rates.) Judging from comparative morphology, apes diverged much faster and further than prosimians from their last common ancestor, but the African apes have not changed much since their split from hominids. Taking into account body size differences among gorillas, chimpanzees, and bonobos, they are all anatomically similar (Shea 1985). Fleagle likens gorillas to overgrown chimpanzees, and bonobos to juvenile chimps (1999, 253). We may infer that there was not much evolutionary change after these ape lineages diverged, so the common ancestor of chimps and humans was anatomically like a chimpanzee. The earliest hominid fossils all appear chimp-like (Daniel Lieberman, personal communication). On these grounds, living chimpanzees seem a suitable model for the last chimp-human ancestor.

R. D. Martin, who is especially critical of incautiously treating extant species as "frozen fossils," nonetheless justifies the interpretation of major groups of living primates as being at different "grades" of evolutionary development:

> There are, in fact, good reasons why this gradation should exist in a very general sense. In the first place, most prosimian primates are nocturnal in habits, whereas simian primates are, with only one exception (the owl monkey, *Aotus*), diurnally active. As it is likely that the ancestral primates were nocturnal in habits . . . , it is only to be expected that nocturnal prosimians should have remained generally more primitive than diurnal simians. . . . Among simians, New World monkeys have been somewhat more isolated than Old World monkeys and apes throughout their evolutionary history, so a somewhat slower overall pace of phylogenetic change is to be expected. Finally, the human lineage has clearly been subjected to rather unusual selection pressures that have resulted in a striking divergence from Old World monkeys and apes. Thus, the *Scala naturae* as applied to primates does have some basis in biological reality. (1990, 106)

Such scaling is apparent in the appearance of representatives from the major primate groups (see Figure 5.2), and the visual continuity is even stronger when juveniles are compared. Body size generally increases across the primate series, and the brain enlarges relative to the size of the body. The index of cranial capacity, a measure of brain size controlled for body size, has a median value of 3.3 for prosimians, 6.0 for New World monkeys, 7.3 for Old World monkeys, 7.7 for apes, and 23.0 for humans (Martin 1990, 362). The human brain uniquely continues to grow at a high rate for the first year after birth.

We approximate the evolution of the cerebral hemispheres by comparing brains of prosimians, monkeys, apes, and humans (see Figure 5.3). In the higher primates there is expansion of the cortex, its differentiation into separate lobes, and increased fissuration. (Convolutions increase as a result of the neocortex enlarging faster than the interior of the skull, causing the cortex to fold in on itself.) In higher primates the olfactory bulbs are reduced in size, while areas of the cortex associated with touch and vision are unusually large. This corresponds to the great simian specialization for diurnal life in the trees, elevating stereoscopic sight and touch to the dominant senses while downgrading smell and hearing (Napier and Napier 1985). Each major group of living primates has a characteristic brain architecture, or cerebrotype, determined by the sizes of the major parts of the brain (neocortex, hippocampus, etc.) relative to the total brain. The cerebrotype changes progressively from prosimians to monkeys (with some overlap between New and Old World monkeys) to apes and humans (Clark, Mitra, and Wang 2001). The transition from monkeys to African apes and humans was accompanied by new details of brain anatomy (Hof et al. 2001).

Presumably changes in behavior track neurological changes. Nearly all living prosimians are arboreal, making it likely that the earliest primates were too. The ringtail lemur (*Lemur catta*) is the only living prosimian with a tendency toward terrestrial activity, and still it spends most of its time in trees. Terrestrial life probably began among Old World monkeys. Some extant species remain arboreal; others live partly or wholly on the ground. African apes are mostly terrestrial during the day. The original arboreal lifestyle is reflected in the grasping foot, virtually universal in living primates except humans, and prehensile fingers with ridged digital pads and special tactile sensitivity (Martin 1990, 657–59). The peculiar ability of human newborns to support their own weight with the strength of their grasping hands, an ability quickly lost, is perhaps a vestige of life in the trees.

The reproductive system is centrally important in the evolutionary process, and here too we see changes across the primate series. The uterus of all prosimian females is divided into two sections (bicornuate). These have become fused into an undivided uterine compartment in all simians, a condition that is rare among other mammals. Presumably this change is related to the reduction in usual litter size from two or three in many prosimian species to a single offspring in nearly all living simians, excepting New World marmosets and tamarins, which commonly have twins. Some of the prosimian species have two or three pairs of teats, whereas all simian females have one pair. Menstruation is not found in lemurs or lorises, and occurs only weakly in tarsiers and New World monkeys, while it is easily detected in Old World monkeys and apes (Martin 1990, 439, 464). Copulation expands from the short, well-defined breeding seasons of prosimians to the year-round mating of apes and humans.

Among prosimians it is fairly common to keep infants in nests or tree holes. Nesting has disappeared from the repertoire of living monkeys (Kappeler 1998). All the great apes do make nests, but they use these for sleeping, not for depositing infants, and hastily construct a new one every night.

Figure 5.2. San Diego Zoo photos of, clockwise from upper left, a lemur (*Lemur catta*, ring-tailed lemur), a New World monkey (*Saimiri sciureus*, squirrel monkey), an ape (*Pan troglodytes*, chimpanzee), and an Old World monkey (*Macaca sylvana*, barbary macaque) (From the Zoological Society of San Diego).

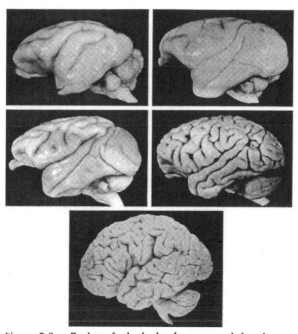

Figure 5.3. Brains of, clockwise from upper left, a lemur (*Lemur catta*, ring-tailed lemur), a New World monkey (*Saimiri sciureus*, squirrel monkey), an ape (*Pan troglodytes*, chimpanzee), a human, and an Old World monkey (*Macaca mulatta*, rhesus macaque); not to scale (From brainmuseum.org, supported by the National Science Foundation).

Possibly there is a common basis for the sleeping nests of apes and the human tendency to prepare sleeping sites, characteristically around hearths.

Primate females are attracted to infants, and mothers often allow other females to participate in "aunt" behavior, including cuddling and grooming the baby, even carrying it some distance from the mother. Aunting is known in New and Old World monkeys and among African apes (Jolly 1972; de Waal 1989).

There is a general prolongation in the stages of life across the primate series. The modal durations of gestation, infancy (until eruption of milk teeth), the juvenile period (until eruption of permanent teeth), and attainment of sexual maturity all increase, though with considerable variation in the major groupings (Martin 1990; Fleagle 1999; Nowak 1999). This lengthening of dependency and postponement of sexual independence is accompanied by more extensive and flexible socialization of the young.

The play behavior of chimpanzee and man is remarkably more complex than that of monkey, with man being the most manipulative and object oriented of all primates in his play. . . . The range of variation in play form and games among chimpanzees is second only to man. . . . When contrasted to chimpanzee play, in which object manipulation is a major feature, monkey play involves predominantly locomotor patterns such as wrestling and chasing with other young. . . . Little, if any, attention is directed to play with objects or to manipulation of many items in the environment. (Jay 1968, 501–502)

An exception to this generalization may be the New World capuchin monkey (*Cebus*), noted for its manipulation of nonfood objects (Moura and Lee 2004), but certainly there is an overall increase in the richness of play through the primate series. The rough-and-tumble chases of young monkeys look frenetic compared with lemur play, which Alison Jolly calls "slow-motion, almost stylized fumbling for each other" (1966, 59).

Intelligence, measured in several ways, becomes more humanlike as we advance through the primate series (Mithen 1996; Byrne 2001). Apes are more adept than monkeys at learning artificial sign "languages" and symbol systems invented by humans (Savage-Rumbaugh, Shanker, and Taylor 1998). The ability to recognize oneself in a mirror, an indicator of self-awareness, occurs in humans and great apes but not in monkeys or prosimians (Inoue-Nakamura 2001). Chimpanzees are like humans in several aspects of "social intelligence." They look into one another's eyes in an affectionate context, practice deception, allow others to take food, probably share food, and cooperate in various ways including hunting. Monkeys and prosimians do not show these behaviors (Matsuzawa 2001).

Monkey-level intellect is sufficient for the intergenerational passage of elementary cultural information. Fifty years ago, when primatologists provisioned a troop of Japanese macaques (*Macaca fuscata*) living by the ocean shore with sweet potatoes and wheat, the monkeys invented customs for eating the foods. Picking up wheat scattered on the beach was laborious. The macaques learned to carry handfuls of mixed sand and wheat into the sea. The sand sank, making it easy to eat the separated wheat. They "washed" sweet potatoes in seawater, perhaps imparting a salty flavor. These customs are still practiced in the troop (Hirata, Watanabe, and Kawai 2001).

It should not be surprising that apes have more elaborate cultures than monkeys, though without the symbolic elements of human cultures (van Schaik et al. 2003). Young chimpanzees, watching their mothers, learn to use tools, including prying with sticks, throwing stones, and wiping themselves with leaves. More impressively, they learn to *make* tools out of natural objects, such as chewing leaves to increase their effectiveness as sponges for sopping up drinking water (Takeshita and van Hooff 2001). They strip and trim twigs for use in catching termites, a favorite food. The chimp inserts the twig into a crevice containing the insects; the termites walk up the twig, and the chimp licks them off (McGrew 1992). Our common ancestor certainly had culture of comparable sophistication.

HUMAN NATURE

It is easy to exaggerate the smoothness of transitions across the primate series. By comparing modal tendencies among major taxa, we ignore occasionally striking exceptions to the basic pattern. Certain species are anomalous and best regarded as uniquely adapted. Owl monkeys, the only New World genus that is nocturnal, must be treated as an aberration from the general pattern of diurnal life in tropical American monkeys. The peculiarly asocial orangutan, acting more like a solitary foraging prosimian than an ape, is another anomaly that defies broader primate trends.

Unique adaptations aside, there are features of primate life that certainly do not develop continuously from prosimians to humans. Mating patterns, for example, show no simple trend (Kappeler and van Schaik 2002). By ignoring discontinuous transitions, we face the danger of circular reasoning, demonstrating continuity through the biased selection of smooth trends. While there is no way to totally avoid this problem, one precaution is to differentiate the sort of feature we expect to change continuously from the sort we do not. This can be done by concentrating on the elements of human nature.

By *human nature*, I mean the set of features that are reliably observed in any human group and are presumably based on an evolved neurophysiological substrate. Put differently, human nature is the normal repertoire of human behaviors resulting in large part from phylogenetic inertia.[3] We should expect most components of human nature, so defined, to emerge smoothly across the primate series.

Features that normally vary from one human society to another are excluded from human nature. Details of human demography, such as population size and age distribution, cannot reflect phylogenetic inertia because they vary so much from place to place and over time. Whether a society is matrilocal or patrilocal, the extent of its home range, the specific content of its culture—all these commonly vary across human groups, so we should not expect them to extrapolate smoothly from prosimians to humans.

The same is true of mating or "family" patterns, which may be invariant in nonhuman species but are diverse among humans. No doubt there is an evolved tendency for a mother and her young to compose a natural and fairly persistent social unit, but human families differ in the way they combine these units with mature males. The monogamous nuclear family idealized in American culture, and found among gibbons, comprises one mother-young unit and one male who is the father. The polygamous or "harem" arrangement of gorillas, also found among humans, combines several mother-young units with a single fully mature male. When the mother-young units have cordial relations with many males but no prolonged connection to a specific male, we obtain the sexual mixing of chimpanzee and bonobo societies, and the "serial monogamy" of some human settings. Among orangutans, contact between mature males and females is essentially limited to the solicitation and consummation of sexual intercourse, another pattern found among versatile humans. The possibilities for combination, as people have discovered, are nearly endless, indicating that in *Homo sapiens*, if not other species, they express environmental or cultural influences, not genetic predispositions.

Variability is, of course, the hallmark of human culture, but cultures are not infinitely variable. Certain universal features are present in all known societies, for example, athletic sports, body adornment, cleanliness training, cooking, courtship, dancing and music, decorative art, division of labor, games, greetings, joking, personal names, religion, sexual restrictions, shelters, tool making, and use of fire (Brown 1991). These universals need not be rooted in our genes or physiology. An arbitrary invention, perhaps religion or decorative art, created at a time when humans were few in number and localized, could have diffused through the population. Other inventions may have been sufficiently obvious and useful that they were invented repeatedly and became established in all human settlements. The universals that we may fairly attribute to our evolved biological nature are those that are common to primates, or at least appear rudimentarily in the primates most similar to humans.

DOMINANCE IN THE PRIMATE SERIES

Dominance hierarchies are a reliable feature of primate societies (Smuts et al. 1987; Muller and Wrangham 2001; Silk 2002). To avoid an overly simple picture of these structures, several qualifications are needed (Bernstein 1981). Status rank may be persistently relevant in species with fairly permanent groups, or only occasionally relevant for animals that forage alone. Rankings are usually but not necessarily transitive. The relative status of two individuals may depend, in part, on the proximity of allies. Sometimes the highest-ranking position is shared by a coalition of two or three animals. Groups vary in the degree to which rankings are apparent to human observers. It is often easier to identify a male ranking than a female ranking. Rankings are usually less clear in the wild than in captive colonies where animals are forced into close contact. Also, some species simply show less overt status behavior than others. Status ranking may become prominent only during the breeding season, as in squirrel monkeys (*Saimiri*) (Baldwin and Baldwin 1981). Given these qualifications, it is still clear that there is a general primate pattern of fairly consistent rank ordering with respect to influence, power, and valued prerogatives.

Among humans, face-to-face status (dominance) hierarchies have corollary features long recognized in classical sociology. Here I enumerate five corollaries and inquire if they are found among nonhuman primates, which would suggest an evolutionary basis.

1. *An individual's rank depends partly on extrinsic attributes that are not obvious prerequisites for status in the group.* Thus a person may have high status in the small group simply by virtue of being older, or male, or coming from a wealthy family. Berger, Cohen, and Zelditch (1972) call these "diffuse status characteristics." Sex and age are reliable status determinants in nonhuman primate groups too, but it seems inappropriate to consider them extrinsic attributes (as we do in humans) since they are clearly correlated with strength, size, experience, and perhaps relevant hormonal differences. More relevant is the tendency, known in several primate species, for an animal's status to be influenced if not fully determined by the rank of its mother. Subsequent alteration of the mother's rank affects the offspring's rank (e.g., de Waal and Lanting 1997; Nakamichi 2001). Broader family connections have similar influence. Troops of Old World monkeys such as baboons, macaques, and vervets are composed of different matrilineal families, each arranged in a stable, linear dominance hierarchy. All females of one matriline outrank all females of another. Female baboons (*Papio hamadryas ursinus*) recognize that a reversal in the status of two matrilines affects their own status (Bergman et al. 2003).

2. *Over the long run, members interact more with others of similar rank ("near-peers") than with members of dissimilar rank* (Homans 1961). This preference for near-peers has not been explicitly studied in animals, but three kinds of incidental observation suggest that it may apply broadly to simian primates. First, interaction usually occurs within sex-age categories (excepting sexual and mother-offspring relations). Since males usually dominate females, and adults dominate juveniles, the effect is to concentrate interaction among near-peers. Second, there are many reports that adults join same-sex coalitions, thereby raising their status higher than they could apparently achieve acting independently. For example, in macaque and baboon troops there is often a central group of males who together dominate all others. Some troops of Old World monkeys contain two or more ranked matrilines where all female members of one matriline outrank or are outranked by all female members of another (Bergman et al. 2003). Chimpanzees form coalitions too, their decisions to give or withdraw support seemingly calculated to earn the rewards of enhanced status (de Waal 1989). "Stable coalitions are characterized by high levels of association between the partners. This means that when one of the pair is in trouble, his ally often happens to be present and thus able to help. Moreover, the very fact that

they are together often inhibits aggression from other males" (Goodall 1986, 419). Third, the accounts occasionally published of pair-wise interactions among troop members (for squirrel monkeys, macaques, and chimpanzees) show more interaction with near-peers than would be expected by chance (Mazur 1973a; also see de Waal 1989, 76, 185). This tendency is not definitely established but clearly deserves more study.

3. *High-ranked members—particularly the leader—perform service and control functions for other members and for the group as a whole.* Leaders of baboon and macaque troops are in the forefront during intertroop combat or in defense against a predator. When a dispute breaks out between troop members, the leader may stop it with a threat, and he protects a mother with an infant who is threatened by another animal.

> High-ranking chimpanzees sometimes adopt a control role, breaking up fights or systematically protecting the weak against the strong. . . . At other times they intervene peacefully or try to calm down one of the participants. . . . In species in which large males defend units of several females, such as Chinese golden monkeys (*Rhinopithecus roxellanae*), the leading male may maintain harmony by interposing himself between female contestants while holding their hands, and stroking or grooming both of them. (de Waal 2000, 589)

4. *Low-ranked members appear more nervous than higher-ranked members; high-ranked members can manipulate the stress experienced by, and thereby the performance of, low-ranked members* (Björkqvist 2001). Early accounts of macaque behavior often describe low-ranking individuals as "nervous, insecure" or "cowering" (e.g., Southwick 1963). Bartlett and Meier trained the members of a rhesus macaque colony to press a bar to obtain fruit. "The more dominant animals seems more 'relaxed' as they bar-pressed, often stopping to eat as the fruit was dispensed, whereas the less dominant animals ate as they pressed the bar and continually glanced around the room as if 'watching out' for the entrance of a more dominant animal" (1971, 217). Low-ranked animals seem more withdrawn and fearful, defecating and urinating more than other members of the group (Peretti and Lewis 1969).

Often after a tension-inducing episode, apes and monkeys "reconcile" by hugging, patting, or grooming to restore calm. The ability of a dominant animal to raise and lower the level of stress is illustrated by Yeroen, the alpha male in a chimpanzee colony at the Arnhem Zoo in the Netherlands.

> In his heyday he would charge straight at a dozen apes, his hair on end, and scatter them in all directions. None of the apes dared to remain seated when Yeroen approached stamping his feet rhythmically. Long before he reached them they would be up, the mothers with their children on their backs or under their bellies, ready to make a quick getaway. Then the air would be filled with the sound of screaming and barking as the apes fled in panic. Sometimes this would be accompanied by blows.

Then, as suddenly as the din had begun, peace would return. Yeroen would seat himself and the other apes would hasten to pay their respects to him. . . . After these "formalities" everyone sat down quietly again, the children wandered away from their mothers and Yeroen relaxed and allowed himself to be groomed. (de Waal 1989, 86)

Such bombastic displays are infrequent among apes. Usually when relative status must be acknowledged, a submissive greeting is adequate. The subordinate animal may lower himself and make short, panting grunts while looking upward at the dominant animal. The greeter may repeatedly bow and sometimes brings objects like a leaf or stick, stretching out a hand to the superior or kissing his neck, chest, or feet. The dominant chimp reacts by stretching himself to full height with his hair standing on end, producing a contrast in the apparent volume of the two apes, even if they are really the same size.

The one almost grovels in the dust, the other regally receives the "greeting." Among adult males this giant/dwarf relationship can be still further accentuated by histrionics such as the dominant ape stepping or leaping over the "greeter." . . . At the same time the submissive ape ducks and puts his arms up to protect his head. This kind of stuntwork is less common in relation to female "greeters." The female usually presents her backside to the dominant ape to be inspected and sniffed. (de Waal 1989, 88)

These deferential gestures avoid or alleviate the tensions that accompany the assertion of dominance.

5. *Humans usually establish and maintain status rank without physical fights, aggressive threats, or overt gestures of submission.* Displays of dominance must be viewed within the broader context of communication. Lower primates are limited, repetitive, and stereotypic in their displays; higher primates are more flexible, using diverse and novel forms of expression.

Prosimians and New World monkeys emit secretions from specialized scent glands to produce primitive olfactory signals.

Ringtailed lemurs have a stylized threat display, in which the male draws his ringed tail through the forearm glands, then shivers it over his head at his opponent like an outraged feather duster. Wild sifakas mark branches with throat glands or urine in the course of territorial conflict. Slow and slender lorises use brachial glands in defense and urine marking both as a territorial sign and in orientation. New World monkeys, such as spider and cebus and woolly monkeys, rub their chest glands on branches and sniff each other's chest glands. Both the lorisoid prosimians and the New World night monkey, squirrel monkey, and cebus mark by dribbling urine onto a cupped hand, then rubbing the hand on the foot of the same side, and finally scrubbing the foot on the branch. This urine-washing sequence is so similar in form and timing among all these animals that it may well be inherited from a common ancestor. (Jolly 1972, 149)

Lemurs have no subtlety in their expressions of dominance, depending on threat, chase, and physical attack, sometimes tearing out fur. Squirrel monkeys assert dominance through chasing, assault, and a stylized penile display. If food is placed between a pair of squirrel monkeys, both go for it and one may steal it from the other. This contrasts with the placement of food between a pair of baboons or macaques, where both animals usually behave as if the food belonged to the dominant of the pair, who picks it up while the subordinate averts his eyes (DeVore 1965). Status differences among baboons and macaques are based on deference as well as dominance. Still, there is considerable overt aggression among competitive monkeys, with frequent resort to overt threat and physical attack.

Apes are capable of violent dominance displays, but these are infrequent. Jane Goodall and her associates, during the years 1976–1979 of their long-running study of the large chimpanzee community at Gombe, observed between 92 and 127 instances *per year* of aggressive attacks—usually hits and pushes, or quick kicks, delivered in passing. Each year, in 15 to 20 of these attacks the violence lasted over half a minute, and serious injuries were inflicted in about a quarter of these prolonged episodes (Goodall 1986, 317).

Violence is an exception to the chimpanzees' usually peaceful behavior. When Goodall began her studies, she found the chimps so uncompetitive that she could not discern their dominance relationships.

> However, when regular observations became possible on the interactions between the various individuals it gradually became evident that the social status of each chimpanzee was fairly well defined in relation to each other individual. In other words, it was often possible to predict, when for example two chimpanzees met on a narrow branch, which animal would gain the right of way; that animal could then be described as the dominant one of the two. (Van Lawick-Goodall 1968, 315)

Commenting on the unassertiveness of female apes, compared to monkeys, Frans de Waal notes,

> Intensive observation of a smallish group of captive macaques will reveal the female hierarchy in only a few days. In the case of our chimpanzees we have to allow many months to arrive at the same conclusions. . . . The female hierarchy in our chimpanzee group seems to be based on respect from below rather than intimidation and a show of strength from above. . . . As among females of other great ape species, acceptance of dominance is probably more important than proving dominance. For example, when orangutan females are placed in a cage together for the first time they immediately, without the least hesitation, establish a stable dominance pattern, without fighting or threatening in any way. (1989, 185–186)

Chimpanzees can be murderous, especially toward out-group individuals, but they are usually tolerant of their own group members, rarely fighting over food and occasionally sharing it (Nishida 1970; Teleki 1973). Gorillas are similar to chimps in deference and tolerance except that they have not been observed to share food. Dominant gorillas often do not assert their rank (Schaller 1993). Bonobos seem even more tolerant and perhaps are second only to humans in the civility of their normal status interactions (de Waal and Lanting 1997).

CONCLUSIONS

Some behaviors that are found reliably across human societies reflect a broader primate pattern. Either they are traceable throughout the primate series, or they appear in rudimentary form as we approach humankind. The prehuman emergence of these universals suggests that they are evolved features of human nature, having proximate causes in our brains and hormones.

Of the three kinds of status structure commonly found in agrarian and industrial societies (chapter 2), only small-group dominance hierarchies are part of the primate pattern. The expression of dominance and deference, as an evolved feature of human nature, must be affected by underlying neurophysiological mechanisms, which I examine in later chapters.

There are corollaries to the basic status ordering. The allocation of rankings in a small group inevitably reflects extrinsic characteristics that are not obvious prerequisites for status. Members interact preferentially with near-peers. Leaders perform service and control functions for other members and for the group as a whole, directing relations with other groups and defense against threats to the membership. Social control within the group, including the allocation of status, is achieved partly by high-ranked members manipulating the stress of low-ranked members. Among humans and apes, though not among all primates, status is normally allocated without overt aggression or serious disruption.

In the next chapters I look more closely at these corollaries, particularly the manipulation of stress to achieve or maintain high rank, and the subtle allocation of status, which often is based on seemingly irrelevant extrinsic signs.

NOTES

1. The stated numbers of genera and species are approximate because there are disagreements over classification, and new species continue to be discovered.

2. Rather than speaking of prosimians and simians [or anthropoids], some taxonomists divide modern primates into two monophyletic suborders, the Strepsirhini
[lemurs and lorises] and the Haplorhini [tarsiers, monkeys, apes, and humans]. This
shift in the position of tarsiers does not affect the present discussion.

3. One may observe rare or manifestly abnormal exceptions to any evolved tendency. Even physical attributes can be overridden by sufficiently countervailing environmental influences like the binding of "lily feet" in traditional China, the use of
rings in Africa to lengthen the neck, terrible birth defects produced by thalidomide,
various cosmetic surgeries, circumcision, and so on.

6

Status Signs

Every individual has certain observable *signs* (or *signals*—I use the terms inter-changeably) that suggest his or her social status is (or ought to be) high or low. Those displaying high-status signs are not guaranteed to hold correspondingly high rank in their group's status hierarchy, but if we know an individual's signs we can make a better than random guess about their actual status.

Some status signs are limited to a particular species, such as the silver hair on the back of a dominant male gorilla. Others are similar across primate species. For example, large size, physical strength, vigor, good health, being adult (vs. being juvenile), being male, and (among the higher primate species) having a high-ranked mother are all signs associated with high status, while their opposites suggest low status. Moving through the primate series from prosimians, through monkeys, to apes with their protocultures, and finally to humans with full cultures, the range of status signs becomes larger, more flexible, and more arbitrary. Wearing expensive and fashionable clothing is a signal of high status among humans. A beautiful wife, desirable to other men, or one with a rich dowry, gives prestige to her husband; a rich or powerful husband or protector elevates a woman's rank.

Among humans, the social position one holds in the larger society—perhaps as a representative of "legitimate" or "official" authority, or by virtue of occupation, wealth, education, family lineage, or race—carries over into face-to-face interaction, although it may have no relevance to that context (Berger, Cohen, and Zelditch 1972). A surgeon and a carpenter, meeting casually outside their professional roles, are likely to rank themselves so that the carpenter defers to the surgeon, even though medical skills are irrelevant to the situation. A famous person, like a visibly wealthy one, can usually dominate an intimate social gathering.

CONSTANT AND CONTROLLABLE SIGNS

It is useful to divide status signs into two categories: *constant* signals that individuals display persistently whether they want to or not, and *controllable* signals that individuals can quickly change by their own (conscious or unconscious) efforts.

Among the constant status signs found in most human cultures are gender, family name, and clan or ethnic markers. Such factors, when inherited, can bias the assignment of whole classes of people toward high- or low-status positions, reinforcing inequality from one generation to another. Reputation is another fairly constant status sign for humans, and also for nonhuman primates, with individuals known to have held high (or low) rank in the past assumed to hold similar rank at present. That is why humans with prestigious reputations purposively enhance and prolong their signs of eminence. Ruling families often fortify their legacy by constructing impressive architecture that communicates through the centuries the stature of their dynasties (Tinniswood 1998).

Among controllable status signs are the various gestures and actions that an individual can change rapidly to convey the impression of being either a dominant person of high status or a deferent person of low status (Guthrie 1976; Weisfeld and Beresford 1982; Weisfeld and Linkey 1985). These may be physical threats or submissive cowering, erect or stooped posture, direct stare or eye aversion, advancing on someone or retreating, relaxed and confident demeanor or nervous fidgeting, growling or grinning (or crying). Among humans, language carries many of these controllable signals either in tone (command vs. request), semantic content ("I came, I saw, I conquered" vs. "I am the dust beneath your feet"), or nonverbal gestures that accompany speech. Items of dress, cosmetics, and accessories also serve humans as controllable status signs. Another status signal is "conspicuous consumption," to use Thorstein Veblen's (1902) term, intended to display the consumer's preeminence, whether by shopping at Cartier's or by the gifting at potlatches once popular among Indians of the Pacific Northwest.

My separation of status signs into *constant* and *controllable* signals is one of convenience, not of inevitability. We can conjure instances when normally fixed status signs are changed, even reversed. This is a familiar theme of classic literature including *Cinderella, The Prince and the Pauper*, and much Shakespearean comedy. Some status signs are neither constant nor fleeting, but of middle duration, such as the furnishings of an executive suite, ownership of an expensive automobile, or the address of one's residence or vacation home. Nonetheless, it is heuristically useful to retain the constant/controllable dichotomy, as we see in examining the face, our most personal sign of status.

FACES

Physiognomy, in its modern sense, is the study of our face and facial expressions and how they affect our social relationships. It must not be confused with discredited claims a century ago that personal traits and mental capacity can be read in one's face. Perhaps overreacting to this pseudo-science, social scientists usually regard people as if they were disembodied actors (for exceptions see Goffman 1963; Glassner 1988). This is despite the well-established fact that beautiful men and women have considerably different life experiences than those who are plain (Berscheid and Walster 1974; Patzer 1985; Hatfield and Sprecher 1986; Cameron et al. 2001).

The face is the most distinctive feature of the human body. As early hominids evolved into modern people, the mouth-containing muzzle receded, and the heavy brow ridge became thinner. The previously sloped forehead became vertical, rising to accommodate an expanding brain. Most recently, the chin developed as a downward projection of the lower jaw, a unique feature of modern humans lacking even in Neanderthals. The combined effect of these changes is the relatively flat and vertical face of modern humans, unlike those of living apes or our dead ancestors. Narrowly spaced nasal holes, common in other Old World primates, are encased in our jutting nose, forming a conspicuous prominence among our otherwise flattened features (McNeill 1998).

We take for granted our ability to remember the faces of an enormous number of people we have met during our lives, enabling us to identify in old photos or chance encounters someone not seen for years, and whom we may have known only briefly. We may forget people's names and nearly everything about them, but their faces ring a bell of recognition, even though aged and surrounded by new hairstyles. This recognition is a gestalt matter, a response to the whole aspect rather than its individual parts. Using general impressions, we fairly accurately distinguish male and female faces, unaware of any one telltale clue. (Numerous facial features are modally different in men and women, but none is definitive [Brown and Perrett 1993].) Usually facial details are unimportant in themselves. Most of us cannot tell a portrait artist how to accurately draw our loved ones because we do not attend closely to specific features of their faces. Yet, strangely, the caricaturist's exaggeration of certain details allows us to identify famous personalities better than we can from accurate portraits (Benson and Perrett 1994).

So accepted is our skill at recognizing faces that eyewitness identification of criminal suspects in a police lineup or at trial is sometimes regarded as the gold standard for implicating evidence. In fact, eyewitness identification is surprisingly inaccurate, especially when the witness's exposure to the perpetrator is fleeting and the circumstances distracting, and when testimony comes a long time after the crime was committed (Loftus and Doyle 1997).

Eyes are the most arresting parts of the face, eliciting more attention from an observer than any other feature. Poetic allusions to these "windows to the soul" emphasize their importance when one person sizes up another. About one-sixth of the eyeball is visible to an observer, and in humans, white surrounds the iris and pupil, making it easy to detect the direction of gaze. The iris enlarges or contracts the pupil, depending on availability of light. Men's pupils dilate when they look at salacious photographs; women's dilate when they look at babies or male nudes. Surprise, joy, and anxiety expand the pupils; boredom and sleepiness contract them. Men judge female faces more attractive when the women's pupils are enlarged than when contracted (Hess 1975).

Eyes are the most potent vehicle for nonverbal communication. The act of staring or gazing at another person can take a variety of meanings depending on how the person staring and the recipient of the stare define the situation. The stare is interpreted as an assertive gesture in a wide range of cultures; however, there are situations in which gazing at another person is likely to be taken as a sign of close bonding or as a request for aid (Watson 1970).

The mouth is the oldest part of the face, present in all chordates as the entryway for food, water, and sometimes air. The mouth with its freely moving lips, along with the eyes and eyebrows, makes the human face exquisitely malleable, producing barely perceptible nuances of expression. The human mouth is narrower than in other animals, usually running no more than the distance between pupils. It is the most plastic feature of the face, crucial for visual signals of emotion—supplemented sometimes by visible teeth or tongue. Essential for the sounds of speech, the lips and mouth also create visible articulation, so it is easier to understand speakers when we watch their lips than when we hear them blindly. The nerve-packed lips encourage kissing, important for social cohesion in chimpanzees and humans.

There are numerous speculations why our noses project outward from the face, and why modern humans have a chin. Whatever the cause, one effect is to add variety to the face, allowing one person to look distinctly different from another. Leonardo Da Vinci claimed there are sixty-four types of nose, as seen from the front, derived from six nasal characteristics: tip (broad or narrow), base (broad or narrow), middle (thick or thin), nostrils (broad or narrow), nostrils (high or low), and openings (visible or hidden), with intermediate qualities allowing many more subtypes (Bambach 2003). Also the chin shows diverse shapes and sizes, apparently without affecting mechanical function—if it has a function beyond visual signaling.

Overall, this package—our face—is admirably suited as both a communication device and an identity label. It should not be surprising that our brain is especially good at recognizing faces and facial expressions. The "fusiform face area," located at the bottom of the neocortex, is maximally active when experimental subjects see human faces as opposed to other stimuli. People with lesions to this area have impaired facial recognition, a condition called prosopagnosia (Cohen and Tong 2001; Barton et al. 2002; Cox, Meyers, and Sinha 2004). Facial expressions showing basic emotions—fear, sadness, anger, happiness, disgust—activate specific but somewhat different areas of the neocortex (Morris et al. 1996; Phillips et al. 1997; Blair et al. 1999; Canli et al. 2002).

FACIAL DOMINANCE

Figure 6.1 shows artist John Hyatt's rendition of two facial displays, one dominant, the other deferent. No one has trouble deciding which is which, though neither display is a pure sign. The dominant face additionally signals menace and anger. The deferent face seems vacantly happy in its submissiveness—an Alfred E. Neumann without buckteeth. (As a mental exercise, visualize expressions of happy dominance and angry deference.)

My distinction between constant and controllable signs is pertinent here. Comparing the temporary expressions on these faces, we see dominance signaled with directly glaring and narrowed eyes beneath lowered brows, taut facial muscles, flared nostrils, and visibly clinched teeth. In contrast, the deferent expression has relaxed musculature, eyes wide open and averted, eyebrows raised, and lips smiling. If these were live faces, their expressions could be reversed in a moment, but doing so would not fully transpose the

Figure 6.1. **John Hyatt's renderings of dominant and submissive faces (Guthrie 1973).**

displays because these faces differ as well in constant features that signal dominance or deference. The left face is bearded, suggesting—though we cannot see it—a square jaw; the face is vertically elongated with rugged, muscular features including a strong brow ridge emphasized by heavy eyebrows; the skin seems coarse. The right face is round, soft, smooth, with pudgy cheeks, perhaps fittingly termed "babyfaced" (Collins and Zebrowitz 1995; Zebrowitz, Olson, and Hoffman 1993). Even with neutral expressions, the constant features of one face convey a more dominant aspect than those of the other.

Our flexibly expressive eyes, brows, and mouth are the critical features for quickly altering visible demeanor, and their manipulation can blatantly or subtly change the meaning read into a facial signal. This was shown in a study of American college students who were instructed, "A dominant person usually tells other people what to do and usually is respected. A dominant person seldom submits to others." The students were then shown pairs of portraits and asked to judge which portrait in each pair showed the most dominant person. Actually, the models for these portraits were posed twice, either with differing eyebrow positions (raised or lowered) or with differing mouth positions (smiling or neutral). This design allowed a comparison of how the same models were perceived when showing different brow or mouth positions. Models were more often judged dominant when their eyebrows were lowered than raised, and when they were posed with neutral mouths rather than smiling mouths (Keating, Mazur, and Segall 1977). American readers easily see these perceptual differences in cartoon faces (Figure 6.2). But do people in different cultures read the same meanings into them?

Psychologist Caroline Keating conducted a cross-cultural test of these brow and mouth effects. Respondents in eleven cultures around the world made dominance judgments about nineteen portrait pairs, each pair showing models in contrasting brow and mouth positions. In every culture, respondents judged models less dominant when posed with a smile than when posed with a neutral mouth. Thus the smile seems a universal signal of deference in humans, perhaps homologous to the submissive "grin" of monkeys and apes (Chevalier-Skolnikoff 1973), and consistent with the tendency of people to smile as a signal of appeasement (Goldenthal, Johnston, and Kraut 1981).

Figure 6.2.   Dominant versus submissive cartoon faces.

However, Keating found no universality in the meaning given brow position. Her respondents in North America, Europe, and the Canary Islands saw lowered brows as a sign of dominance compared with raised brows, as expected, but respondents in South America, Africa, and Thailand saw little or no difference in the brow positions. Apparently the brow signal is limited to relatively Western cultures, though it is difficult to guess why that is so (Keating, Mazur, and Segall 1981; Keating et al. 1981).

A serendipitous result from this study shifts our attention back to constant signs in the face. Keating noticed that respondents from diverse cultures usually agreed on which models were most dominant looking—independent of their brow or mouth positions—and which models looked nondominant. A face judged dominant in one culture is similarly judged in other cultures. Apparently there are universal perceptions of dominant and deferent faces.

This finding immediately posed a new question: Do the dominant-looking people of the world have discernibly different life experiences from those who look submissive? Perhaps they have an advantage moving up status hierarchies, at least in societies where mobility is possible. If we followed the careers of members of a university graduating class, would we see those with dominant faces advancing further and faster than their deferent-looking classmates? Such research is complicated because graduates pick dissimilar careers with incommensurate goals (one a lawyer, one a journalist, another a musician). And they leave school with unequal assets and debts, different family connections, and diverse interests and training, so we cannot easily tell if face per se has any net effect on career attainment.

Ulrich Mueller and I avoided some of these difficulties by studying cadets who graduated in 1950 from the U.S. Military Academy at West Point, which then prepared officers for both the army and the air force. Selective entry into the academy and then four years of schooling (with high attrition) produced a relatively homogeneous class of physically fit men, similarly trained, and following similar careers. In many ways their background differences had been erased. West Point's socialization practices, still including hazing at that time, foster an unusual amount of social leveling among cadets of diverse family and regional background. The government is another equalizer, paying all education and career expenses. Graduates remaining in service beyond the obligatory period have more or less the same goals for advancement, pursuing well-defined promotions. As uniformed officers they usually work, and with their wives socialize, in circumscribed military communities, again minimizing prior social differences. Indeed, there was virtually no effect of regional or family background, even of having a father of high military rank, on a graduate's career advancement (Mazur, Mazur, and Keating 1984; Mazur and Mueller 1996a, 1996b; Mueller and Mazur 1996, 1997). Under these special circumstances, it is easy to trace any effect of facial appearance on rank attainment.

MILITARY RANK ATTAINMENT

The U.S. Army and Air Force are two of many formal organizational hierarchies that are characterized as meritocracies, where career advancement is supposed to be determined mostly by one's ability to achieve institutional goals. Critics have long claimed, however, that promotion in a meritocracy is inevitably affected by factors separate from competence. Moore and Trout (1978) contrast "performance theory," which says that promotion in the military goes to those who perform best, with their preferred "visibility theory," which stresses the importance of being seen and known and of having contacts with peers and mentors who can influence one's upward mobility.

The most salient aspect of visibility is literally how one looks. Journalist Rick Atkinson writes of the "lantern jaw and chiseled features prized in military officers" (1989). Lucian Truscott IV, a West Point graduate later turned novelist, describes a fictitious first captain at the academy:

> He had one of those young Gregory Peck faces, the dark handsome good looks of a born general. It had always seemed there was an unwritten requirement that first captains and other high-ranking cadets be attractive . . . not just good looking, but . . . idols. Statues to the American ideal of *cadet* . . . At 6'1", 185 pounds, a letterman in soccer and lacrosse, he was the ideal first captain. There was a certain awkwardness—intimidation—in his presence. (Truscott 1978, 414).

To see if looks really influence promotion, we measured facial dominance in a crude but serviceable way. West Point has a yearbook, the *Howitzer*, and like other college yearbooks of the time, it carried graduation portraits in a uniform format using a small number of stereotyped poses. These were shown to judges who independently rated faces on a seven-point scale of dominance-submissiveness (1 = very submissive, 7 = very dominant). Median scores ranged from 2 (moderately submissive) to 6 (moderately dominant), with a median value of 4 (neutral). Figure 6.3 shows four cadets of varying facial dominance, and formal portraits of the same men after all had achieved the rank of general.[1]

The Class of 1950 entered West Point as formally undifferentiated plebes. The first time they were given ranks was in junior year when nearly half were elevated to corporal, the rest remaining privates. As seniors they were ranked again, with one-quarter of the class named cadet officers and the rest sergeants.

At graduation everyone received the rank of second lieutenant, and most entered one of the army's several branches (e.g., infantry, engineers) while 25 percent went into the air force. About half participated in the Korean War, which began only weeks after graduation, and most of the others joined the Cold War in Europe. Within three years, 8 percent of the classmen were dead. By 1956, 17 percent of the class had resigned, and by 1964 another 5

Figure 6.3. Men of varying facial dominance who became high-ranked generals, shown as cadets and in late career. From left: Wallace Nutting (facial dominance score as cadet = 6), Charles Gabriel (5), John Wickham Jr. (4), and Lincoln Faurer (3). Cadet portraits are from the West Point yearbook, *The Howitzer 1950;* officer portraits are from Pentagon archives.

percent had done so, for various reasons including attractive jobs outside the military, family considerations, and dissatisfaction with a military career. Nearly all who remained in the military through the 1950s stayed for twenty years (or more) in order to retire with benefits.

Promotion of young officers is nearly automatic through the rank of captain, being determined primarily by amount of time served, although more rapid advance can come in wartime situations such as Korea. Most young officers earn advanced degrees and seek a variety of assignments in command and staff positions, and in combat zones if there is a war, obtaining broad experience that is considered necessary for the highest ranks. Early promotion to major is regarded as an indication of special merit. The sorting of men begins early, separating those who will reach the top from those who will not, as occurs in many other occupational hierarchies.

By 1963, nearly everyone remaining on active duty had been promoted to major. During the early 1960s, roughly three-quarters of these men were invited to spend an academic year at the army's Command and General Staff College to receive training at the level of battalion command or division staff. This was a critical branch point because men who did not attend staff college were almost certain to advance no higher than lieutenant colonel.

Graduation from a staff college is an essential but not sufficient requirement for an invitation to a war college, the second crucial branch point. Less
than half of the graduates from staff college were admitted to war college,
usually during the late 1960s, to receive training at the level of division command. All war college graduates reached the rank of colonel. More importantly, since World War II, no one has become a general officer without first
graduating from war college.

Many of the classmen served in Southeast Asia during the Vietnam War,
but only seven were killed, reflecting the relative safety of their higher ranks.
Nearly everyone in the class who remained in the military had been promoted at least to lieutenant colonel by 1970, the first year in which they were
eligible for retirement with benefits. Many lieutenant colonels retired in 1970
or soon afterward, some because of attractive opportunities outside the military and others because they had twice been passed over for promotion.

Of the graduates of 1950, 8 percent became generals, making them by this
measure one of the most successful of modern-day West Point classes. Most
of these generals remained on active duty into the 1980s, filling the highest
ranks of the American military. All had retired by 1987.

It is convenient to envision military careers as a set of "channels" running
through the promotion system (Figure 6.4). The least successful officers

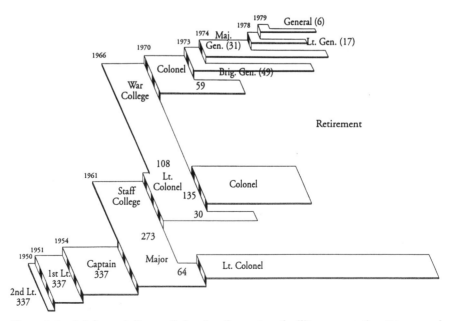

**Figure 6.4. A "channel diagram" showing the routes of military promotion (Mazur and
Mueller 1996a).**

flowed through the "nearest" channel toward retirement as lieutenant colonels, a relatively low rank for a West Point graduate. Others were shunted into higher channels via the two critical branch points: (1) whether one attends military staff college, and (2) whether one attends war college. These are shown as "left turns" in the channel diagram. Unless an officer passes through these shunts, upward mobility is unlikely.

Did looks affect promotion? At West Point they did. In junior year, cadets with the most dominant-looking faces were twice as likely to make corporal as those with the least dominant-looking faces. In senior year the promotion rate of the most dominant-looking men was five times that of their least dominant-looking classmates. (Varsity athletes also had a great advantage in these promotions.)

Out of West Point, the dynamics of rank attainment changed. Facial dominance did not predict promotion to major or lieutenant colonel, or selection to staff or war colleges, nor did it predict the rapidity of these advancements. What did count was the rate of advance; some men were on a fast track, racing through successive promotions ahead of their classmates, but these men did not have especially dominant faces. Promotions in midcareer are decided impersonally by boards of officers who do not know the candidates but look at their dossiers.

Colonels who entered war college before 1971 make up the pool from which the four grades of general are drawn. Nearly everyone who reaches this stage has an excellent record, so personnel files do not differentiate very well. The pool is relatively small, about 108 men for the Class of 1950. At this level in the hierarchy, someone on the promotion board almost certainly knows each candidate personally and would have heard of others by reputation or through advice from mentors and colleagues. Promotions at this stage are similar to the selection of cadet officers back at West Point in the sense that those making the selection know the men as individuals rather than from paper records. Therefore, it is not surprising that the criteria for selection to the highest ranks are again highly personal, including whether the man *looks* like a leader, and whether he was a star athlete at the academy. (Of the football lettermen who remained in the military, 58 percent became generals, compared with 13 percent of their classmates.) For war college graduates, the number of promotions beyond colonel increased with facial dominance (Figure 6.5).

POWERFUL FACES

Considering that cadet faces were rated by strangers looking quickly at yearbook portraits, it is remarkable that these scores predict promotions made twenty or more years after the portraits were taken. Surely a fuller and more

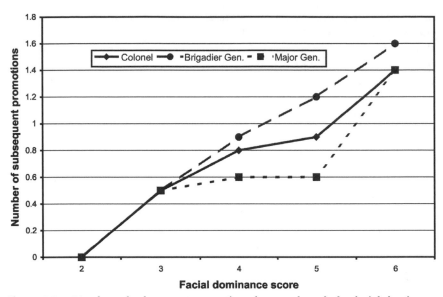

Figure 6.5. **Number of subsequent promotions from each rank, by facial dominance (war college graduates only, Mueller and Mazur 1996).**

contemporaneous evaluation of dominant appearance, including not only one's face but one's body, one's postures and gestures, and one's voice, would predict more strongly the decisions of promotions boards.

A question that inevitably arises is, what do dominant faces look like? Everyone knows because anyone can sort portraits on that basis, but facial dominance is a gestalt concept, difficult to describe in simple terms. Dominant faces often seem muscular, with prominent as opposed to weak chins, and with heavy brow ridges and deep-set eyes. Submissive faces are often round or narrow, with ears "sticking out," while dominant faces are oval or rectangular with close-set ears. Faces identified as dominant are more likely to be handsome than not, though with striking exceptions. Many rate Arnold Schwarzenegger's face as dominant but not handsome, and Hugh Grant's face as handsome but not dominant.

Faces change with age, often losing some of their earlier perceived potency (Zebrowitz, Olson, and Hoffman 1993). Thirty men from the Class of 1950 provided portraits taken in middle age. Dominance ratings of these pictures were lower than the scores the same men had received when evaluated as cadets. However, their *relative* dominance rankings were moderately persistent (r = .36, p = .05; Mazur and Mueller 1996).

My exploration of the face in this chapter relies heavily on rank attainment in a formal organization. Before I take up status signs in informal dominance hierarchies, it is worth looking at an unusual and impressive example from another formally organized status structure.

For Romania's 1996 presidential election, sixteen official candidates competed for votes during the first round of voting. The formerly Communist nation had no tradition of free elections, and these candidates were largely unknown to the public. On the last day of campaigning, the candidates participated in a nationally televised debate. All were white males ranging in age from their forties though their sixties and were similarly dressed.

James Schubert and his colleagues (1997) showed short video segments from the debate to Americans who did not speak Romanian and knew nothing of the parties or issues in the election. Based on this superficial exposure to each candidate's visual appearance and unintelligible speech, the Americans scored each man on multiple scales of electability—with remarkable accuracy! American ratings of the candidates, and the number of votes each received from the Romanian electorate, correlated at r = .6. In American presidential elections too, most notably in televised debates, the visual and personal impressions conveyed by candidates may be as important as their party identification or their stand on the issues in determining a winner (Masters and Way 1996).

NOTE

1. Students rated these portraits for dominance when they were projected in front of college classes. A dominant person was defined as someone who tells other people what to do, is respected, influential, and often a leader; submissive or subordinate people are not influential or assertive and are usually directed by others. On 85 percent of the rated portraits, at least half the judges' choices fell within two adjacent scale points, indicating more clustering than would be expected if choices were uniformly distributed across the seven-point scale. Additional information about the cadets was collected from public records of promotion and by a questionnaire mailed in 1990 to men from the class for whom recent addresses were available. Of 416 classmen who served twenty or more years in the military, complete data were obtained on 337 (81 percent), including virtually all the generals.

7

Allocating Ranks

Dominance hierarchies, once set, are fairly stable. But when a new group forms, there must be an initial allocation of ranks, and in established groups some individuals occasionally alter their positions. How are these initial rankings, and later changes in rank, determined? The short answer is that ranks are allocated either *cooperatively*, by consensus of those involved, or *competitively*, when there is disagreement over who should be superior.

Primate species vary in the degree to which they allocate ranks competitively. Among the prosimians, as well as baboons and macaques, rank allocation within newly formed groups, and changes of rank within established groups, are usually accompanied by overt conflict that produces a victor and vanquished. Among apes and humans, rank allocation is often cooperative, and when there is competition it usually stops short of physical attack.

COOPERATIVE RANKING

We may explore the decision to compete or cooperate by visualizing two individuals (Ego and Alter) meeting for the first time. If their interaction is very brief or casual, the notion of ranking may never arise. In more extended or serious meetings, each appraises the status signs of the other, forming some idea of their relative standings. If Ego perceives that Alter's status signs exceed his own, he may defer to Alter without any dispute. In the American court system, for example, when jury members elect a foreman, they favor men with prestigious occupations, although sex and occupation are irrelevant to the foreman's task (Strodtbeck, James, and Hawkins 1957). Ego, in explaining such concessions, may offer that Alter *belongs* in the higher rank,

79

or that Alter *deserves* it, or that Alter *could easily take* it if Ego resisted, or that Alter will be more *competent* in the duties of high rank.

Even when no obvious status signs distinguish participants from each other in a newly formed group, they still tend to stratify cooperatively and often very quickly. In a study by Fisek and Ofshe (1970), fifty-nine discussion groups were formed, each comprising three unacquainted college students undifferentiated by sex, age, or race. Within the first minute of conversation, half these groups formed a hierarchy that lasted for the duration of the discussion. This was a surprising finding when first reported because sociologists did not recognize that barely perceptible status signs, like those emanating from the face, convey ranking information as effective as blatant markers like sex and occupation.

The signaling capability of an eye glance is demonstrated with the following experiment devised by Strongman and Champness (1968). Start with three unacquainted subjects. Taking two at a time, there are three possible pairs. Seat each pair of subjects at a table so they are face-to-face but with a screen blocking their view of each other. Remove the screen, telling subjects to get to know one another. Typically, as the screen is removed, the pair makes eye contact. One person holds the glance longer than the other, and we describe this person as "out-glancing" the other. Repeat the procedure for the other two pairs. A transitive ordering occurs if one person out-glances the other two, one person out-glances one but is out-glanced by another, and one person is out-glanced by two others. Strongman and Champness found a nearly transitive eye-glance hierarchy among ten subjects, matched pair-wise in a round robin tournament. Eugene Rosa and I found perfect transitivity in a round robin tournament of six subjects.

Rosa went further, asking if rank in this momentary eye-glance hierarchy predicts rank in the status hierarchy that emerges when the same subjects are brought together in prolonged discussion. He ran twenty groups, each composed of three unacquainted college students undifferentiated by age, race, sex, or social class; half the groups were male, half female. First Rosa put each threesome through a pair-wise round robin to establish the eye-glance hierarchy. Later he brought the three subjects together in a half-hour discussion, measuring each person's status by the amount he or she talked during the discussion. (He corroborated this ranking by afterward asking subjects to rate who contributed the most ideas and best guidance to the group.) Sixteen of the twenty groups formed a transitive eye-glance hierarchy. In these transitive groups, Rosa found that eye-glance rank significantly predicted status ranking in the following discussion (Rosa and Mazur 1979).

Eye glance is only one of many facial gestures that can signal dominance or deference (Anderson and Willis 1976; Kalma 1991, 1992; Mazur and Cataldo 1989), and these are usually accompanied by parallel signals in speech and body posture, producing an integrated presentation of high or low status. The impact of such displays on other people is nicely demonstrated by an experiment in which a trained confederate changes his demeanor from dominant to deferential. In his dominant guise, the confederate

> spoke with a "firm voice"; he also spoke more loudly . . . and at a faster pace. His speech contained few hesitations, and he spoke without stumbling over his words. His posture appeared to be relaxed, and he always looked up as he spoke. He periodically lowered his eyebrows to assert a point. Visible dress consisted of a sport jacket and dress shirt with no tie. . . .
>
> [In deferential guise, the confederate] spoke more softly and slowly. . . . He had the greatest number of hesitations and avoided introducing a "firm" tone in his voice. Pauses in his speech were filled pauses (e.g., "ummn," "uh," "well"). He frequently stumbled over words. Seating posture was rigid. The intention was to produce the effect of tenseness. Movements indicating nervousness (e.g., grooming behavior, wringing of hands) were sometimes used. He would occasionally lose eye contact with his audience by looking down, and occasionally raise his eyebrows indicating uncertainty. Visible dress consisted of a T-shirt. (Lee and Ofshe 1981, 78)

This confederate and other actors played the roles of a mock jury deliberating in a civil suit. Following a script, the confederate argued that the plaintiff should be given a very low award, only two thousand dollars, while the other actors pressed for a higher award of fifteen thousand dollars. Two versions of the deliberation were videotaped. In one the confederate assumed his dominant guise; in the other version he acted his part deferentially. (The other actors appeared the same in both versions.)

Subjects were shown one version or the other and asked, how much compensation should the plaintiff be awarded? Those who saw the confederate-dominant video were far more likely to accept the confederate's argument for a low amount. On average, they awarded the plaintiff seven thousand dollars less than did subjects who heard the confederate voice the same argument deferentially.

People do not always accept influence so easily. Ego's decision to comply or compete depends on his motivation to dominate. An individual who has experienced a recent rise in stature, perhaps from a victory or by passing through puberty, may be unusually pugnacious and challenge someone with impressive status signs. When Ego is on home territory, or protecting group members or valued possessions, and Alter is an intruder, then Ego is particularly likely to rise to a challenge. Among humans, a substantive disagreement—perhaps over a point of information or ideology—may escalate into a dominance competition so that winning becomes an end in itself, with the original substantive disagreement relegated to secondary importance. If both Ego and Alter decide to compete, their relative ranks are then determined by the outcome of one or more short *dominance contests* between them.

DOMINANCE CONTESTS

A very high-stakes dominance contest, between an Israeli interrogator and a Palestinian terrorist suspect, is described by former Shin Bet agent Michael Koubi (2004):

> At the beginning he was totally silent. He didn't answer any questions. Then I said to him, I know you are a religious man. . . . Let's have a competition. I'll ask you a question about the Koran, and if I win I can ask you another about any subject and you have to answer. He was sure he would know it better than me. . . .
>
> When you are in prison you forget things. For example, I asked him to tell me the name of the only sura out of the 114 in the Koran that did not contain the letter mim. He didn't know. I asked him how many verses there were in the Baqarah sura, the longest in the Koran. He had forgotten. So I won, and I sat with him for hundreds of hours while he talked about the ideology of Hamas. He even told other detainees to cooperate with me, because he respected me. If he could he would have killed me, but he respected me.

Nonhuman primates often establish and maintain their dominance hierarchies through a series of short face-to-face competitions between members of the group. Usually these are pair-wise contests, but occasionally they involve more than two individuals at once. Some competitions involve fierce combat to determine victor and vanquished. Others are mild, as when one animal is obviously the more powerful or assertive, or the other appears fearful. In such cases, a simple stare by the powerful animal, followed by the fearful animal averting its eyes or yielding something of value (perhaps food or a sitting place), may suffice to determine the winner. Sometimes a single contest is all that is needed to allocate ranks or to verify a preexisting status relationship, but often the outcome is settled only after a series of contests.

A mechanism postulated to operate across this range of competition is the manipulation of discomfort levels during these contests. In this model, a threat or attack is an attempt by one animal to "out-stress" or intimidate the opponent, by inducing fear, anxiety, or other discomfort. The animal that out-stresses its adversary is the winner.

At first glance, the model seems inappropriate to humans, who usually form status hierarchies politely. Chimpanzees, bonobos, and gorillas—the primates most like us—are more subtle in their status competition than monkeys or prosimians, and humans continue that trend. The emotional distribution of status occurs less stressfully among us than among nonhuman primates, but stresses are not wholly absent.

The model becomes clearer if we consider a concrete example. The eyes of two strangers, Ego and Alter, meet by chance across a room. Let us say that Ego decides to hold the glance. The chance eye contact now becomes a dominance encounter. Ego's stare makes Alter uncomfortable. Alter may avert his eyes, thus relieving his discomfort while in effect surrendering, or he may stare back, making Ego uncomfortable in return. In the latter case, the stare-down continues with each individual trying to out-stress the other until finally one person succumbs to the discomfort (and to the challenger) by averting his eyes. The matter thus settled, the yielder usually avoids further eye contact, though the winner may occasionally look at the loser as if to verify his victory.

In this example, Ego's stare is assumed to cause stress in Alter. Alter's eye aversion is assumed to relieve his own felt stress. Typically in stare-downs of this kind, the levels of discomfort are low, and the adversaries may be barely aware of their contest.

In this context, staring is an assertive sign of high status. Eye aversion is a deferent sign associated with low status. In other words, a dominant act (staring) elicits stress in the recipient; a deferent act (eye aversion) relieves stress in the actor. A central assumption of the model is that most dominant and deferent acts work this way, inducing or relieving stress, respectively. These actions are the means through which adversaries wage their dominance contest, aiming "darts" at one another. When the stress becomes too great for one, he switches from dominant to deferent actions, thereby relieving his stress and simultaneously signaling his acceptance of the lower rank.

Figure 7.1 diagrams a dominance contest between Ego and Alter. (Only Ego is shown in detail.) We may assume they are strangers, having just met.

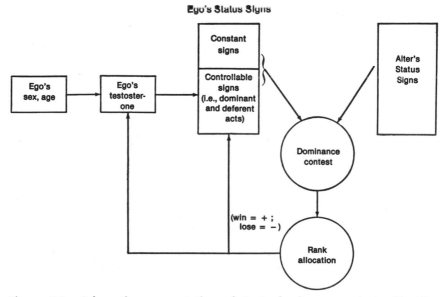

Figure 7.1. Schematic representation of Ego's dominance contest with Alter (Mazur 1985).

Each has appraised the status signs of the other, and neither is sufficiently impressed to cede the high rank, so they compete for the position. Both Ego and Alter display an array of status signs, some of them constant signals, but more important are the controllable signals. Each musters as many dominant acts as are appropriate. Each is stressed by the other's actions. Finally one of the adversaries—let us say Ego—feels that the high-ranked position is not worth his discomfort, so he switches from dominant actions to deferent actions, an acquiescence to Alter.

Normally a dominance-seeking person stresses adversaries through means that are polite or at least socially acceptable, and within the norms of business or sports competition. The wag Stephen Potter, savant of *gamesmanship* ("the art of winning games without actually cheating"), proposes as an axiom of competition that the first muscle stiffened in one's opponent is the first point gained. Potter advises players to create a state of anxiety in the adversary, as in the situation where your tennis opponent drives over to pick you up for the match.

> Your procedure should be as follows: (1) Be late in answering the bell. (2) Don't have your things ready. Appearing at last, (3) call *in an anxious or "rattled" voice* to wife (who need not, of course, be there at all) some taut last-minute questions about dinner. Walk down path and (4) realize you have forgotten shoes. Return with shoes; then just before getting into car pause (5) *a certain length of time* . . . and wonder (i) whether racket is at the club or (ii) whether you have left it "in the bath-room at top of the house."
>
> Like the first hint of paralysis, a scarcely observable fixing of your opponent's expression should now be visible. Now is the time to redouble the attack. Mapplay can be brought to bear. On the journey let it be known that you "think you know a better way," *which should turn out, when followed, to be incorrect and should if possible lead to a blind alley.* (Potter, undated, 21)

STRESS

Stress is an organism's subjective-plus-physiological responses to threatening or demanding stimuli. Subjectively, this response is experienced as discomfort, whether as anxiety, fear, anger, annoyance, or depression. Physiologically, it involves a complex response of the neurohormonal system: release of adrenocorticotrophin from the anterior pituitary, glucocorticoids from the adrenal cortex, epinephrine (adrenaline) from the adrenal medulla, and norepinephrine from the sympathetic nerves of the autonomic nervous system, all of which produce effects on other parts of the body (Axelrod and Reisine 1984).

This total reaction is often called the "fight-or-flight response" because it admirably prepares the organism to flee or face up to the threat. The central nervous system is aroused, the body provides glucose for quick energy, skeletal muscle increases contractility and loses fatigue, heart output increases, blood is shunted from viscera and the periphery of the body to the heart, lungs, and large muscles, and there is increased ventilation (Henry 1992). This is not a wholly stereotyped pattern, its different components coming more or less into play depending on the character of the threat and the previous experience of the organism (Ekman, Levenson, and Friesen 1983; Stemmler et al. 2001).

The model assumes that during status contests, Ego's dominant actions are perceived as threatening by Alter and therefore produce a stress response in Alter. That this occurs during violent contests involving overt threats and attacks can hardly be doubted. The occurrence of milder stress responses during more subtle contests, such as stare-downs, is less obvious although well supported by experimental evidence. A decrease in thumb blood volume is a convenient indicator of stress, showing the shift of blood from the periphery of the body to the skeletal muscles, an important feature of the fight-or-flight response. Human subjects engaged in a stare-down report feelings of discomfort, and they experience a significantly greater decrease in thumb blood volume than do subjects in control conditions of no stare or of unreciprocated stare (Mazur et al. 1980). This effect is illustrated in Figure 7.2a.

In a variant of this study, subjects were unknowingly paired in a stare-down with an experimental confederate. Depending on a random draw, the confederate either raised or lowered his eyebrows while staring. Subjects' thumb blood volume decreased significantly more when the confederate lowered his brows, intensifying his dominant aspect, than when his brows were raised (Figure 7.2b).

The model assumes that Alter can relieve felt stress by shifting his own dominant actions to deferent ones, in effect yielding the high-status rank to Ego. Alter's stress is relieved in part because Ego is likely to withdraw his threat, having won the victory. Furthermore, the simple action of making a deferent sign appears to relieve stress on the actor. Human subjects experiencing stress during a stare-down show recovery in thumb blood volume and a reduction of discomfort when they avert their eyes (Mazur et al. 1980). Other deferent acts such as cowering, crying, slumping in posture, smiling, allowing oneself to be displaced by a dominant individual—all signs of submission—presumably serve the function of relieving the actor's own felt stress. Submission is the price one pays to relieve stress-induced feelings of discomfort.

With stress a central variable in the biosocial model, we can explain some of the corollary features of status hierarchies (chapter 5). In most species, the low-ranked members of a group show more stress symptoms than

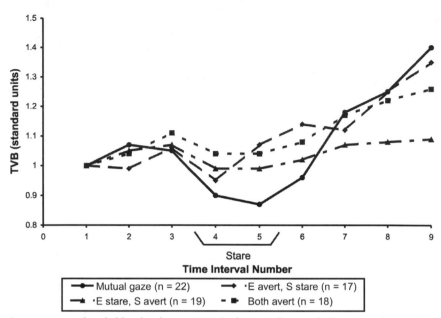

Figure 7.2a. Thumb blood volume (TBV) is depressed more during stare-downs than during other gaze conditions (Mazur et al. 1980).

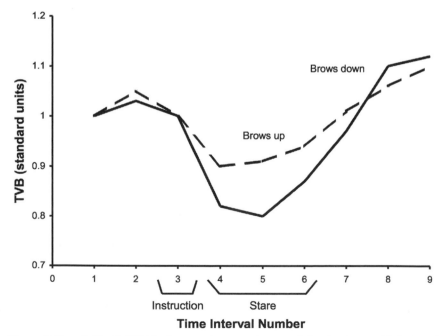

Figure 7.2b. Subject's TBV is depressed more when confederate stares with lowered than with raised eyebrows (n = 21 in each condition; Mazur et al. 1980).

higher-ranked members during common interaction. Often the low-ranked are described as "nervous, insecure" while those of high rank appear "relaxed, confident." We now see that the processes of rank allocation, especially dominance contests, encourage the upward movement of those group members most able to withstand stress and best equipped to impose stress on others, while those with the most difficulty handling stress, or the least interest in stressing others, move downward. Thus, there is a natural sorting that places individuals who are comfortable with stress near the top of the hierarchy and those who are "nervous" at the bottom.

Top-ranked individuals are well equipped with high-status signs and can easily impose stress on those down the hierarchy, enforcing compliance if it is not freely given. The imposition of stress is not only a powerful sanction on those below; it directly inhibits their performance as well. While the stress response admirably equips the body for the gross actions of fight or flight, it also produces muscle tension and tremor that interfere with finer actions, such as those required for controlled accuracy in sports or weapons competition. By intimidating our opponent in a duel or tennis match, we degrade his body's usual level of skill, diminishing his chances of scoring against us. Extreme stress can enervate an organism and, if chronic, cause physical morbidity. It is difficult for one of low rank to act dominantly toward a higher-ranked individual, for such an action is "presumptuous" (in human terms) and therefore may produce more stress on the low-status actor than on his higher-status target.

The stress variable also explains why the leaders rather than the low-ranked members of the group are most likely to face external threats such as predators, strange intruders, or hostile conspecifics. Those who handle stress most comfortably have been sorted into the high ranks, so they, rather than the low-ranked nervous individuals, are least intimidated by external threat and therefore most likely to advance against it. In human groups, the individuals who best handle stress are not only prone to become leaders but also, depending on circumstances, may be the thrill seekers and those most willing and able to violate laws or other norms.

CORTISOL

Cortisol is often called the "stress hormone" because in primates it is the major glucocorticoid produced during stress (Coe, Savage, and Bromley 1992). Released from the adrenal cortices into the bloodstream, cortisol flows to the brain and other organs, where it mobilizes the body's physical resources in preparation for fight or flight. (Cortisol may also mobilize a *social* response—the joining of protective coalitions—but this speculative topic is deferred to the appendix.)

The dissemination of cortisol throughout the body is preceded by a chain of events. First the sense organs perceive some threat or other distressing situation, sending an alarm to various parts of the brain including the amygdalae. These signal the hypothalamus at the brain's base to send the chemical messenger CRF (corticotrophin-releasing factor) to the closely connected pituitary gland. The pituitary then releases ACTH (adrenocorticotrophin hormone), which flows in the blood to the two adrenal glands (located near the stomach), stimulating the production and release of cortisol. It takes minutes for all this to occur and for cortisol to suffuse through the body, activating its target organs. If we had to wait for a cortisol response before responding to a sudden threat, we would have a poor chance at survival.

Fortunately, the amygdalae and hypothalamus also trigger an autonomic nervous response, which might better be called an "automatic" nervous response because it is instantaneous and instinctive. This rapid first response comprises a shot of adrenaline (epinephrine) from the core (medulla) of the adrenal glands, startled arousal, and protection (by shielding or escape) of vulnerable body parts. Usually this immediate reaction buys sufficient time for the hypothalamic-pituitary-adrenal axis to come online, facilitating a more consciously planned and prolonged effort to escape the stressor or defend against it (LeDoux 2002).

Like many other hormones, cortisol is controlled by a feedback system. When the brain senses that cortisol is sufficiently elevated, it stops the hypothalamus-pituitary nexus from releasing ACTH into the bloodstream. Lacking this prod, the adrenal cortices throttle back. If the cortisol level drops too far, the hypothalamus-pituitary releases more ACTH, thereby accelerating the adrenal cortices. During a period of calm, the various emergency hormones are cleared from the blood and excreted, returning the body to normal.

The stressors that especially concern us here are those surrounding competition for status. Dominance contests are intrinsically stress inducing. Cortisol reliably elevates among competitors, no matter whether they are challenging one another in physically vigorous sports or sedentary chess matches or trading personal insults (e.g., Booth et al. 1989; Elias 1981; Salvador et al. 1987; Gladue, Boechler, and McCaul 1989; Suay et al. 1999). Stress is the vehicle in which dominance is contested, and the process of status allocation places those who are most able to handle these stresses near the top of the hierarchy, while the most nervous individuals are found near the bottom. Furthermore, individuals who are chronically shy or nervous, hence usually unassertive, have relatively high cortisol levels (Kagen, Reznick, and Snidman 1988; Mazur 1994).

We should expect from all this that there is generally an inverse relationship between status and cortisol. If we know the rank ordering of group members, and we measure their hormones, we ought to find that top-ranked members have lower cortisol levels than do those at the bottom of the hierarchy. Such a relationship is clearly present among members of a university tennis team whose cortisol was measured at six intercollegiate meets over the course of a season (Figure 7.3). There is a strong and consistent tendency for the lowest-seeded players to have the highest cortisol levels (Booth et al. 1989).

Despite this impressive example, an inverse correlation between rank and cortisol is not inevitable (Muller and Wrangham 2004). In a meta-analysis of results on stable dominance hierarchies in several primate species, Abbott et al. (2003) conclude that the inverse relationship is most likely when subordinates are subjected to high rates of stressors, and when subordinates have few opportunities for social support (also see Barrett et al. 2002). When the status hierarchy is unstable, and high-ranked individuals are competing for dominance, they may have higher cortisol levels than low-ranked members.

Even with a stable hierarchy, there are situations in which top-ranked members experience the greatest stress, as when the group faces an external threat. Then, typically, leaders come forward as protectors, placing themselves between the source of danger and the rest of the group. Whenever a human group is confronted with a collective task, leaders have the greatest responsibility for accomplishing it successfully, which places them under unusually high stress. In such circumstances, we should expect the highest cortisol levels among those atop the hierarchy (Mazur 1985).[1]

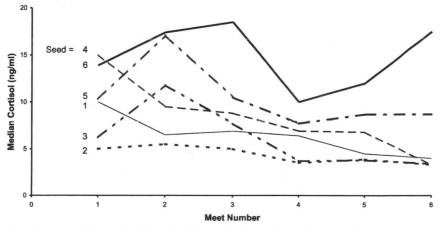

Figure 7.3. Median cortisol levels of six seeded members of a tennis team, across the season's meets (Booth et al. 1989).

MODES OF COMPETITION

An ape has numerous actions in its behavioral repertoire that communicate dominant intent, from biting and pummeling, to glaring, to a relaxed glance. The range of deferent acts is as great, from cowering and screaming, to presenting oneself to a dominant animal for mounting, to eye aversion and grinning. In observing behavioral sequences between apes, these acts are not completely intermingled but, rather, cluster into separable modes of communication (Berdecio and Nash 1981). One can distinguish an overt threat-and-attack mode where violent bites, lunges, screams, and intense activity define the interaction. At the other extreme is a quiet mode, without violent action, where glances and eye aversion, sexual mounting, and the slow movement of one animal to displace another are more typical expressions of status competition. It would be difficult to specify precise boundaries for these modes, and one mode can change into another, as when quiet competition escalates into violence, but it is nonetheless clear that separable modes exist, at least among the higher primate species.

All modes of communicating status that commonly appear among nonhuman primates (except scent marking) occur among humans too. The violent threat mode is illustrated in a Pulitzer Prize–winning photograph taken by Horst Fass during the Vietnam War (Figure 7.4). A South Vietnamese soldier is interrogating a suspected Viet Cong collaborator. The soldier, with taut muscles, glares at his prisoner, gripping him by the neck and displaying a classic "threat face" with lowered brows, lips drawn back, and teeth showing. The prisoner crouches, his hands raised and unclenched, his head lowered, his eyes upturned, looking indirectly at his captor. Probably these gestures predate language and conveyed the same meaning to early hominids as they do to us. Also shown are cultural symbols that amplify the dominant and deferent roles: a knife in the captor's hand, his clean uniform compared to the muddy pajamas of the captive. "The knife was a threat," writes the photographer, "and I think he used it" (quoted in Rubin and Newton 2000, 55).

Excepting warfare, modern societies discourage violent threat-and-attack as a mode of allocating status, but it remains common among adolescent males and outlaws. Violent competition, like most human activity, is usually governed by culturally specific norms. Homer's account of the Trojan War, where success in personal combat was the preeminent means of attaining high status among noblemen, emphasizes the correct method of fighting, proper ways of winning and losing, and honorable and dishonorable means of disposing of the loser's armor and body (Rouse 1938). Chivalric jousting between knights and duels between samurai were code governed, although one could abandon the rules when attacking someone deemed unworthy of respect. Even rival youth gangs have some shared understanding of accept-

Figure 7.4. South Vietnamese soldier questioning suspected Viet Cong collaborator (Horst Fass 1964, Associated Press).

able behavior in a street fight. Harvey Logan's exclamation to Butch Cassidy—"no rules in a knife fight!"—is an anomaly in real-life combat between respected foes.

Gentler modes of human competition also have rules, such as whether or not blinking is permissible in a stare-down. If the stare-down involves potential sexual partners, propositions communicated by the gaze may depend for their understanding on cultural expectations about permissible liaisons. Many primates allocate status in a play mode (Baldwin and Baldwin 1981), which in humans takes form in a variety of competitive games and sports.

Humans seem limited only by their ingenuity in devising novel modes of competition that are mutually understood. Examples of famously unusual competitions may be drawn from classic films. In *Rebel Without a Cause* (1955), James Dean and a competitor play "chicken" by racing their cars toward the precipice of a cliff. Dean is first to jump from his car, and therefore the loser, but the competitor's victory is short lived as he drives off the cliff and crashes on rocks below. Another classic duel, from *Casablanca* (1942), is set in Rick's Café. Nazi officers rise to sing "Die Wacht Am Rhein," a patriotic drinking song. The proud French resistance leader, Victor Laszlo (played by Paul Henreid), strides to the stage and leads the mostly French patrons in "Le Marseillaise"—drowning out the Germans, who sulk in defeat. It is a stirring scene.

The concept of modes is important in fitting humans into a general primate model because our most important style of communication is conversation, which is qualitatively different from the behavior of any other primate. Theorists have the choice of treating language-using humans as unique, to be explained on our own terms, or of treating language as simply one of several alternate modes of action whereby primates communicate with conspecifics. I have chosen the latter course, seeing in the evolutionary development of the primates a general broadening in the range and flexibility of available modes of communication, especially among the apes and reaching its extreme—to include language—among humans. The commonalities across the status hierarchies of humans and nonhuman primates seem to me a compelling reason for this choice, so I now turn to conversation as a mode of competition.

NOTE

1. The relatively "cool" individuals who often reach the top of dominance hierarchies may, in other social contexts, be those most likely to violate laws or social norms, or to take unusual risks. Norm violation and risk taking are stress-inducing activities, prohibiting most of us from doing them. Several studies show that criminals and other norm breakers, as well as high risk takers, experience relatively low physiological arousal, including low cortisol, low heart rate, and dry palms (e.g., Tremblay et al. 1998; Raine, Venables, and Williams 1990, 1995; McBurnett et al. 2000).

8

Conversation

Language is one of several candidates nominated over the years as the essential difference between humans and the rest of the animal world. Others are bipedalism or upright posture, having a soul, tool use (until animals were seen using natural objects to perform tasks), tool making (until chimps were observed modifying twigs and leaves for use as tools), a sense of awe (though it is not clear how anyone could know), and singing and dancing. Humans are noted as first among the primates for brain size (not counting Neanderthals, whose brains were bigger), penis size (no Neanderthal fossil survives for comparison), and least hairy body (the "naked ape"). It is perennially offered that we are the only species trying to define its uniqueness.

Today there is nearly a consensus that language is the sine qua non for humanity. More specifically, it is the recursive feature of language that is uniquely human, our ability to produce and understand an infinite variety of sentences from a limited number of words (Hauser, Chomsky, and Fitch 2002). Apes taught an artificial "language" of symbol manipulation communicate impressively—for apes—but do not seriously challenge the singularity of our own linguistic capability.

THE NATURE OF LANGUAGE

In the mid-twentieth century when behaviorism was the prevailing view of American psychology, language was regarded as a cultural skill that was learned like reading and writing, through repetition, reinforcement, and imitation. The revolution in linguistics attributed to Noam Chomsky (1957) replaced this view with an assertion that human brains are prewired for a universal grammar, a system of principles enabling children to easily and unconsciously absorb any spoken language and use it to produce and understand an infinite number of novel sentences.

The nub of Chomsky's argument is that any language's rules for sentence formation are too complicated to be acquired from scratch by a three-year-old. Therefore at least some basic principles or constraints on rule construction must have been in the child's head from the start (Jackendoff 1994). Chomsky's argument is more or less persuasive depending on how great a learning capacity we attribute to children. Youthful virtuosos perform incredible feats on the piano or violin or acrobatic apparatus, reminding us that they are much better than adults at acquiring certain skills. Toddlers acquire new syntactic constructions and word meanings with astounding accuracy, far beyond the capability even of teenagers.

Hardly anyone but a linguist who has investigated a language in depth can expect to explicate its sentence rules, yet all normal speakers of the language use them implicitly in conversation. Each toddler unconsciously extracts the rules anew from utterances heard during the first years of life. Some get a lot of linguistic input from parents and other children, others get little, yet virtually all master speech by the age of three. In the process, toddlers make faulty hypotheses, producing sentences like *I doed it, Mommy!* These are corrected or laughed at by listeners, helping the child to winnow incorrect inferences, but Chomsky and others have argued that such experiences are insufficient to learn sentencing without some instinctual command of grammar.

Chomsky's view introduces problems of its own, especially the failure so far to discover the specific principles of a universal grammar. Certain rules that are logically possible are seemingly *absent* from all languages. For example, no language forms questions by reversing the order of words within a statement, like *Built jack that house the is this?* (Pinker 1994, 233). Chomsky's claim is that human minds are innately incapable of acquiring such constructions unconsciously, though they may acquire many other complex structures without difficulty.

Whether or not there is a universal grammar, it is clear that all languages have features in common. All have words for things and people (nouns), words for actions or states of nouns (verbs), words for relationships, and words or inflections for modifying other words. In all languages, words are strung together into grammatical (rule-based) sentences that convey meaning. For example, English speakers understand *John loves Mary* and know it is different from *Mary loves John.* (*Mary John loves* or *Loves Mary John* is ungrammatical as well as meaningless in English.) All languages allow phrases to serve the same purpose as a single word, for example, a single noun can be replaced by a noun phrase, a single verb by a verb phrase. If John is a blond man with a tattoo, and Mary is a short woman with pearly white teeth, and we elaborate the meaning of "love," our sentence becomes, *A blond man with a tattoo feels enormous affection and heart palpitations for a short woman with pearly white teeth.* Any speaker over the age of five can do these recursions, producing novel comprehensible sentences of considerable length. In all languages the ambiguity of sentence meanings can be reduced through facial expressions and voice modulations, especially when mothers speak to infants. For example, speakers often signal the focal word in a question by raising their eyebrows and inflecting their voice upward. Thus, in English, *Does John love Mary?* takes four different meanings depending on which word is flagged with raised brows and upwardly pitched voice.

Commonalities among the world's five thousand or so languages may seem less impressive than their differences. The meaning of an English sentence depends on word order, subject-verb-object, as in *John loves Mary.* To obtain the same meaning in Japanese the order would be *John Mary loves*; in Classical Arabic it would be *Loves John Mary*; and in Malagasy it would be *Loves Mary John.* Some languages allow almost any ordering, differentiating subject from object by inflecting the words. Not all languages require a sentence to have a subject, as English does. In some languages, but not English, nouns fall into gender classes like the masculine and feminine nouns of the Romance tongues (Smith and Wilson 1979; Pinker 1994). Furthermore, the rules of any language change over time, as amply illustrated in the history of English. All this variation shows that universal grammar must allow considerable syntactic flexibility. On the other hand, one might regard these differences as minor and limited to specific points, so that variation among languages is not as great as it may seem on the surface.

About the time Chomsky asserted that humans have innate grammar, Eric Lenneberg (1967) argued on different grounds that language is biologically based. He described the child's language capacity in terms of broad developmental milestones, listed in Table 8.1. The chronological ages of these milestones are approximate, but they reliably follow one after the other. The same is true of motor development milestones, which correlate highly with language milestones. Children in diverse cultures display these same correspondences, suggesting that the emergence of language is one aspect of the general biological maturation of the child. One cannot say this about major cultural inventions like reading, writing, cooking, playing a musical instrument, or religious observance; these do not develop naturally along a nearly invariant sequence in virtually every child.

There are substantial physical changes in the brain during the first years of life, its weight increasing roughly 350 percent from birth to the age of two, whereas from ages two to twelve there is a weight increase of only 35 percent, and after age twelve there is practically no weight increase at all. Cortical neurons grow considerably in volume during the first two years, and then growth rate decreases until by puberty little change occurs. There are similar rates of change in the decreasing packing density of neurons.

Table 8.1. Correspondence between Motor and Language Milestones

Approximate age	Motor development milestone	Language development milestone
3 months	Supports head when in prone position; hands mostly open; no grasp reflex.	Less crying than at 8 weeks; smiles and coos when talked to; sustains vowel-like cooing for 15–20 seconds.
4 months	Plays with rattle placed in hands; head self-supporting.	Responds to human sounds; turns head; eyes seem to search for speaker.
6 months	Sits using hands for support; unilateral reaching.	Cooing changes to babbling resembling 1-syllable utterances; most common utterances sound like ma, mu, da, or di.
1 year	Stands; walks when held by one hand.	Signs of understanding some words; applies some sounds regularly to signify persons or objects.
1.5 years	Prehension and release fully developed; gait propulsive; creeps downstairs backwards.	Repertoire of 3–50 words not joined in phrases; trains of sounds and intonation patterns resembling discourse; good progress in understanding.
2 years	Runs (with falls); walks stairs with one foot forward only.	More than 50 words; 2-word phrases most common; more interest in verbal communication; no more babbling.
2.5 years	Jumps with both feet; stands on one foot for 1 second.	Every day new words; utterances of 3 or more words; seems to understand almost everything said; still many grammatical deviations.
3 years	Tiptoes 3 yards; walks stairs with alternating feet; jumps 12 inches.	Vocabulary of some 1,000 words; about 80% intelligibility; grammar of utterances close approximation to colloquial adult language, though mistakes still occur.
4 years	Jumps over rope; hops on one foot; walks on line.	Language well developed; grammatical anomalies limited to unusual constructions.

Lenneberg inferred that there is a critical period for language acquisition that begins at about the age of two, when the brain has reached sufficient maturity, and ends sometime before puberty, when the brain has lost most of its adaptive ability. Children who receive damage to one hemisphere before the onset of speech still have a good chance for normal development, irrespective of whether the damage is to the left or right side. It appears that when the left hemisphere is damaged at this early age, the right hemisphere is able to take over the language functions. Damage to the left hemisphere of an older child is much more likely to result in disturbed speech than damage to the right (Lenneberg 1967).

SPEECH AND GESTURE

Speech is so obviously the method of choice for human communication that it has been considered essential for language. Debates about the extent of Neanderthal language often focus on whether or not the larynx had sufficient sound-producing capability, as indicated by fossils (Jordan 1999). But perhaps Neanderthal "language" was based on gestures rather than speech (Corballis 1999). Language resides in the brain, not the voice box. Signing systems are found in all communities of deaf people, each a distinct and full language with the same sort of grammar rules found in spoken languages (Senghas, Kita, and Özyürek 2004). Furthermore, the grammar of a true sign language is unrelated to surrounding spoken languages. American Sign Language (ASL), commonly used by the deaf community in the United States, resembles neither spoken English nor British Sign Language but has features reminiscent of Navajo and Bantu (Pinker 1994).

When two psychologists, Cathy and Keith Hayes, brought a baby chimp named Viki into their home and raised her like a human baby, they too equated language with speaking. Since Viki did not pick up English on her own, her "parents" used special techniques to teach her by age two to say close approximations of "mama," "papa," and "cup" (indicating she wanted a drink). In six years Viki learned only four English words and a few additional sounds used for specific requests (Hayes 1970; Gardner and Gardner 1969). The project, no doubt disappointing for the Hayeses, convincingly demonstrated that speaking is not a successful avenue for chimpanzees, probably because their vocal anatomy is poorly suited to produce many of the sounds used by humans.

Meanwhile observers of chimpanzees in the wild were noticing their richly gestured communication based on facial expressions, hand positions, and body postures. Pursuing this line, another pair of psychologists, Allan and Beatrice Gardner (1969), began training a year-old chimp named Washoe in a "sign language" of the deaf—a crude version of American Sign Language.

Adults conversed in the sign language in Washoe's presence, they named objects to her, and sometimes they shaped her fingers into correct positions. By the time Washoe was three years old, she could make thirty-four signs and apparently use them in appropriate situations. Sometimes she would put two signs together, suggesting the language level of a two-year-old human. Eventually Washoe was adopted by one of the Gardners' graduate students, Roger Fouts (1997). She continued learning new signs, sometimes stringing three or four together.

Ape language studies have evoked bitter controversy and severe criticism of their research methods, with charges that the words produced by Washoe and other apes are like tricks performed for rewards by dogs, seals, and parrots. The semantic content of ape "sentences," according to critics, comes more from wishful thinking of investigators than from the linguistic ability of the animals (e.g., Terrace 1979). In response, ape researchers have tightened their methods, making the apes' actions less susceptible to investigator bias. Sue Savage-Rumbaugh has performed some of the best of the new studies, using bonobos, thought by some to be smarter than chimpanzees. She has her animals communicate by pressing symbols on a computer keyboard, thereby demonstrating, for example, that one bonobo can tell another where to find a key that will liberate a banana they can share. A male named Kanzi is Savage-Rumbaugh's most impressive subject, learning the meaning of several keyboard symbols from watching his mother's training sessions. The mother was an inept student, but Kanzi was excellent, perhaps because he was younger, acquiring a vocabulary of two hundred symbols by the age of six, and constructing elemental "sentences" by combining a word with a gesture or occasionally putting two or three words together (Savage-Rumbaugh, Shanker, and Taylor 1998).

We have always known animals are intelligent in their own terms, coping with problems of their natural environment and lifestyle. The language apes were challenged with human-style problems: contrived laboratory tasks, tests of logic, and routines in an American household. On these tasks they demonstrate far better "human" thinking than many of us initially expected.

Nonetheless, these apes do not use language remotely like humans do. Even assuming Washoe performed as her trainers suggested, she never came close to using ASL, which is not simply a collection of signs but a fully grammatical human language. Apparently, apes—even Kanzi—simply do not have the mental ability for language, whether via gestures, speech, or computer symbols. Humans can and do express themselves linguistically through multiple channels. More importantly, language is not part of the ape's normal social repertoire. Among humans, conversation is the major vehicle for social interaction.

To a sociologist, Chomskyan theory, in its concern for the individual's unconscious knowledge of grammar, seems oddly asocial. Normal use of grammatical knowledge, in conjunction with other knowledge such as the rules of conversation (see below), implies interaction between people, and, in fact, such use can function perfectly well even without explicitly formed sentences. The following fictional dialogue is fully comprehensible, conveying information and commentary while solidifying the social relationship.

Hey!

What's doin'?

Nothin' much—how you?

Fine.

Heard from Bill?

Yah, broken thumb.

Shit!

Real pisser.

How?

Firecracker.

Firecracker! His own fault?

Damn straight.

Whatta dumb ass!

Yep.

Well, say "hi" for me.

OK—gotta go.

Me too—Ciao!

Ciao!

This script ignores body postures, facial cues, and hand movements that give added meaning to—and may convey more information than—the exchange of words. Altogether, the features of conversation allow effective communication and functional social interaction even without language. On the other hand, language capability does not imply the capacity to converse. Children with the variant of autism known as Asperger's Syndrome pass the normal linguistic milestones, yet they cannot carry on a normal conversation, having difficulty with eye-to-eye gaze, facial expression, and body gestures that regulate the exchange. An Asperger's child might speak articulately about something of interest, then walk away when someone else begins talking, without recognizing his departure as inappropriate. Thus, conversation is a considerably different ability than language per se and probably appeared far earlier in hominid evolution.

RULES OF CONVERSATION

The biosocial model of status works independently of the mode of communication used between Ego and Alter, as long as they can distinguish dominant (high-status) acts from deferent (low-status) ones. To include language as a mode of communicating dominance and deference, we need only specify how the speaker and listener (or signer and recipient) recognize dominant and deferent actions during conversation. One obvious way is through the words that each person speaks, since these may carry lexical meaning indicating that the speaker (or listener) is a high- or low-status person. We can understand these meanings only by knowing the language:

> "Where do you come from?" said the Red Queen. "And where are you going? Look up, speak nicely, and don't twiddle your fingers all the time."
>
> Alice attended to all these directions, and explained, as well as she could, that she had lost her way.
>
> "I don't know what you mean by *your* way," said the Queen: "all the ways about here belong to *me*—but why did you come out here at all?" she added in a kinder tone. "Curtsey while you're thinking what to say. It saves time."
>
> Alice wondered a little at this, but she was too much in awe of the Queen to disbelieve it. . . .
>
> "It's time for you to answer now," the Queen said, looking at her watch: "open your mouth a *little* wider when you speak, and always say 'your Majesty.'"
>
> "I only wanted to see what the garden was like, your Majesty—"
>
> "That's right," said the Queen, patting her on the head, which Alice didn't like at all: "though, when you say 'garden'—I've seen gardens, compared with which this would be a wilderness."
>
> Alice didn't dare to argue the point, but went on: "—and I thought I'd try and find my way to the top of that hill—"
>
> "When you say 'hill,'" the Queen interrupted, "*I* could show you hills, in comparison with which you'd call that a valley."
>
> "No, I shouldn't," said Alice, surprised into contradicting her at last: "a hill *can't* be a valley, you know. That would be nonsense—"
>
> The Red Queen shook her head, "You may call it 'nonsense' if you like," she said, "but *I've* heard nonsense, compared with which that would be as sensible as a dictionary!"
>
> Alice curtseyed again, as she was afraid from the Queen's tone that she was a *little* offended. . . .
>
> Lewis Carroll, *Through the Looking Glass*

Since conversations also carry meaning in their form and action—apart from the particular string of words—we often recognize the relative status of conversing foreigners even though we do not understand their speech. It is these features of form and action, independent of grammar or lexicon, that I describe here as a set of rules that are usually followed in natural conversation (Goffman 1967; Schwartz and Jacobs 1979).

Some of the rules are asymmetrical, specifying different actions for a high-status actor than a low-status one. If an individual in conversation takes the high-status role, then he is displaying a dominant sign, whereas if he acts the low-status part, then he displays a deferent sign.

Other rules are symmetrical, applying without regard for the status of the actor. It is the *violation* of these rules that signals a dominant act, whereas strict conformity to them—while others are violating—signals deference (or politeness). The obvious underlying assumption here is that the dominant actor is most likely to assume the prerogative of violating the norms, whereas the deference person would not dare. (To act dominantly toward one's superior is presumptuous and therefore stressful on the actor.) As in all modes, a dominant act is assumed to stress the recipient of the act, and a deferent act relieves stress on the actor. Thus, for Ego to violate any of the following rules would place stress on Alter. Alter would relieve this stress through strict conformity to the rules. These stresses are assumed to be subtle, and the actors may barely be aware of their motivating qualities.

Most conversation between familiars is *not* concerned with achieving or exhibiting status differences, so these rules are usually adhered to, producing relaxed, polite, noncompetitive conversations. Violations occur primarily during dominance contests, or when high-status individuals choose to emphasize their superior positions.

Conversation between Ego and Alter is, by definition, a series of turns in which each talks to the other in a language that both understand. The first two rules govern turn taking (Duncan and Fiske 1977).

1. *If one individual is speaking, the other should remain quiet* (Sacks, Schegloff, and Jefferson 1974). If Ego interrupts Alter's speech, Ego has acted dominantly (Zimmerman and West 1975). Sometimes the interruption is inadvertent, as when speaker Alter pauses and Ego, mistaking the pause for an ending, begins to talk, only to have Alter continue speaking. If Ego realizes Alter is not done and aborts a premature speech, Ego has deferred to Alter. If both continue speaking, they are vying for dominance.

2. *A listener who is offered the floor should speak.* A speaker can conclude talking without passing the floor, or may explicitly offer it, as by asking a question of the listener, or by directing his eyes to the listener after concluding a speech (Kendon 1967). If Ego remains silent after Alter offers the floor, Ego has acted dominantly, stressing Alter. If silent Ego then offers the floor back to Alter (by looking at Alter and waiting for Alter to speak), and Alter speaks (relieving his own stress), then Alter has deferentially complied with the same rule that Ego has just violated.

3. *Do not look into another individual's eyes when no one is speaking* (unless in a romantic context or at a distance well beyond normal conversational

spacing). The violation of this rule, silent staring, is a common dominant act among primates, whereas rule-following eye aversion indicates deference. Conversation complicates these common signals since all listeners, whatever their status, look directly at a speaker's face to maximize comprehension; thus the rule applies only during silent periods and is the converse of the next rule (Argyle and Cook 1976; Exline 1972).

4. *Look at the speaker's face, particularly if the speaker is looking at you* (Goodwin 1980). To look away, suggesting inattention (unless it is to look at an object of obvious concern), is very hard to do if you respect the person speaking to you (Ellyson, Dovidio, and Fehr 1981). If the person is of minor consequence, it is easy to violate the rule, thus showing your dominance. This rule is inoperative when the listener's averted eyes are a clear signal of submission, as when a child's eyes are downcast while the child is being reprimanded by an adult.

5. *Do not speak loudly, sternly, or angrily.* Shouting matches and arguments are obviously dominance contests.

6. *The speaker should direct the listener's actions by request rather than command and should avoid a stern or stubborn tone.* To speak in a commanding or inflexible way implies that the listener is of lower status.

7. *The listener should respond to the speaker's directions for action.* Frequently, the listener responds to the speaker's requests while the speaker continues to hold the floor, as by head nods, laughs, or brief vocalizations. Refusing a request is an assertion of status; refusing a command is an outright challenge.

The next two rules are asymmetrical, treating the high-status participant differently than the low-status person. To take the high-status role is a dominant act; to relinquish it is deferential. If both participants assume the high-status role, there is an obvious dominance contest.

8. *The high-status person sets the pace and mood of the conversation, and the low-status person follows.* The dominant person sets these with smiles, jokes, frowns, exclamations, volume, and rapidity of speech (Chapple 1970; Feldstein and Welkowitz 1978; Gregory 1983). High-status Ego may sustain a lagging conversation by asking questions or otherwise eliciting responses from Alter. If Ego tells a loud joke, Alter can deferentially comply with a loud laugh, or can challenge by substituting an inappropriate response.

9. *The high-status person introduces and terminates major topics of conversation.* This rule, like the previous one, indicates that the high-status person can take control of the conversation, which is the essence of having high status. If the relative status of the participants is not already set, then either one who assumes control is acting dominantly. If both attempt to control the conversation, there is a dominance contest.

These rules operate within a context of linguistic interaction, and the words actually spoken are an important part of the whole display (Derber

1979). When we deferentially compliment someone, our own words are said in strict accordance with the rules, whereas our verbal insults gain emphasis when spoken in violation of the rules of conversation. Also, we accompany our speech with appropriate gestures, perhaps glaring for dominance or smiling for deference. This full array of actions—words, gestures, and rules—constitutes the status display.

We turn again to the movie *Butch Cassidy and the Sundance Kid* to illustrate how language and accompanying demeanor are mobilized during status competition. The scene is a pickup poker game among strangers. The Sundance Kid is one of the players and has won several hands. Finally he is challenged by a player across the table:

CHALLENGER: You're a hell of a card player, fella. I know 'cause I'm a hell of a card player. And I can't even spot how you're cheatin'.

(Sundance freezes, looks at Challenger; other players leave the table. Challenger rises, his hand poised over his gun.)

CHALLENGER: The money stays, and you go.

BUTCH (*entering the scene*): Well, we seem to be a little short on brotherly love around here.

CHALLENGER (*to Butch*): If you're with him, you better get yourselves out of here.

BUTCH (*to Challenger*): We're on our way. (*To Sundance*) Come on.

SUNDANCE (*staring at Challenger*): I wasn't cheating.

BUTCH (*to Sundance*): Come on.

SUNDANCE (*to Butch, while staring at Challenger*): I wasn't cheating!

CHALLENGER: You can die. For that matter, you can both die.

BUTCH (*to Sundance*): You hear that?

SUNDANCE (*still staring*): If he asks us to stay then we'll go.

BUTCH (to Sundance): We were ready to go anyway.

SUNDANCE (*still staring*): He's got to invite us to stick around!

BUTCH (*to Sundance*): He'll draw on you—he's ready—you don't know how fast he is.

(*Sundance continues staring at Challenger.*)

BUTCH (*politely to Challenger*): What would you think about maybe asking us to stick around?

CHALLENGER (*incredulously*): What?

BUTCH (*approaching Challenger*): You don't have to mean it. Just ask us to stick around. I promise you—

(*Challenger pushes Butch back, stopping him in mid-sentence.*)

BUTCH (*to Sundance*): I can't help you, Sundance.

CHALLENGER (*averts his eyes, speaks hesitantly*): I didn't know you were the Sundance Kid when I said you were cheatin'.

(*Sundance stands.*)

CHALLENGER: If I draw on you, you'll kill me.

SUNDANCE: There's that possibility.

BUTCH: No, you'll be killin' yourself. So why don't you just invite us to stick around? (*Coaxingly*) You can do it easy. Come on, come on.

CHALLENGER (*long pause, eyes downward, speaking softly*): Why don't you stick around?

BUTCH: Thanks, but we've gotta get goin'.

(*Butch sweeps money from table into his hat, Sundance finishes his drink. They walk toward the door.*)

CHALLENGER (*calling after Sundance*): Hey Kid, how good are ya'?

(*Sundance wheels, draws, shoots Challenger's gun off his belt and across the floor. He re-holsters, turns, and walks off, ending the scene.*)

Even in this classic Western showdown, the goal is not to outshoot one's opponent but to out-stress him, not to cause physical harm but to make the adversary sufficiently uncomfortable—psychically and physiologically—that he capitulates. Sundance, with Butch's help, won the contest through conversation. The gunplay on his way out was an unnecessary flourish, a superfluous show of bravura.

Most of us do not live so dangerously. The language of status competition is usually innocuous, sometimes embarrassing, occasionally degrading, but rarely hazardous. It may be contemptuous or excessively polite; it may be erudite or feign ignorance. Quick wit and an acute sense of irony are potent weapons. Satire, a caustically witty attack in writing, may be called "sharp as a rapier," but that is not literally true since it targets the emotions rather than drawing blood.

Often the content of humorous barbs, or bon mots, is culturally specific, reflecting regional prejudices or a historical era, as in this classic joke from the 1930s:

During his first visit to Manhattan, Mr. Hicks from Kansas is introduced to Mr. Cobb, a Wall Street broker. Cobb asks pompously, "Do you know what we do with hicks in New York?" "No," responds Hicks, "but I know what we do with cobs in Kansas."

Every culture has characteristic means for verbal sparring, for example, Yiddish's multitudinous "sh" nouns conveying personal derision: *shikker* (drunk), *shlemiel* (clumsy person), *shlimazel* (unlucky person), *shlooche* (slut), *shlub* (jerk), *shlump* (untidy person), *shmegegi* (fool), *shmendrik* (nincompoop), *shmo* (goof), *shmuck* (prick), *shnook* (patsy), *shnorrer* (beggar), and *shtunk* (stinker).

No dominance repartee is wittier than lower-class black men skillfully "playing the dozens." Performed for a street audience, this war of words puts a premium on quick and clever insults ("snaps") about one's opponent, his girlfriend, his relatives, and especially his mother. Snaps often have standard openings to which are appended original endings crafted to the individual, as in examples posted by IS/OOP Group's *Online Magazine*:

> You're so dumb, it takes you an hour to cook Minute Rice.
> You're so dumb, you think Taco Bell is a Mexican phone company.
> You're so ugly, you couldn't get laid if you were a brick.
> Your girlfriend is so dumb, the first time she used a vibrator she cracked two teeth.
> Your sister is so stupid, she went to the baker for a yeast infection.
> Your mother is so fat her blood type is Ragu.
> Your mother is so fat, she broke her arm and gravy poured out.
> Your mother is so old, she knew Burger King when he was a prince.

Dozens players may stand nose-to-nose but without touching. A snap may be reinforced with a hip shake, a stare, or a lewd gesture. An attack is strengthened with the delivery of a series of snaps in rhythm (and traditionally in rhyme, foreshadowing modern rap lyrics). In past years, mother insults were the ultimate blow, but today they have become ritualized and have no special importance. As always, maintaining a cool demeanor is essential for a win.

ARGUMENTATION

Most oral arguments are dominance contests, producing stress in the contestants (Brinkerhoff and Booth 1984; Rejeski et al. 1989, 1990). Sometimes the competition is blatant, with disagreements uttered so vehemently there is no doubt of an assault on the listener, who may barely be listening, being so intent on formulating a counterattack. Sometimes the contest is subtle, camouflaged as a polite or intellectual exchange of views. Every professor has had the experience of speaking to a scholarly audience and then, in the question period, facing hostile inquiries intended to display the intellectual superiority of the questioner over the presenter.

I am not suggesting that rational argumentation is epiphenomenal, a veneer overlying some more essential joust for personal victory. That is implied only under the false dichotomy that debate either is, or is not, a purely unemotional exchange of ideas. In reality, debaters strive for personal victory while at the same time striving to present a logically or empirically cogent case.

The famous courtroom confrontation between Clarence Darrow and William Jennings Bryan illustrates the futility of pigeonholing oral debate as *either* rational argumentation *or* dominance contest, for it is a beautiful example of both. In 1925 the state of Tennessee had enacted a law preventing the teaching in public schools of any theory that denies the Biblical story of creation. Opponents of the law, seeking to test its legality, recruited a young high school teacher named Scopes to lecture his class on evolution. As agreed, his friends informed state authorities, and Scopes was indicted (Darrow 1987).

The Northern press generated national interest, playing the coming "monkey trial" as an example of the South's backwardness. William Jennings Bryan, an orator and supporter of women's suffrage, three times the unsuccessful Democratic candidate for president of the United States and informal leader of the nation's fundamentalist movement, volunteered to assist the prosecution. Clarence Darrow, at that time America's most famous trial lawyer, volunteered to help the Scopes defense. The case became a crusade, for Bryan against Darwinism, for Darrow against religious fanaticism. Their arena was a small-town courtroom during the heat of summer, its daily proceedings reported by journalists who had come for the battle. Toward the end of the trial, Bryan suggested himself as an expert witness on the Bible. Darrow was entitled to cross-examine Bryan on his qualifications:

> Darrow: Do you claim that everything in the Bible should be literally interpreted?
>
> Bryan: I believe everything in the Bible should be accepted as it is given there. . . .
>
> Darrow: Does the statement, "The morning and the evening were the first day . . . ," mean anything to you?
>
> Bryan: I do not think it necessarily means a twenty-four hour day. . . .
>
> Darrow: Then, when the Bible said, for instance, "and God called the firmament heaven. And the evening and the morning were the second day," that does not necessarily mean twenty-four hours?
>
> Bryan: I do not think it necessarily does. . . .
>
> Darrow: You think those were not literal days? . . .
>
> Bryan: I think it would be just as easy for the kind of God we believe in to make the earth in six days as in six years or in 6,000,000 years. . . . My impression is

they were periods, but I would not attempt to argue as against anybody who wanted to believe in literal days.

DARROW: Have you any idea of the length of the periods?

BRYAN: No, I don't.

DARROW: Do you think the sun was made on the fourth day?

BRYAN: Yes.

DARROW: And they had evening and morning without the sun?

BRYAN: I am simply saying it is a period.

DARROW: They had evening and morning for four periods without the sun, do you think?

BRYAN: I believe in creation as there told, and if I am not able to explain it I will accept it. . . .

DARROW: The creation might have been going on for a very long time?

BRYAN: It might have continued for millions of years.

DARROW: Yes, alright. Do you believe the story of the temptation of Eve by the serpent?

BRYAN: I do.

DARROW: Do you believe that after Eve ate the apple, or gave it to Adam, . . .that God cursed Eve, and that time decreed that all womankind thenceforth and forever should suffer the pains of childbirth in the reproduction of the earth?

BRYAN: I believe what it says, and I believe the fact as fully—

DARROW: That is what it says, doesn't it?

BRYAN: Yes. . . .

DARROW: And you believe that is the reason that God made the serpent to go on his belly after he tempted Eve?

BRYAN: I believe the Bible as it is, and I do not permit you to put your language in the place of the language of the Almighty. You read that Bible and ask me questions, and I will answer them. I will not answer your questions in your language.

DARROW: I will read it to you from the Bible: "And the Lord God said unto the serpent, because thou hast done this, thou art cursed above all cattle, and above every beast of the field; upon thy belly shalt thou go and dust shalt thou eat all the days of thy life." Do you think that is why the serpent is compelled to crawl upon its belly?"

BRYAN: I believe that.

DARROW: Have you any idea how the snake went before that time?

BRYAN: No, sir.

DARROW: Do you know whether he walked on his tail or not?

BRYAN: No, sir. I have no way to know. (Laughter in courtroom.) . . . Your honor, . . .the only purpose Mr. Darrow has is to slur at the Bible. . . .

DARROW: I object to your statement. I am . . . [questioning] you on your fool ideas that no intelligent Christian on earth believes.

JUDGE: Court is adjourned until 9 o'clock tomorrow morning.

This is a short fragment from the lengthy exchange that was fully telegraphed to the nation's newspapers. Darrow had made Bryan look a fool, by using cold logic and controlling the exchange. Five days after the trial, Bryan died in his sleep; perhaps humiliation was a contributing factor. All this did no good for Scopes, who was found guilty by a jury of churchgoers, though the Tennessee Supreme Court later reversed his conviction on a technicality. The antievolution law stayed on the Tennessee statute book until its repeal in 1967.

CONCLUSIONS

Conversation, unique among humans, is normally our primary mode of communication. Spoken words—reinforced and modified by inflections, prosody, facial expressions, and body postures—convey information and define social relationships, including dominance and deference. Whereas humans retain nearly all the status signs found among other primates, we give priority to conversation as our means for displaying and competing for status.

Conversational acts, like all status signs, indicate that the signer is or ought to be of either higher or lower status than the recipient. It is usually clear during polite conversation which person holds the higher rank and which the lower. This is because conversation is governed by normative rules for the speaker and the listener, and during polite interaction these rules are adhered to. Some of the rules are asymmetrical, assigning one form of behavior to the high-status person, another form to the low-status person. Thus, we easily perceive who is playing the elevated role and who is taking a deferent position. This happens whether the conversation is between two parties or among more.

Occasionally participants in a conversation do not agree on their relative status. Then they may compete for high rank (and the prerogatives that go with it). Sometimes competition is overt; sometimes it is so subtle that it is barely perceptible even to the contenders. In any case, their conversational actions become dominant signs that stress the recipient. As usual in dominance contests, these stressors are exchanged until one person relieves his or her felt discomfort by switching to deferent actions, thereby signaling acceptance of the subordinate position in the hierarchy.

9

Testosterone

In theory, testosterone is the key hormone involved in dominance and deference interactions, at least among mature males. Unfortunately, empirical research is equivocal, neither firmly sustaining nor refuting the theory. Interpretations of this work inevitably vary. The respected testosterone researcher James Dabbs (2000) believed testosterone has already been demonstrated to be a primary cause of dominant and excessively macho behavior in humans. I am warier of weak and inconsistent findings, and of confirmatory results reported by investigators (including myself) with a personal commitment to the theory.

DOMINANCE, AGGRESSION, AND ANTISOCIAL BEHAVIOR

Numerous animal experiments, especially on rodents, show that raising testosterone increases aggressiveness (Svare 1983; Monaghan and Glickman 1992). In interpreting this work, it is important to distinguish aggressive behavior from dominance behavior. An individual is said to act *aggressively* if its apparent intent is to inflict physical injury on a member of its species. An individual acts *dominantly* if its apparent intent is to achieve or maintain high status—that is, to obtain power, influence, or valued prerogatives—over a conspecific. Rodents typically dominate aggressively, but that is not true among the higher primates (see chapter 5).

It may be difficult to appraise the intentions of an animal in order to distinguish dominance from aggression. But when we study humans—the focal species here—it would be naively Skinnerian to deny our ability to read people's intentions, a skill that is the very basis for human sociability. Much of interpersonal behavior is overtly or subtly concerned with managing dominance and subordination without causing physical harm. Sports, spelling bees, elections, criticism, competitions for promotion, and academic jousting all involve domination without aggression. It is harder to identify instances of aggression devoid of a dominating motive, but examples are infanticide; purely instrumental killings such as sometimes occur in the execution of felons, murder for hire, or religious sacrifice; circumcision and ritual mutilation; euthanasia, surgery, and dentistry; suicide and self-flagellation; and knowingly causing collateral casualties from military attack. We may usually distinguish actions intended to dominate from those intended to injure a target person. We understand that there are different motivations for dominance and aggression, which sometimes work concurrently.

The distinction between aggression and dominance is particularly important for humans, because we usually assert our dominance without any intention of causing physical injury. It may be the case that testosterone is related primarily to dominance among men and not to aggression except in situations where dominance happens to be asserted aggressively. Ehrenkranz, Bliss, and Sheard (1974), found that socially dominant but nonaggressive prisoners had relatively high testosterone, not significantly different from the testosterone levels of aggressive prisoners. Nearly all primate studies that have been interpreted as linking testosterone to aggression may as easily be interpreted as linking testosterone with dominance (Mazur 1976). It is doubtful that among humans, testosterone is related to aggressiveness per se (Archer 1991; Albert, Walsh, and Jonik 1994).

On theoretical grounds, dominating mechanisms—whether aggressive or nonaggressive in form—would confer an evolutionary advantage in helping an individual acquire valued resources, especially in competition for mates, resulting in enhanced production of offspring.[1] This is not simply a matter of a dominant man taking what he wants; women regard men who *look* dominant as attractive (Townsend 1993, 1998). Teenage men rated by naive judges as having "dominant-looking" faces (often with prominent chins, heavy brow ridges, muscular rather than fleshy or skinny faces) report copulating earlier than their submissive-looking peers, presumably in part because they have an easier time finding willing partners (Mazur, Halpern, and Udry 1994).

It is not obvious why there would be selective advantage in aggressiveness per se, apart from its dominating function. (Predation for food is a different matter, unrelated to testosterone.) We therefore frame our inquiry around dominating (and deferential) behavior as being theoretically prior to aggressiveness, leaving for the next chapter the important but subsidiary question why men sometimes dominate with intent to harm.

An important variant of dominant behavior occurs in settings like schools, prisons, the military, families, or work groups, where authority figures require behavior to conform closely to rigid standards. In these circumstances, dominant-acting individuals who hold subordinate roles are relatively likely to break restrictive norms and codes of conduct. Such actions, opposed or hostile to social institutions and laws, are conventionally defined by sociologists as *antisocial behavior*, and are labeled by those in authority as rebellious or even criminal. We believe antisocial actions are often attempts to dominate figures in authority (teachers, policemen) or, more abstractly, to prevail over a constraining environment. Therefore our inquiry focuses on the relationship of testosterone not only to dominant and aggressive actions, but also to antisocial behavior.

A PRIMER ON TESTOSTERONE

Testosterone is the primary *androgen*, a class of steroid hormones that develop and maintain masculine features. Although testosterone is made in the adrenal cortex and ovary of females, it is produced in far greater amounts by the Leydig cells of the testis. Testosterone in men is secreted into the bloodstream in spurts, so measured levels can change considerably within a few minutes. The hormone has a circadian rhythm in both sexes, highest and most variable in the morning, lower and more stable during the afternoon (Dabbs 1990).

Synthetic modifications of testosterone are pharmacologically more useful than testosterone itself because they are absorbed more easily when taken as pills or, in the case of esters such as testosterone propionate, have longer-lasting effects when injected. Beside its *androgenic* (masculinizing) effects, testosterone also has *anabolic* (protein-tissue-building) qualities that have therapeutic value (Bhasin et al. 1996). The anabolic steroids used by athletes to build muscle mass, reduce fat, and improve performance are synthetic derivatives of testosterone, designed to maximize protein synthesis and minimize masculinizing effects; however, virilization by anabolic steroids is never wholly eliminated (Kochakian 1993).

Many effects that we explain today by testosterone deficiency have been obtained since ancient times by castration of men and animals, which has been practiced not only to prevent fertility but also to prevent the development of secondary sexual characteristics, produce docility, reduce sex drive, and—in butchered animals—to produce fatter, more tender meat. (Among men, testosterone is inversely correlated with body fat [Mazur 1995].) Castrating a male chick, for example, makes its adult flesh more edible, and the capon fails to develop the rooster's head furnishings (red comb and wattles—markers of reproductive competence), does not crow or court hens, and does not fight other cocks. In Asia, eunuchs were presumed to be safe harem guards because of their lack of both interest in copulating and the ability to do so. Male sopranos and contraltos, emasculated to maintain their prepubescent voice range, were prominent in the opera and church music of seventeenth- and eighteenth-century Europe.

Our modern understanding began in the 1930s with the isolation and identification of testosterone. Reminiscent of the Curies' heroic extraction of minute amounts of radium from a ton of pitchblende, Koch and his coworkers mashed tons of bull testicles to fractionate ounces of material sufficiently pure to make the combs of capons grow bright red (de Kruif 1945). (Butenandt distilled twenty-five thousand liters of policemen's urine to obtain fifteen milligrams of another androgen, androsterone [Kochakian 1993]). Identification and synthesis followed quickly, enabling experimenters to replace or enhance testosterone in animal subjects and human patients. An example is the classic study of hen pecking orders by Allee, Collias, and Lutherman (1939), who injected testosterone propionate into low-ranking hens. These injected females became aggressive, and each rose in her status hierarchy, some to the top position. Furthermore, their comb size increased (a male characteristic), egg laying was suppressed, some began crowing (rare in hens), and a few began courting other hens.

Until the availability of radioimmunoassay in the 1960s, the measurement of endogenous testosterone was elusive because it is produced by the body in tiny amounts (Nieschlag and Wickings 1981). A normal man has about one hundred-thousandth gram of hormone per liter of blood (i.e., ten nanograms/milliliter); women have roughly one-seventh as much. Soon it was practical to measure *free* testosterone (i.e., testosterone not bound to protein, which is assumed to be the physiologically active portion) in saliva, with a concentration of about one-hundredth that of total testosterone in blood (Wang et al. 1981; Riad-Fahmy et al. 1982; Dabbs et al. 1995). Collection of saliva rather than blood has facilitated research outside of medical settings. These remarkable improvements in method, plus the recent availability of studies including thousands of men, have expanded our knowledge greatly.

TESTOSTERONE WORKS DIFFERENTLY
PERINATALLY, AT PUBERTY, AND IN ADULTHOOD

It is now clear that testosterone affects human males importantly but differently at three stages of life: perinatally (in utero and shortly after birth), during puberty, and in adulthood. This chapter focuses on the adult stage, but a brief review of earlier effects is worthwhile.

The mammalian fetus of both XX and XY individuals begins with undifferentiated sexual parts. A gene on the Y chromosome has been identified that causes the asexual gonads to develop as testes; lacking this gene the gonads become ovaries. So far as we know, the sex chromosomes have little more to do with sex differentiation, which hereafter is driven by hormones produced in the now sex-specific gonads. The testes produce testosterone during gestation, and production peaks again a month or two after birth, then declines by six months of age to the low range seen in later childhood (Winter et al. 1976). Testosterone and other testicular secretions cause the external genitalia to form into penis and scrotum rather than clitoris and labia, and internal ducts take the male form. The central nervous system is masculinized in rats and probably in humans too. The general rule, somewhat simplified, is that early exposure to greater amounts of testosterone produces more male characteristics (masculinization) and fewer female characteristics (defeminization), while less exposure to testosterone produces the reverse. Perinatal manipulation of animal subjects, and developmental abnormalities among humans, show convincingly that even genetic females show male forms if dosed early enough with testosterone, and genetic males show female forms if deprived of the hormone (Breedlove 1992).

Perinatal testosterone exposure affects behavior in a number of animal species (Breedlove 1992). For example, young male rhesus monkeys normally engage in more threats and rough-and-tumble play than do females, but when testosterone is administered to pregnant monkeys, their pseudohermaphroditic female offspring exhibit male-type play behavior. Furthermore, by limiting testosterone administration to the later part of gestation, female offspring are produced who exhibit male-type play but retain female-appearing genitals, showing that behavioral masculinization is independent of genital masculinization (Goy, Bercovitch, and McBrair 1988). Studies of human children exposed perinatally to abnormally high or low levels of testosterone are hampered by methodological problems and are not fully consistent but may be construed to support the primate results (Collaer and Hines 1995).

Many perinatal hormone effects are regarded as *organizing* the architecture of the body and brain, and the distribution of hormone receptors, into a relatively male-like configuration. When male testosterone increases later in life, it *activates* these preexisting structures. Thus, behaviors derive from the interaction of long-term organizational and shorter-term activation effects.

The testes greatly increase production of testosterone at puberty, elevating prepubescent serum levels from under one hundred nanograms per deciliter to adult levels ten or more times higher. This promotes growth of the penis, larynx (and deeper voice), muscles, beard and body hair, sex interest, and perhaps combativeness (Romano et al. 2004). Boys who are hypogonadal or castrated before puberty do not experience these changes, but they can be induced by testosterone replacement therapy.

One of the earliest and best-known studies of testosterone and aggression among adolescent boys is that of Olweus and his colleagues in Sweden

(Olweus et al. 1980, 1988; Mattsson et al. 1980). Since reviewers sometimes interpret these results more strongly than do the original investigators, it is worth examining them closely. A group of forty delinquent boys, ages fourteen to nineteen years (mean = sixteen years), living in an institution for serious recidivist youth offenders, was compared with a group of fifty-eight nondelinquent high school students, ages fifteen to seventeen years (mean = sixteen years). The result: Testosterone of the delinquents was slightly but not significantly higher than that of the nondelinquents.

Attempts to relate testosterone to aggressiveness *within* the delinquent sample produced marginal results. Boys who committed the most violent crimes had slightly but not significantly higher testosterone than boys who committed only property crimes. Ratings of the boys' aggressiveness by institution staff were not related to testosterone, nor were evaluations of aggressiveness by a psychiatrist. The boys completed several paper-and-pencil inventories of personality. Four scales measured forms of aggressiveness, and a fifth measured dominance/assertiveness. Only one of these five scales correlated significantly with testosterone. By comparing the eight delinquents with highest testosterone and the eight with lowest testosterone, one additional scale reached significance. For the delinquent sample overall, the investigators conclude, relationships between testosterone and their behavioral and personality variables are small in degree.

Comparable attempts were made to relate testosterone to aggressiveness within the nondelinquent sample of high school boys. Student peers rated the boys on three forms of aggressive behavior, none of which significantly related to testosterone. The boys completed pencil-and-paper inventories, mostly the same ones given to the delinquents. Four scales measured forms of aggressiveness, and a fifth measured antisocial behavior. Only two of these scales correlated significantly with testosterone. The investigators, summarizing their results for the nondelinquent boys, noted that inventory items that most clearly correlate with testosterone were those involving an aggressive *response to provocation* ("When a teacher criticizes me, I tend to answer back and protest") as opposed to expressions of unprovoked aggression ("I fight with other boys at school"). This interpretation associates testosterone with responses to challenge rather than with aggressiveness per se, but as we have seen, the empirical results are ambiguous. Acknowledging this uncertainty, the Swedish investigators suggest that the causal effects of testosterone be evaluated further using a longitudinal design.

Perhaps the reason the Swedish link between testosterone and aggression has been so often repeated and exaggerated is that it fits preconceived notions that the sharp adolescent rise in boys' testosterone fuels a nearly simultaneous rise in male aggressiveness. Before examining this possibility, it is worth emphasizing that physical aggression by boys does *not* generally rise during adolescence (Tremblay 2000; Rowe et al. 2004). Actually, it is littler boys who are most prone to physically assault their peers, though they lack the muscle or weapons to do much damage. The well-documented rise in boys' antisocial behavior with puberty is due mainly to nonviolent delinquency such as vandalism and status violations (Rutter, Giller, and Hagell 1998).

Later attempts to evaluate the contribution of testosterone to adolescent social problems produced mixed findings (Udry et al. 1985; Udry 1988, 1990; Susman et al. 1987; Inoff-Germain et al. 1988; Drigotas and Udry 1993; Halpern et al. 1993; Constantino et al. 1993). These are difficult studies to conduct because investigators must untangle the direct effect of testosterone from other physical changes in the boy's body at puberty, which affect how people respond to him. Also, there are important *social* changes during the early teen years—entry into high school, taking a job, prolonged absence from parents, more dependence on peer approval—any of which may affect behavior independently of hormonal effects.

The primary lesson of this research is that one cannot assess the effect of hormones on behavior without taking into account the social context. An adolescent's behavior is importantly affected by relationships with parents and peers. In a study of boys ages eight to eighteen years old, the correlation of testosterone to risk taking depended on the quality of the boy's relationship with his parents; the hormone-behavior link was strongest when the son-parent link was weakest (Booth et al. 2003). Rising testosterone might have a different effect on a boy in a delinquent gang than on a member of the Boy Scouts.

Newer work has overcome some of these methodological problems, not least by increasing sample size, as in a recent study of Rowe et al. (2004) using 713 boys, ages nine to fifteen years. The empirical picture emerging from this research, and from Tremblay and his associates (Tremblay et al. 1998; Schaal et al. 1996), and Booth and his associates (Booth et al. 2003), is that the adolescent rise in testosterone does *not* lead simply and directly to increased problem behavior among teenage boys. But once the social context is taken into account, we *do* see an effect of testosterone on dominance *in a direction consistent with the behavior of peers.* This was most dramatically shown when Rowe et al. (2004) considered whether boys did or did not have deviant peers. Boys with high testosterone committed a large number of "conduct disorders" (usually nonviolent antisocial actions like lying or breaking in) *if* they had delinquent peers, but there was no testosterone-disorder relationship among boys without delinquent peers. As if in mirror image, boys with high testosterone were more likely to be chosen by other children as team leaders if they did *not* have delinquent peers, but there was no testosterone-leader relationship among boys with delinquent peers. (These relationships were not diminished by controlling on physical maturation or chronological age.)

By the late teens, with puberty over, the physical shape and organization of the body and neurohormonal system are established (until the degradations of old age), so our concern during adulthood is solely with the behavioral effects of testosterone circulating in the blood, available to receptors in the brain and other organs (McEwen 1981). Testosterone levels peak in the late teens and early twenties, and then typically decline slowly as men age and put on weight. (Testosterone does not decline in men who maintain constant body fat [Mazur 1998].) There are similar age trends for male libido, aggressiveness, and antisocial deviance, all being highest among teenagers and men in their early twenties, then diminishing (Wilson and Herrnstein 1985; Laumann et al. 1994). However, the causal connection from hormones to behavior remains open to question.

Does high circulating testosterone make a man sexier than average in his behavior? The common occurrence of penile erection in prepubertal boys shows that vaginal penetration is possible with little circulating testosterone. Most researchers agree that a full repertoire of male sexual behaviors, including libidinous feelings and ejaculation, is unlikely without some minimal level of testosterone (e.g., Bagatell et al. 1994). Otherwise, variation in the level of circulating testosterone explains at most modest variation in sexual behavior (Carter 1992; Sadowsky et al. 1993). The usual decline in testosterone with age does not seem to be the reason for diminished sexual activity by older men (Tsitouras, Martin, and Harman 1982; Davidson et al. 1983; Mazur, Mueller, and Krause 2002). Overall, fluctuations in testosterone (within the normal range) have little effect on men's sexual behavior as long as a minimum amount of hormone is present. May the same be said for testosterone's effect on dominance?

DOMINANCE AND AGGRESSION IN ADULTHOOD

By the end of puberty, usually about age sixteen years, the physical form of a boy has changed into that of a man, so testosterone can no longer influence behavior through major reorganization of the body. However, the level of testosterone circulating in the bloodstream may affect dominating or aggressive behavior by activating receptors in organs or the nervous system.

Because of the practical and ethical difficulties in observing or even allowing high aggression in human subjects, researchers are often tempted to measure aggression, or aggressive or hostile *feelings*, by administering paper-and-pencil tests. A few positive correlations have been reported between testosterone and such measures, but more typical are failures to find this relationship. Testosterone is not related in any consistent way with aggression as measured on common personality scales. Furthermore, performance on these paper-and-pencil tests is not always correlated with actual aggressive acts, and there is little evidence of their relevance to violent or dominant behavior (Mazur and Booth 1998). I agree with Archer (1991) that studies based on self-assessment of aggressive traits or predispositions have limited relevance.

Focusing on more concrete indicators of behavior, and on males who have passed through puberty, there are reports of relatively high testosterone among dominant, aggressive, or antisocial men in jail. Other studies on non-incarcerated subjects show mostly corroborative results. Some of these findings are based on small samples and are methodologically dubious. (For a detailed review, see Mazur and Booth 1998; also see Salvador et al. 1999.) More trustworthy are studies based on an unusually large sample of 4,462 male army veterans in middle age. Several investigators using this database have shown testosterone to be significantly correlated to diverse antisocial behaviors including childhood truancy, trouble as an adult on the job and with the law, marital disruption, drug and alcohol abuse, violent behavior, and military AWOL—mostly indicators of rebelliousness and assertive norm breaking (Dabbs and Morris 1990; Booth and Osgood 1993; Booth and Dabbs 1993; Mazur 1995).

Overall, there is considerable evidence from a variety of settings that in men, circulating testosterone is correlated with dominant or aggressive behavior and antisocial norm breaking. Of course, correlation does not imply causation, and the question remains: Is high testosterone a *cause* of dominant and antisocial behavior? This could be answered with a double-blind experiment, comparing the behavior of normal men whose testosterone was raised pharmaceutically with a control group receiving a placebo. If dominant actions increased under the testosterone treatment, that would implicate the hormone as a cause of the behavior.

There have been recent experiments roughly of this kind, some spurred by interest in testosterone as a male contraceptive (Anderson, Bancroft, and Wu 1992; Bagatell et al. 1994; Tricker et al. 1996; Finkelstein et al. 1997; Yates et al. 1999; O'Connor et al. 2002; O'Connor et al. 2004). These studies use paper-and-pencil measures of self-reported (occasionally partner-reported) aggressiveness, and of angry, hostile, and irritable moods, as the dependent measures. While the results are mixed, overall they show little if any increase in anger/aggression/irritability due to supplemental testosterone. Unfortunately, this work has limited value for testing the testosterone-dominance hypothesis because, as noted above, pencil-and-paper tests of moods and traits poorly reflect dominance behavior. These experiments would better test the hypothesis by incorporating established laboratory methods for measuring dominant or assertive actions.

Kouri et al. (1995) first moved in this direction but with only six subjects. These were normal young men given increasingly high doses of testosterone cypionate or placebo using a double-blind, randomized, crossover design.

Each subject was tested for "aggressive" behavior by being placed in a lab setting and paired with another (fictitious) subject. The experimenter explained that each member of this pair could, by pushing an appropriate button, reduce the cash that would be paid to his opposite number. The subject was then made to believe that his fictitious opposite was indeed taking this punitive action against him. In this provocative situation, subjects made significantly more punitive button pushes while receiving testosterone than placebo. (Nonpunitive button pushes did not differ between testosterone and placebo conditions.) A second study by the same researchers used fifty-six men ages twenty to fifty years. In a similar crossover design, the investigators administered weekly doses of testosterone for six weeks and placebo for six weeks, separated by six weeks of no treatment. Again the subjects made significantly more punitive button pushes while receiving testosterone than when receiving placebo. Puzzlingly, the effect was due to a small group of competitive responders, only 16 percent of all subjects, while the majority of subjects showed no behavioral effect of the testosterone (Pope, Kouri, and Hudson 2000).

We must await additional controlled experiments to decisively test whether or not testosterone is a cause of dominant behavior in men. At present, in my view, this remains an unconfirmed hypothesis.

RECIPROCAL CAUSATION

If there is a link between testosterone and dominance, primate studies suggest a reciprocity of effects. Not only does testosterone affect dominance, but changes in dominance behavior or in social status cause changes in testosterone level (Rose, Bernstein, and Gordon 1975). We have stronger evidence on this *reverse* effect in humans because studies of it require no drug administration and can therefore be done by researchers other than physicians; also, testosterone levels can be obtained from subjects' saliva, which is easily collected. By now there have been several reports of testosterone changes in young men during athletic events, which are convenient research settings because they are stylized dominance contests involving face-to-face competition with a clear winner and loser.

Male testosterone varies in predicable ways both before and after competitive matches. First, athletes' testosterone rises shortly before their matches, as if in anticipation of the competition (Campbell, O'Rourke, and Rabow 1988; Booth et al. 1989; Suay et al. 1999; Salvador et al. 2003). This precompetition boost may promote dominant behavior, increasing the chance victory. Second, for one or two hours after the match, testosterone of winners is usually high relative to that of losers (Mazur and Lamb 1980; Elias 1981; Campbell, O'Rourke, and Rabow 1988; Booth et al. 1989), although this difference does not appear in every study of athletes. (For insignificant or null results, and possible reasons, see Salvador et al. 1987; Mazur, Booth, and Dabbs 1993; Suay et al. 1999; and Gonzalez-Bono et al. 1999.) Both testosterone effects, the prematch rise and the postmatch difference between winners and losers, are illustrated in Figure 9.1, using data from a men's varsity tennis team.

These testosterone effects were obtained in physically taxing sports. Perhaps more interesting is the less vigorous competition of everyday social interaction and symbolic changes in social status (Kemper 1990; Mazur 1985). Additional studies show the same pattern of male testosterone responses during nonphysical contests or ritual status manipulations. First, testosterone rises shortly before chess matches (Mazur, Booth, and Dabbs 1992) or laboratory contests of reaction time (Gladue, Boechler, and McCaul 1989), and in subjects confronted with a symbolic challenge from an insult (Nisbett and Cohen 1996). Second, testosterone levels of winners are high relative to those of losers following chess matches (Mazur, Booth, and Dabbs 1992) and contests of reaction time, especially if subjects' moods are appropriately positive or negative (Gladue, Boechler, and McCaul 1989; McCaul, Gladue, and Joppa 1992). Similar effects occur among sports fans who are not themselves

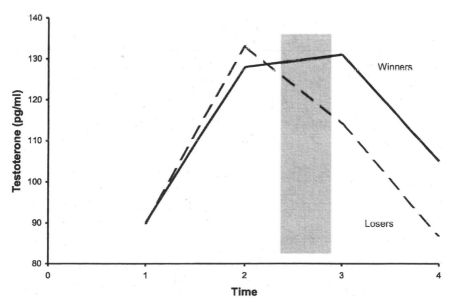

Figure 9.1. Testosterone of male university tennis-team members, before and after their matches. Winners (n = 20) are compared to losers (n = 16). Time 1 is the day before the match, time 2 is about 15 minutes before the match, time 3 is immediately after the match, and time 4 is the next day. The match is indicated by a gray bar (adapted from Booth et al. 1989)

participants in the physical competition. Following the 1994 World Cup soccer tournament, in which Brazil beat Italy, testosterone increased significantly in Brazilian fans who had watched the match on television, and decreased in Italian fans (Fielden, Lutter, and Dabbs 1994).

The hormone-depressing effect of status loss is shown in a study by Kreuz, Rose, and Jennings (1972), who found that the testosterone of officer candidates was abnormally low during the early, most degrading weeks of Officer Candidate School, but their testosterone returned to normal during the relaxed weeks just prior to graduation. Similarly, testosterone among prisoners dropped after admission to an incarceration program modeled after military boot camp (Thompson, Dabbs, and Frady 1990). Mazur and Lamb (1980) found that testosterone of medical students rose after their graduation ceremony, at the time when their mood was elated. During the first days of freedom for fifty-two Americans who had been held captive in Iran for fifteen months, a period of elation over their improvement in status, the former hostages' testosterone was highly elevated (Rahe et al. 1990). Thus, the testosterone pattern appears in nonphysical as well as physical competition, and in response to symbolic challenges and status changes among men.

The rise in testosterone following a win is associated with the subject's elated mood. If the mood elevation is lessened because the subject has won by luck rather than through his own efforts, or because he does not regard the win as important, then the rise in testosterone is lessened or does not occur at all (Mazur and Lamb 1980; McCaul, Gladue, and Joppa 1992). Men who truly want to win are more likely to experience a rise or fall of testosterone, depending on if they succeed or fail, than do men who care little about winning (Schultheiss and Rohde 2002; Schultheiss, Campbell, and McClelland 1999). Soccer players show higher pregame testosterone levels when playing extreme rivals compared to moderate rivals, and they have higher pregame testosterone at home games than away games, a finding consistent with the oft-noted "home advantage" (Neave and Wolfson 2003).

TESTOSTERONE IN WOMEN

Despite considerable speculation that testosterone is associated with aggression or status in women (e.g., Kemper 1990), the empirical literature shows no consistent picture. There are reports of relatively high testosterone in women with high-status occupations (Purifoy and Koopmans 1979) or who score highly on self-reports of dominance (Grant and France 2001) or who are relatively aggressive (Ehlers, Rickler, and Hovey (1980). In a series of studies on women in prison, Dabbs and his associates report both positive and null relationships, depending on the measure of dominance or aggressiveness (Dabbs et al. 1988; Dabbs and Hargrove 1997; Banks and Dabbs

1996). Others find testosterone to be negatively related to aggression or status in women (Gladue 1991; Cashdan 1995). Furthermore, female testosterone does not respond to competition with the same pattern found in men (Rejeski et al. 1990; Mazur, Susman, and Edelbrock 1997; Booth and Dabbs 1995; Kivlighan, Granger, and Booth 2005). Women on a college rugby team showed a pregame rise in testosterone, but changes after the game were not related to winning or losing (Bateup et al. 2002), The lack of consistency among these findings is a caution to await further research.

MOMENTUM

In a dominance contest, Ego's decision to compete with Alter, or to defer, depends on his motivation to dominate, which hypothetically depends on his testosterone level (among other factors). A man who has experienced a recent rise in testosterone, perhaps from a prior victory or a symbolic elevation in status, should be unusually assertive and may challenge someone of relatively high status. If both Ego and Alter decide to compete, their subsequent ranks are determined according to who successfully out-stresses whom.

If the winner (say, Ego) experiences rising testosterone as a result of his victory, this should sustain or increase his assertiveness and his display of dominant signs such as erect posture, sauntering or striding gait, and direct eye contact with others. Thus bolstered, Ego may seek out new dominance encounters and is primed to win them. The feedback between high testosterone and dominant demeanor may explain the momentum often associated with strings of triumphs. Success begets a high testosterone response, which begets more dominant behavior, which begets more success. This sequence has been verified in mice but not in men (Trainor, Bird, and Marler 2004).

On the other side Alter, the loser, experiences a drop in testosterone, reducing his assertiveness and increasing his display of deferential signs such as stooped posture, smiling, or eye aversion. Faced with a new dominance encounter, he is now at a psychic and physiological disadvantage. One defeat begets another. Alter is more likely than before to retreat or submit. This may be an adaptive response, saving Alter from further losses and perhaps from additional damage.

HONOR SUBCULTURES

Nisbett (1993; Nisbett and Cohen 1996) has attributed the historically high violence in the American South, compared to the North, to its "culture of honor" whereby Southern men, when challenged by insults to themselves or their families, are required to defend themselves as virtuous warriors or else lose face. Apparently as a result, Southern men are unusually alert to possible insults, reacting dominantly—sometimes violently—to speech or actions that might not be perceived as injurious in other cultures.

Leaving aside the particular historic roots of the South, there may be a general hypersensitivity to insult in *any* subculture that is (or once was) organized around young men who are unconstrained by traditional community agents of social control, as often occurs in frontier communities, in gangs, among vagabonds or bohemians, and after breakdowns in the social fabric following wars or natural disasters. When young men place special emphasis on protecting their reputations, and they are not restrained from doing so, dominance contests become ubiquitous, the hallmark of male-to-male interaction (Thrasher 1963; Sanchez-Jankowsky 1991).

The leading student of street behavior in America's inner cities, sociologist Elijah Anderson (1994), vividly portrays the importance of dominance contests and their constant presence for poor young black men:

> [M]ost youths have . . . internalized the code of the streets . . . , which chiefly [has] to do with interpersonal communication . . . , [including] facial expressions, gait, and verbal expressions—all of which are geared mainly to deterring aggression. . . .
>
> Even so, there are no guarantees against challenges, because there are always people looking for a fight to increase their share of respect—of "juice," as it is sometimes called on the street. Moreover, if a person is assaulted, it is important, not only in the eyes of his opponent but also in the eyes of his "running buddies," for him to avenge himself. Otherwise he risks being "tried" [challenged] or "moved on" by any number of others. To maintain his honor he must show he is not someone to be "messed with" or "dissed."
>
> . . . The craving for respect that results gives people thin skins. Shows of deference by others can be highly soothing, contributing to a sense of security, comfort, self-confidence, and self-respect. . . . Hence one must be ever vigilant against the transgressions of others or even appearing as if transgressions will be tolerated. Among young people, whose sense of self-esteem is particularly vulnerable, there is an especially heightened concern with being disrespected. Many inner-city young men in particular crave respect to such a degree that they will risk their lives to attain and maintain it. (88–89)

The honor subculture, emphasizing defense of one's reputation from insult, has been amply demonstrated by social scientists to be a feature of life for young men in the inner city (Anderson 1978, 1991; Horowitz 1983; Katz 1988).

We know that testosterone rises in men awaiting a contest, regardless of the eventual outcome of that contest. Generalizing to the street, hormone levels should be elevated in young men who are constantly vigilant against challenges to their reputations. Of course, testosterone is also affected by the outcome of the contest, so persistent losers might be hormonally depressed, but most men—those with mixed outcomes or better—should have elevated testosterone.[2]

This hypothesis provides an interpretation of reported racial differences in testosterone. A comparison of black and white boys ages six to eighteen years, mostly preteens, showed no significant race difference in testosterone (Richards et al. 1992). But by adulthood, as Ellis and Nyborg (1992) have shown, black males do have significantly higher testosterone levels than white males (also see Ross et al. 1986). Possibly this difference reflects the higher defensive demands on black men during young adulthood.

The data used by Ellis and Nyborg came from 4,462 U.S. Army veterans, ranging in age from thirty to forty-seven, and permit a finer-grain analysis. Among veterans older than the median age of thirty-seven years—too old to be involved in inner-city honor cultures—the testosterone of blacks is no higher than that of whites (Figure 9.2). Furthermore, among younger veterans who have gone to college—and thus are unlikely to be inner-city residents—there is no significant race difference in testosterone. Only among *younger veterans with little education* do we find testosterone in blacks to be unusually high, significantly higher than in whites. These younger black men, poorly educated, most of them urban residents, are most likely to participate in the honor subculture, and that may be the reason for their elevated testosterone.

The reciprocal linkage between hormones and behavior suggests that if testosterone levels among young men in the inner city are heightened by their continual defensive posture against challenge, then these high hormone levels in turn encourage further dominance contests.[3] Feedback between challenge and testosterone may create a vicious circle, sometimes with lethal effects.

BASAL VS. RECIPROCAL MODELS: DIVORCE AND MARRIAGE

A *basal model* is usually implied in describing the causal effects of testosterone on behavior. Each man's testosterone measurement reflects his basal level, which is genetically determined and more or less constant from year to year. Consistent with this model, reliabilities from $r = .50$ to $r = .65$ are reported for testosterone measurements taken (at the same time of day to control for circadian variation) over periods ranging from days to six years (Booth and Dabbs 1993). Thus, men with relatively high testosterone at one time tend to be relatively high at other times too. On the assumption that basal hormone levels are consistent, they necessarily predate any postadolescent behavior and so cannot be a consequence of that behavior. Furthermore, since basal levels are stable, it follows that they can be adequately

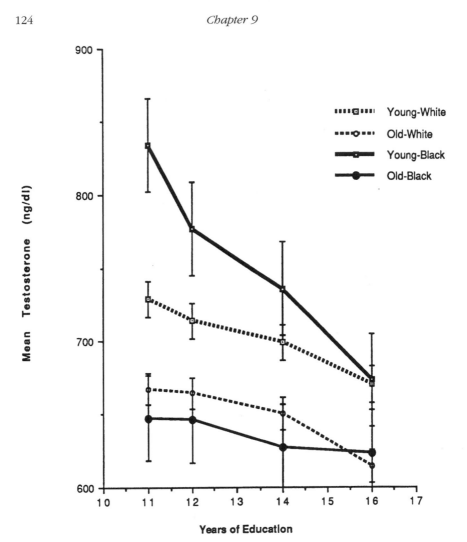

Figure 9.2.   Testosterone of male army veterans by education, age, and race. Vertical bars represent standard errors (Mazur 1995).

measured at any time, whether before or after the behavior, and therefore can be adequately assessed in a cross-sectional study. Going further, basal hormone level is regarded as a prima facie cause of any postadolescent behavior that it predicts, especially if the effect persists after controlling for alternate explanations.

We must contrast the static basal model with a dynamic *reciprocal model* in which testosterone and status competition influence one another, going up or down together. The observed reliability of a man's testosterone measurements from year to year may reflect his stable social position rather than his genetically determined basal level. Current data are insufficient to choose one model over the other, so both are viable and heuristically useful.

The power of the basal model is illustrated by its ability to predict behavior from testosterone measured at a single point in time. It suggests, for example, that men with high basal testosterone tend toward dominating or antisocial behavior that disrupts family functioning, leading eventually to divorce. Pursuing this reasoning, Julian and McKenry (1989) found in a small sample of men that testosterone levels are negatively related to marital satisfaction. A more extensive analysis of data from 4,462 former military servicemen in middle age showed that males with higher testosterone (measured once) were less likely to marry and more likely to divorce (Booth and Dabbs 1993). The likelihood of never marrying was 50 percent higher for men whose testosterone was one standard deviation above the mean compared to those one standard deviation below the mean. Similarly, among men who had married, those at the higher level of testosterone were 43 percent more likely to divorce than those at the lower level. Once married, men with higher testosterone were 31 percent more likely to leave home because of troubled relationships with their wives, 38 percent more likely to have extramarital sex, and 13 percent more likely to report hitting or throwing things at their spouses. In addition, high-testosterone men were more likely to report a lower quality of marital interaction. The occurrence of these behaviors increased continuously with testosterone; it was not limited to men with exceptionally high testosterone.

Using the same sample of men, correlations between testosterone and education, and between testosterone and income, are significantly negative but small in magnitude. Dabbs (1992) coded the status of the occupations of these men, using U.S. Census categories, and showed a correlation with testosterone of $r = -.11$ ($p = .001$). Professional and technical workers had lower levels of testosterone than service and production workers. The unemployed had the highest level of testosterone. There was no evidence of a threshold effect.

Men with higher levels of testosterone are more likely to be arrested for offenses other than traffic violations, to buy and sell stolen property, incur bad debts, and use a weapon in fights (Booth and Osgood 1993). Those with a testosterone level one standard deviation above the mean were 28 percent more likely to engage in criminal behavior than those one standard deviation below the mean. Again, no evidence of a threshold effect is observed. In addition, those who were delinquent as juveniles were more likely to commit crimes as adults if they had higher levels of testosterone.

An analysis of factors that predict exposure to military combat reveals that testosterone increases the likelihood of exposure (Gimbel and Booth 1996). It is unclear whether high-testosterone individuals take an active role in seeking out combat or if those in command recognize behaviors that make the individual a better combatant and assign him accordingly. It is also possible that high-testosterone individuals are antisocial enough to get combat assignments as punishment. In any case, the basal model shows impressive predictive ability.

Unfortunately these findings, based on data measured at a single point in time, cannot tell us whether the men with marital and other difficulties always had relatively high testosterone, as assumed in the basal model, or if discord surrounding their problems produced elevated testosterone, which in turn exacerbated the discord, as assumed in the reciprocal model.

An unusual opportunity to compare the two models is presented by a panel study of 2,100 male air force veterans who received four physical examinations, roughly three years apart, over a decade (Wolfe et al. 1990; Mazur and Michalek 1998). Correlations between testosterone levels measured in any two exams range from r = .47 to r = .61, showing the expected consistency across years.

There was little behavioral measurement in this study, but marital status was determined at each examination. Testosterone, as measured four times during the decade, could accordingly be correlated with marital status at each exam. Among the sixteen possible correlations, ten were significantly positive, replicating Booth and Dabbs's (1993) association of high basal testosterone with divorce. However, testosterone as measured *right after* the divorce is the best predictor, giving a correlation roughly twice as large as does testosterone when measured five years away from the divorce. This indicates that the reciprocal model is also at work.

Furthermore, men who divorced during the decade of the study had elevated testosterone in the examinations just before and after their breakups, compared to examinations further removed in time. The testosterone of men who married during the decade fell as they made the transition from bachelor to husband, and testosterone remained low among stably married men. Thus, testosterone is highly responsive to changes in marital status, falling with marriage and rising with divorce (Figure 9.3).

These results have an easy interpretation in the reciprocal model. Normal marriages are secure and supportive, freer from stress than single life, consistent with the relatively low cortisol found in married air force veterans. Single men are more likely than married men to face confrontations and challenges, and, lacking the social support of a spouse, they are more likely to face situations where they must watch out for themselves, acting defensively and adopting protective postures. These are precisely the kinds of situations in which testosterone rises. A marriage ceremony is the culmination of a longer and more gradual period of courtship and engagement, in which a man accepts the support of his partner, removing himself from the competitive area in which he has operated with his fellows. It is for this reason, perhaps, that testosterone declines with marriage (Burnham et al. 2003).

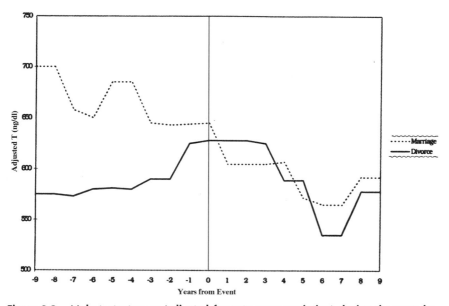

Figure 9.3. Male testosterone (adjusted for extraneous variation) during the years before and after a marriage or a divorce (Mazur and Michalek 1998)

Similarly, a divorce is discrete in time, but the breakup of a marriage is a process usually spanning years both before and after the legal announcement (Booth and Amato 1991). Typically it is accompanied by arguments and confrontations, the kinds of events associated with high testosterone, both as cause and effect (Booth et al. 1985). Most men undergoing this level of challenge, unless persistently defeated, experience rising testosterone, which in turn encourages further confrontation with their estranged wives. Reciprocity is thus an appealing model here, but we also need the basal model to explain why men initially high in testosterone have more propensity to divorce.

SUMMARY STATEMENT

Perinatally and during puberty, the effects of testosterone on behavior appear to work primarily through long-term reorganizations of the body and neurohormonal system, and only secondarily through short-term activation. By the end of puberty, usually around age sixteen years, the body is nearly at its adult form, so behavior is affected primarily by the level of testosterone circulating in the bloodstream and available to activate steroid receptors.

I share doubts expressed by Archer (1991) and Albert, Walsh, and Jonik (1994) that circulating testosterone directly affects human aggression—the intentional infliction of physical injury. I favor instead the hypothesis that high or rising testosterone encourages dominant behavior intended to achieve or maintain high status (implying power, influence, and valued prerogatives). Usually humans express dominance nonaggressively. In the next chapter, I take up the important question of why men sometimes dominate with intent to harm.

When military, school, or legal authorities require the behavior of subordinates to conform to rigid norms or laws, those people in subordinate roles who are motivated to act dominantly are likely to do so by breaking these norms or laws. In such settings, high or rising testosterone encourages actions conventionally regarded as rebellious, antisocial, or even criminal.

Studies using various paper-and-pencil self-reports of aggressive/hostile moods or personalities have not been generally successful in demonstrating relationships to testosterone. Using more direct indicators or inventories of behavior, studies in both prisons and free settings fairly consistently show significant correlations between testosterone and dominating behaviors (with or without aggressiveness), and between testosterone and diverse antisocial or rebellious actions. Although the *correlation* between testosterone and dominant or antisocial behavior is well established, heightened testosterone has not been established as a *cause* of these behaviors. We are just beginning to see proper double-blind experiments testing the effect of testosterone on dominant behavior as measured with established laboratory procedures.

There is strong correlational and experimental evidence that testosterone responds in predictable ways both before and after competitions for status. First, testosterone rises shortly before a competitive event, as if in anticipation of the challenge. Second, after the conclusion of competition, testosterone in winners rises relative to that of losers. Testosterone also rises after status elevations, and it falls after status demotions. These effects require the presence of appropriate mood changes—elation or dejection—accompanying the status changes. Limited evidence suggests that this pattern of testosterone responses is specific to men.

"Honor subcultures" are communities in which young men are hypersensitive to insult, rushing to defend their reputations in dominance contests. Challenges are pervasive and have the effect of elevating testosterone among those who participate in them (unless they are persistently defeated). Heightened testosterone may in turn encourage more challenge behavior, producing a vicious circle.

This *reciprocal model* implies feedback between testosterone and dominance, each reinforcing the other. It contrasts with the customary *basal model* in which an individual's basal level of testosterone is presumed to be a fairly stable trait that predicts his behavior. Most studies cannot distinguish between the basal and reciprocal models because their data are collected at one point in time. An exception is a study of marital status among 2,100 male air force veterans who received four medical examinations over a ten-year period. Among these men, testosterone levels fall and remain low with marriage, and rise with divorce, rather than remaining constant. These results, although limited in scope, favor the reciprocal model over the basal model. The basal model, on the other hand, better explains the propensity for divorce among men who were initially high in testosterone. At present, both models are viable.

The reliable association of high testosterone with antisocial behaviors, including marital disruption and violent criminality, raises an interesting puzzle. These negative behaviors foster downward social mobility. Under the basal model, which assumes testosterone level to be a persistent trait, we should expect an accumulation of *high testosterone* men in the lower ranks of society. Indeed, as noted, correlations between testosterone and various measures of socioeconomic status (occupation, income, education) are significantly negative. But they are slight in magnitude. Thus, leaving aside honor subcultures, we find little concentration of men with high testosterone in the lower classes. Why? One possibility is that the downward mobility of high testosterone antisocial men is nearly balanced by the upward mobility of high-testosterone prosocial men. This hypothetical stream of high-testosterone prosocial men remains invisible to us, so far, perhaps because past studies have used as subjects mostly working-class men or convicts, who have limited opportunities for legitimate advancement.

The nearly uniform distribution of testosterone across social classes is less puzzling under the reciprocal model, which regards testosterone as malleable rather than a stable personality trait. Again excepting honor subcultures, where challenges are exceptionally common, dominance contests probably occur nearly as frequently among elites as in the working class, as often in the boardroom as on the shop floor. Therefore, testosterone responses to challenge, and to winning and losing, should be distributed fairly evenly across classes. Under this reciprocal model, we would expect little accumulation of testosterone at the bottom levels of society.

The applicability of one model or the other would be elucidated by studying the relationship of testosterone to behavior among upper-class men who have favorable social opportunities and strong incentives for prosocial behavior.

NOTES

1. See Ellis (1995) for a meta-analysis of empirical tests of this supposition.
2. Stressors such as weight loss, surgery, or military training sometimes depress testosterone (Strauss, Lanese, and Malarkey 1985; Booth, Mazur, and Dabbs 1993). If

all stressors depressed testosterone, then the stressful challenges of inner-city street life should lower the hormone, not elevate it. However, not all stressors are the same, and social challenges in particular evoke hormonal responses different from those due to surgery or weight loss. Indeed, we have already seen that testosterone reliably *rises* in the face of competitive challenges, even while cortisol goes up as well (Booth et al. 1989; Elias 1981; Salvador et al. 1987; Gladue, Boechler, and McCaul 1989). Thus, stress effects do not negate the hypothesis that street challenges elevate male testosterone.

3. See Banks and Dabbs (1996) for a similar difference in testosterone between white college students and white delinquents of the same age.

10

Violence

In everyday life, dominance contests are based on the manipulation of psychological and physiological stress, not on causing or even threatening physical harm to one's adversary. Most adult humans experience little violent confrontation. Only 28 percent of American men and 15 percent of women report ever having been hit after childhood (Davis, Smith, and Marsden 2003).

Occasionally face-to-face competition escalates to a violent stage not originally intended or foreseen. This happens more often among males than females, and more in some cultural settings than others. There is a modern predilection to blame high testosterone or misuse of synthetic steroids for violence by males, with accompanying images of "'roid rages" and "testosterone poisoning." While good evidence suggests that testosterone encourages dominant behavior, there is no strong indication that the hormone in either natural or synthetic form produces violence per se (but see Pope and Katz 1990; 1994).

We do not profoundly understand why dominance encounters sometimes devolve into violent attacks.[1] The importance of this unsolved problem warrants brief excursions into the dominance-related topics of murder and warfare.

MURDER

Assistant District Attorney Kenneth Rosso said Salgado [age 23] shot Lee [age 21] twice in the right side of the head, then discovered he still had six rounds of ammunition in the handgun, stood over Lee and fired an additional six shots into the left side of Lee's head. Rosso said Lee and Salgado knew each other and the shooting apparently stemmed from an earlier confrontation in a local nightclub where Salgado had bumped into Lee and the two exchanged angry words. (*Syracuse Post-Standard*, June 8, 2002)

Illegal killing occurs for diverse reasons including drug marketing, robbery, jealousy, mental derangement, religious or ideological commitment, and cash payment. Here I focus on what criminologist Jack Katz (1988) calls the most numerous type of criminal homicide, the impassioned killing of someone for what the killer regards as a good moralistic reason, perhaps the defense of his family, his property, or his good name.

Usually these murders of passion occur without premeditation. The episodes Katz had in mind develop quickly, occurring without thought of legal consequences. Often the killers are surprised by the unintended fatality, regarding the outcome as an accident. Reflecting their lack of forethought, many killers do not attempt to escape, or do so ineptly. Police make arrests in roughly 80 percent of homicide cases—usually within a day of the crime—compared to arrests in about 25 percent of robberies and 15 percent of burglaries.

The desired end point of an impassioned attack is not necessarily death so much as hurting or physically punishing the victim. Whether an attack ends as a criminal homicide or an aggravated assault may be incidental, depending on such chance factors as the time to reach an emergency room, the quality of medical service, whether a gun was used, whether the falling victim's head hit concrete, and so on. While there is little reason to think such killings differ much from impassioned attacks whose victims survived, murders are better documented than nonlethal assaults and therefore more amenable to analysis.

Murderers are more often young men, in their teens or early twenties, than any other sex or age category (Daly and Wilson 1988; Archer 1994). A major reason is that young men are far more likely than any other age-sex category to engage in overt dominance contests, some inevitably escalating to violence. But this cannot be the entire explanation because men are more violent than women even when dominance is not involved. In all nations with adequate statistics, men more frequently kill themselves, although women more frequently *threaten* suicide without carrying it out (Maris 2000). Males, young or old, are persistently more likely than females to hunt, to play violently, and to be interested in weapons. Relatively high alcohol use by young men contributes to their hazard level. Alcohol reduces inhibitions, encourages recklessness, and inflames confrontations, violence, and other harmful behavior (Campbell and Gibbs 1986).

Victims are usually relatives or friends of, or at least acquainted with, their killers. Criminologists have repeatedly replicated Marvin Wolfgang's (1958) classic study of homicide, showing that fatal aggression between men is usually precipitated by a trivial altercation, perhaps an insult, curse, or jostling. This is followed by an escalation of hostile verbal actions that may look no different from many nonfatal arguments, as in the following episode:

> Vice President Cheney. . . , serving in his role as president of the Senate, appeared in the chamber for a photo session. A chance meeting with Sen. Patrick Leahy, D-Vt., the ranking Democrat on the Judiciary Committee, became an argument about Cheney's ties to Halliburton Co., an international energy services corporation. . . . The exchange ended when Cheney offered some crass advice.
> "F— yourself," said the vice president.
> Leahy's spokesman, David Carle, Wednesday confirmed the brief but fierce exchange. "The vice president seemed to be taking personally the criticisms that Senator Leahy and others have leveled against Halliburton's sole-source contracts in Iraq," Carle said. . . .
> Cheney said Friday he was in no mood to exchange pleasantries with Leahy because Leahy had "challenged my integrity" by making charges of cronyism between Cheney and his former firm. . . .
> Tuesday's exchange began when Leahy crossed the aisle at the photo session and joked to Cheney about being on the Republican side. . . . Then Cheney, according to Carle, "lashed into" Leahy for the Halliburton remarks. (Dewar and Milbank 2004, A7)

There was no prospect of murder in this case, but the intensification of hostile remarks is of the kind that often precedes fatal attacks.

A fuller escalation is described in a homicide case cited by Katz. Here the victim and attacker began their evening as friends in a bar. The attacker paid for a cab and some beer, expecting to continue drinking at the victim's home and to spend the night there. On arrival, the victim told the attacker to leave. They exchanged curses and threats as the attacker moved to depart:

> The dude said, "That's right, get your fucking ass out of here now," and pushed me once more. I said to myself, "Fuck it, that's it, I'm going to fuck him up." I hit him with a right hook, went berserk, and grabbed a lamp and busted him over the head and downed him. I yelled, "You punk motherfucker, I'll kick your eyes out of your head" and stomped him in the face. (1988, 39)

Sometimes the altercation continues through a series of exchanges, each broken off when one or both adversaries depart to recoup or enlist allies or fetch a weapon, returning to the fray with a better chance of victory or when continuation cannot be avoided.

Often the killer feels provoked by the victim, the target of an insult, the butt of a joke, or an object of humiliation. "From the killer's perspective, the victim either teases, dares, defies, or pursues the killer. . . . That the killer feels compelled to respond to a fundamental challenge to his worth is indicated as well by the frequent presence and the role of an audience" (Katz 1988, 20).

In about 60 percent of U.S. homicides, males kill males. Women killing women account for less than 3 percent. Most remaining cases involve men killing women, usually their wives or girlfriends. No doubt there are occasions when sadistic men attack subservient women, but more often the male attacker feels provoked by his female partner asserting independence (Wilson and Daly 1993). Here is another of Katz's cases:

> I told her if she stopped with the divorce, I would promise to act better . . . but she wouldn't buy any of it. I got angrier and angrier. . . . I looked at her straight in the face and said, "Well, you better start thinking about those poor kids of ours." She said, "I don't care about them. I just want a divorce." My hate for her exploded then, and I said, "You dirty, no-good bitch," and started pounding her in the face with my fist. She put her arms up and covered her face, so I ran and got my rifle and pointed it at her. I said, "Bitch, you better change your mind fast or I'm going to kill you." She looked up and said in a smart-ass way, "Go ahead then, shoot me." I got so mad and felt so much hate for her, that I just started shooting her again and again. (1988, 33)

Here, apparently, the enraged murderer failed at all nonlethal means of asserting his dominance and took the ultimate step to halt his wife's defiance. The refusal of either party to stand down requires that both reach for more potent stressors to settle the matter. Presumably, although we cannot be certain, if one adversary in an ultimately fatal dominance contest had surrendered by signaling deference, the violence would have de-escalated and the killing been avoided.

Extreme anger (rage) heightens the potential lethality of competition by shifting the adversaries' intentions from dominating to damaging the opposition. The red face of anger, with its raised voice and universally recognized facial gestures and body postures, likely entails particular neurophysiological actions. These cannot be studied easily because of the practical difficulty of finding subjects in an enraged state, and because of ethical restraints against enraging psychology undergraduates simply for the purpose of study. As noted in chapter 4, emotions—including anger/rage—use portions of the brain loosely termed the limbic system, including the amygdala and hypothalamus. A number of neurotransmitters and hormones seem implicated in anger, including serotonin, prolactin, norepinephrine, and dopamine (Suarez et al. 1998; Siegel et al. 1999; Davidson, Putnam, and Larson 2000). Alcohol may intensify the normal neurophysiological effect of rage.

Rage may develop gradually, as a confrontation escalates, or suddenly. It can be triggered by an "inappropriate" violation of social norms, by an assault on one's pride or reputation (Weisfeld 1994). People who are humiliated often become enraged at the person who humiliated them. The classic gentlemanly duel was precipitated by an affront to honor, perhaps a slur on one's manhood, or an aspersion on one's lady or family name. Such improprieties elicited a glove in the face, often too rashly and later regretted. The subsequent duel, in contrast to the initiating challenge, was (ideally) conducted politely, following precise rules, with arrangements handled formally by seconds (whose presence inhibited anyone from running away). A duelist who relied on a precision weapon had an edge if he remained cooler, less emotional, than his opponent. The killing was itself no affront to the victim. To the contrary, death on the dueling field was an affirmation of the victim's bravery, if not his skill (Johnson 1991).

Impassioned homicide sometimes involves multiple victims, but that is unusual. The seriousness of murder as a social problem stems not from the number of victims in any episode, but from the number of episodes, which fall heavily on impoverished communities with honor cultures. In the United States there were sixteen thousand homicides in 2003, a large portion the result of clashing egos (FBI 2004).

WARFARE

Violence of even greater magnitude sometimes grows out of personal dominance contests in an entirely different way, through warfare, which tragically engulfs victims who were not even trivially involved in the inciting episode. Wars, large and small, are a continuing feature of the global scene. In any given year, one can count dozens of national armies engaged in combat operations. It would be absurd to claim that *all* modern wars are seeded by a clash of personalities, or that any war is *nothing but* a dominance contest writ large. Avoiding these extremes, I propose that personal dominance motives play an important role in warfare. In the past century, small-group dominance competition repeatedly nucleated war-fighting situations in which populations actually or potentially suffered the gravest consequences.

Why do men *want* to go to war? One important reason is that the warrior is a glorious figure, admired since the beginning of literature:

> In their midst was Achilles, arming himself in the armor that [the god] Hephaistos had made. . . . First he clasped over his legs those fine greaves with their silver ankle-guards. Next he put the corselet about his chest and slung the silver-studded sword over his shoulders. Then he took up the great shield, which gleamed like another moon. . . . Then he lifted the strong helmet and set it upon his head, shining like a star and nodding its golden plumes. Achilles tried himself in the armor, to see if it fitted and if his limbs had easy play—it seemed to lift him up in the air like wings. (Homer, translated by Rouse 1938, 235)

> The judges had now been two hours in the lists, awaiting in vain the appearance of a champion. . . . It was, however, the general belief that no one could or would appear [to defend] a Jewess accused of sorcery. . . . At this instant a

knight, urging his horse to speed, appeared on the plain advancing toward the lists. A hundred voices exclaimed, "A champion!—a champion!" . . .

"I have come hither to sustain with lance and sword the just and lawful quarrel of this damsel. . . ."

"The stranger must first show," said Malvoism, "that he is a good knight and of honorable lineage. . . ."

"My name," said the knight, raising his helmet, "is better known, my lineage more pure, Malvoism, than thine own. I am Wilfred of Ivanhoe." (Sir Walter Scott 1962, 454)

The Seventh Ulany Brigade held its annual officers' affair at the Europa Hotel . . . [which] brought out the cream of Warsaw. Gabriela . . . entered the ballroom on Martha's arm. Both of them saw him at the same time. In fact, every pair of eyes seemed set on the door as the epitome of a Polish cavalry officer, Lieutenant Andrei Androfski, entered. . . .

"Isn't he yummy," Martha said.

Gabriela was still staring. (Leon Uris 1961, 33–34)

The warrior is the most romantic of male images, whether as tragic Greek demigod, chivalric knight, or dashing hussar. If there is a better way to spend one's youth than as a hero, I don't know it.

Preparation for war can be an exhilarating experience. Often young men join up in a rush, urged on by young women and their elders, anticipating the grandest adventures of their lives. Not everyone wants to go to every war; otherwise there would be no need for conscription. The Vietnam War was eventually so unpopular that some Americans fled to Canada to avoid service. During the American Civil War, wealthy young Northerners paid poorer men to take their places in the draft. Still, the eve of war can be an invigorating time, as in the opening days of World War I when soldiers on both sides became suddenly popular, treated with gifts of food and beer and kisses as they strolled the streets in their new uniforms, greeting friends and showing off to the ladies.

Even when bloodless preparation gives way to the reality of killing, some still find pleasure in the contest of arms, which, in the following passage by famed test pilot Chuck Yeager, is transparently a dominance contest played out with lethal machines.

I knew that dog-fighting was what I was born to do. It's almost impossible to explain the feeling: it's as if you were one with that Mustang, an extension of the damn throttle. . . . With experience, you knew before a kill when you were going to score. Once you zeroed in, began to outmaneuver your opponent while closing in, you became a cat with a mouse. You set him up, and there was no way out: both of you knew he was finished. . . . You picked your spot: slightly below, so you could pull up, lead him a little, and avoid being hit by metal when he disintegrated. When he blew up, it was a pleasing, beautiful sight. There was no joy in killing someone, but real satisfaction when you out-flew a guy and destroyed his machine. That was the contest: human skill and machine performance. . . . The excitement of those dogfights never diminished. For me, combat remains the ultimate flying experience. (Yeager and Janos 1985, 66–67)

Another American warrior, President Theodore Roosevelt, expressed similar thoughts more poetically when he said, "Every man who has in him any real power of joy in battle knows that he feels it when the wolf begins to rise in his heart" (1926, 306).

Dogfights, tank duels, and bayonet attacks are all instances of personal competition for dominance, using the most violent mode of signaling. However, these cannot be equated with warfare between nations because they are nothing more than constituent elements within a greater theater of combat. Hostilities between large agrarian or industrial societies are at base clashes between formal organizations, between the officially structured armies and navies of the opposing sides. In much of modern warfare, combatants never see or even closely approach their adversaries. Today's soldiers often pursue the "fight" by monitoring radar screens, filling out reports, maintaining equipment, and shipping supplies; few actually shoot at anyone, and when they do, it is more likely to be a distant and anonymous target than a recognizable person.

The distinction drawn in chapter 2 between a face-to-face group and a formal organization applies here. It would seriously confuse levels of analysis to explain any major war as if it were an interpersonal dominance competition between nations. If we move above the level of face to face combat, then international warfare—its causes, pursuit, and outcome—must be understood mostly in organizational terms of logistics and supplies, communications, tactics and strategy, operational flexibility, preparedness, public support, and financial and industrial resources, or in geopolitical terms such as control for scarce resources, clash of cultures, or control of the means of production.

It is critical for cogent explanation to keep these levels separate. There is "on the ground" (or in the air) a level of face-to-face combat properly conceived as a personal dominance contest. Above that is the army-to-army (or government-to-government) level of conflict, properly conceived as competition between formal organizations. At this organizational level it makes no sense to explain behavior in terms of facial gestures, stress signals, or hormones.

Having taken pains to distinguish personal combat between individual soldiers trying to dominate one another from organizational competition between armies, I need to backtrack a bit. At the very top of competing organizations are individuals who recognize and regard one another as personal foes. Saddam Hussein and either of the Presidents George Bush compose a recent example. Many wars between nations are meaningfully regarded, at least in part, as personal clash between leaders. Days before the outbreak of what Israel calls the "Six Day War," and Arabs call the "June 1967 War," Egyptian Defense Minister Amer told one of his generals, "Between me and Moshe Dayan there is a feud going back to . . . [the 1956 war in Sinai]. This is my opportunity to teach him a lesson he won't forget and to destroy the Israeli Army" (Oren 2002, 160). But in the opening hours of battle, Egypt's air force was eliminated; its army was broken as a fighting force within a week. In a few days more, the disgraced Amer was dead, apparently a suicide. Dayan with his signature eye patch was lauded as conquering hero in Israel and the United States.

Thus, face-to-face competition between warring adversaries occurs not only in dogfights and trenches, but also at the top of the command pyramid. The crucial common feature is that adversaries compete with one another as recognizable individuals. A tragicomic example is the exchange of telegrams on the brink of World War I between Kaiser Wilhelm of Germany and Tsar Nicholas of Russia, each trying to convince the other to stand down.

During the summer of 1914 Europe was so volatile that any spark could ignite a conflagration. At the end of June a Serbian nationalist assassinated Archduke Franz Ferdinand, the heir to the throne of Austria-Hungary. As punishment, Austria-Hungary gave Serbia, a small country on its southern border, a degrading ultimatum, threatening invasion if it were not met. Serbia mobilized to repulse the attack, and in response, Austria-Hungary formally declared war.

Kaiser Wilhelm was closely allied with Austria-Hungary, and Tsar Nicholas regarded himself as protector of his fellow Slavs in Serbia. With Austria and Serbia entering a state of war, Germany and Russia were under intense pressure to support their respective allies. But the Kaiser and the Tsar knew that by entering the fight they would trigger preexisting alliances, drawing the rest of Europe and Turkey into an enormous conflict.

Wilhelm and Nicholas each hoped to win limited goals from the other, but neither wanted bloody hostilities. To the contrary, they were first cousins (as was King George of Britain) and on friendly terms. Standing on the brink yet hoping to avert a larger conflict, the monarchs exchanged secret telegrams, addressing one another as Willy and Nicky. These are given here in abridged and edited form (Bernstein 1918).

Tsar to Kaiser, July 29:

Am glad you are back. In this serious moment, I appeal to you to help me. An ignoble war has been declared [by Austria] to a weak country [Serbia]. The indignation in Russia shared fully by me is enormous. I foresee that very soon I shall be overwhelmed by the pressure and forced to take extreme measures that will lead to war. To try and avoid such a calamity as a European war I beg you in the name of our old friendship to do what you can to stop your allies from going too far.

Nicky

Kaiser to Tsar, July 29:

I received your telegram and share your wish that peace should be maintained. But . . . I cannot consider Austria's action against Serbia an "ignoble" war. . . . Austria does not want to make any territorial conquests at the expense of Serbia. I therefore suggest that it would be quite possible for Russia to remain a spectator of the Austro-Serbian conflict without involving Europe in the most horrible war she ever witnessed. . . . Of course military measures on the part of Russia would be looked upon by Austria as a calamity we both wish to avoid and jeopardize my position as mediator, which I readily accepted on your appeal to my friendship and my help.

Willy

Tsar to Kaiser, July 30:

Thank you heartily for your quick answer. . . . The military measures that have now come into force were decided five days ago for reasons of defense on account of Austria's preparations. I hope with all my heart that these measures won't in any way interfere with your part as mediator, which I greatly value. We need your strong pressure on Austria to come to an understanding with us.

Nicky

Kaiser to Tsar, July 31:

On your appeal to my friendship and your call for assistance, I began to mediate between your and the Austro-Hungary government. While this action was proceeding your troops were mobilized against Austro-Hungary, my ally, thereby, as I have already pointed out to you, my mediation has been made almost illusory.

I have nevertheless continued my action. I now receive authentic news of [Russia's] serious preparations for war on my eastern frontier. Responsibility for the safety of my empire forces preventive measures of defense upon me. In my endeavors to maintain peace of the world I have gone to the utmost limit possible. The responsibility for the disaster . . . now threatening the whole civilized world will not be laid at my door. In this moment it still lies in your power to avert it. Nobody is threatening the honor or power of Russia, which can well afford to await the result of my mediation. . . .

The peace of Europe may still be maintained by you, if Russia will agree to stop the military measures that must threaten Germany and Austro-Hungary.

Willy

Tsar to Kaiser, July 31:

I thank you heartily for your mediation, which begins to give one hope that all may yet end peacefully. It is *technically* impossible to stop our military preparations, which were obligatory owing to Austria's mobilization. We are far from wishing war. As long as the negotiations with Austria on Serbia's account are taking place my troops shall not make any *provocative* action. I give you my solemn word for this. I put all my trust in God's mercy and hope in your successful mediation in Vienna for the welfare of our countries and for the peace of Europe.

Your affectionate Nicky

Kaiser to Tsar, August 1:

Thanks for your telegram. I yesterday pointed out to your government the only way by which war may be avoided. Although I requested an answer by noon today, no [. . . answer] has reached me yet. I therefore have been obliged to mobilize my army.

Immediate affirmative, clear and unmistakable answer from your government is the only way to avoid endless misery. Until I have received this answer, alas, I am unable to discuss the subject of your telegram. As a matter of fact, I must request you to immediately order your troops on no account to commit the slightest act of trespassing over our frontiers.

Willy

It required four years and ten million deaths—including the murder of Tsar Nicholas and his family by Lenin's Bolsheviks after the Russian Revolution—before Kaiser Wilhelm conceded defeat.

RULING CLIQUES

No ruler governs alone. To focus on a monarch, a president, or a dictator as the embodiment of a national or imperial government is to ignore the influential clique of advisors, administrators, and hangers-on who inevitably surround the ruler. Important decisions by heads of state follow discussion and debate within a privy council. Among Tsar Nicholas's closest advisers was his wife, Tsarina Alexandra, and she was under the sway of the charlatan monk, Gregory Rasputin, whose special power was based on his apparent ability to control her son's hemophilia. With the war in progress and Nicholas absent at the front, Russia's worsening domestic crisis fell under the misguidance of Alexandra and her mountebank confidant. Finally members of the innermost tsarist circle rebelled, murdering the monk, but it was an ineffective cure, too late to prevent the Bolshevik revolution.

The Tsar's Communist successors, Lenin and Stalin, were each in turn the alpha male within a small ruling clique—the Soviet Politburo (from 1952 to 1966 called the Presidium)—that forged and implemented imperial policy. It could not be otherwise because the requirements of government are beyond the capacity of a single person, and apart from that, even dictators need friends and companions.

Joseph Stalin was perhaps the most autocratic ruler of modern Europe, presiding over a clique of sycophants and henchmen who persistently jockeyed for position, sometimes winning favor with their overlord, sometimes losing it and being dispatched. Perched atop the Communist Party, Stalin and the Politburo oversaw the transformation of the Soviet Union from an agrarian society into an industrial superpower and along the way committed atrocities rivaling Hitler's. Privately owned farms were eliminated, their lands combined into state collectives that in theory—not in practice—were more efficient producers of food. The more prosperous among the peasants, the *kulaks*, resisted surrendering their property. They slaughtered their animals and held back on planting. In response, Stalin eliminated the kulaks as a class. Millions were killed or sent to labor camps. These agricultural disruptions led to catastrophic famine in 1933, claiming millions more lives.

Stalin's terror soon turned inward on the Communist Party and the Red Army. In the "Great Purge" of 1936–1938 the paranoid dictator and his minions searched out anyone who might be disloyal. The army's senior officer corps was decimated with roughly 60 percent of its 684 highest-ranking commanders arrested. In 1937 and 1938 alone, more than 1.5 million were arrested on political grounds, and nearly 700,000 executed. At the Communist Party's congress of 1939, only 37 survivors were present from among the 1,827 delegates who had attended the prior congress in 1934. (Johnson 1983; Taubman 2003).

As powerful as the Politburo was in the larger society, its members were toadies in Stalin's presence. Nikita Khrushchev, who would be Stalin's successor, recalled get-togethers of the leadership during the dictator's final years.

We would meet either in his study at the Kremlin or, more often, in the Kremlin movie theater. We would watch movies and talk about various matters between reels. . . . He liked [American] cowboy movies especially. . . . When a movie ended, Stalin would suggest, "Well, let's go get something to eat, why don't we?" The rest of us weren't hungry. By now it was usually one or two o'clock in the morning. . . . But everyone would say, yes, he was hungry, too. . . .

Whenever we had dinner with him, Stalin wouldn't touch a single dish . . . until someone else had tested it. . . . He didn't even trust the people serving him. . . . We always had his favorite dishes, and the cooks prepared them very well. . . . But we had to eat according to the following routine.

Let's say Stalin wanted something to eat; everyone was assigned a dish which he was supposed to try before Stalin would taste it.

"Look, here are the giblets, Nikita. Have you tried them yet?"

"Oh, I forgot." I could see he would like to take some himself but was afraid. I would try them and only then would he start to eat them himself. . . .

These dinners were frightful. We would get home from them early in the morning, just in time for breakfast, and then we'd have to go to work. During the day I usually tried to take a nap in my lunch hour because there was always a risk that if you didn't take a nap and Stalin invited you for dinner, you might get sleepy at the table; and those who got sleepy at Stalin's table could come to a bad end. There were often serious drinking bouts, too. I remember Beria, Malenkov, and Mikoyan had to ask the waitresses to pour them colored water instead of wine because they couldn't keep up with Stalin's drinking. . . .

Stalin found it entertaining to watch the people around him get themselves into embarrassing and even disgraceful situations. . . . I remember once Stalin

made me dance [a Ukrainian folk dance] before some top Party officials. I had
to squat down on my haunches and kick out my heels, which frankly wasn't
very easy for me. But I did it and I tried to keep a pleasant expression on my
face. . . . When Stalin says dance, a wise man dances. (1970, 297–301)

After Stalin suffered a massive stroke in early 1953, the Politburo members
kept vigil at his bedside, some fearing his death, others hoping for it. "As
soon as Stalin showed signs of consciousness on his face and made us think
he might recover, Beria threw himself on his knees, seized Stalin's hand, and
started kissing it. When Stalin lost consciousness again and closed his eyes,
Beria stood up and spat" (Khrushchev 1970, 318). Lavrenti Beria, a murderer,
torturer, and serial rapist, was chief of the secret police and second- or third-
ranked in the hierarchy. Khrushchev was slightly below Beria (Taubman
2003, 240).

Georgy Malenkov, another high-ranked Politburo member, seemed likely
to become the new head of Soviet government with Beria the power behind
the throne. But within three months of Stalin's death, Khrushchev had secretly engineered a split between Beria and Malenkov, leading to Beria's ar-
rest and execution. By 1955 Malenkov and other contenders were subordi-
nated, and Khrushchev held the top position in the Politburo and hence in
the Soviet Union.

To look at him, Khrushchev seemed an implausible replacement for Stalin.
Short, fat, and bald, uneducated and crude in behavior, his image was more
like a buffoon than a leader of men. If he had one physical sign of dominance, it was his eyes.

> They are piercingly bright and penetrating, fully concentrated on the task at
> hand. Those same eyes struck a boyhood friend of Sergei Khrushchev's when
> he first met Sergei's father in the 1950s. The friend was stunned by the contrast
> between Khrushchev's unimpressive figure and the burning intensity of his
> eyes. "All you had to do to understand how Khrushchev could have become so
> powerful was to look in his eyes." (Taubman 2003, 95)

Certainly Khrushchev had nonphysical attributes of leadership. He was
bright and hardworking, had an excellent sense of humor, made friends and
alliances easily, and he could be intensely domineering. Still, it was surprising that he emerged victorious when the Politburo members scrambled for
leadership after Stalin's death. (The Soviet Union had no formal method for
selecting a successor.) Biographer William Taubman suggests that his colleagues in the inner circle, despite their long association, underestimated
Khrushchev, and this gave him a tactical advantage (2003, 241).

> When push came to shove, the short fat man was able to unsheathe withering
> tirades. At the time Khrushchev became Soviet leader he knew little about for-
> eign affairs but quickly concluded that the creation of stress was as effective a

tool in diplomacy as it was in the Politburo. In 1956, when Israel, France, and Britain wrested control of the Suez Canal, Khrushchev threatened military intervention on Egypt's behalf. In fact, it was American rather than Soviet pressure that forced the invaders to retreat from Egypt, but Khrushchev saw it as a victory for intimidation. He told an Egyptian journalist, when "we dispatched an ultimatum to London and Paris, [U.S. Secretary of State] Dulles was the one whose nerves broke. . . . [Those] with the strongest nerves will be the winner. . . . The people with the weak nerves will go to the wall." (Taubman 2003, 360)

Khrushchev harangued heads of both Communist and Western nations, not least President Dwight Eisenhower, aborting a U.S.-Soviet summit in Paris with the revelation that American pilot Gary Powers had been shot down over-flying the Soviet Union in a U-2 spy plane and was being held captive. Even the well-seasoned Eisenhower, known for his smooth handling of outbursts by vain allied generals during World War II, could barely resist rising to Khrushchev's challenge.

THE CUBAN MISSILE CRISIS

John F. Kennedy was a handsome man, and though young for a president, he looked and debated like a leader. But Khrushchev appraised Kennedy as inexperienced and regarded him as a tempting target for confrontation.

Priding himself on his ability to out-argue Western leaders more educated and better mannered than he, he must have particularly relished the thought of trouncing a rich man's boy who was "younger than my own son." . . . For Kennedy, Khrushchev represented an equally vexing challenge. . . . As a boy, Kennedy was often weak and sickly. Yet his father insisted that he excel and mocked him when he did not. . . . [T]he fact that he strained every fiber to become the sort of tough, macho leader his father wanted made it all the more important to stand up to Khrushchev. . . . What Kennedy told his aide Kenneth O'Donnell was: "I have to show him that we can be just as tough as he is. . . . I'll have to sit down with him, and let him see who he's dealing with." (Taubman 2003, 485)

Kennedy had barely taken office when cosmonaut Yuri Gagarin became the first person to orbit the earth—a stunning success for Soviet technology. At nearly the same time, a force of Cuban exiles, secretly backed by the CIA, invaded Castro's Cuba at the Bay of Pigs with complete failure, partly because Kennedy, after giving the go-ahead, refused to provide air cover. The young president became depressed over the Cuban debacle, fearful that Khrushchev would regard him a weakling.

Apparently to show a stronger face, Kennedy invited Khrushchev to meet face-to-face in Vienna in early June 1961. Soviet expert Averill Harriman advised Kennedy, "Don't let him rattle you, he'll try to rattle you and frighten you, but don't pay any attention to that. . . . His style will be to attack and then see if he can get away with it. Laugh about it, don't get into a fight." French President Charles de Gaulle warned Kennedy, "Your job, Mr. President, is to make sure Khrushchev believes you are a man who will fight. Stand fast. . . . Hold on, be firm, be strong" (Taubman 2003, 494). But Kennedy took a beating at Vienna. At the end of the summit, the president described his two days with Khrushchev:

> Roughest time in my life. . . . I think he did it because of the Bay of Pigs. I think he thought that anyone who was so young and inexperienced as to get into that mess could be taken. And anyone who got into it and didn't see it through had no guts. So he just beat the hell out of me. . . . I've got a terrible problem. If he thinks I'm inexperienced and have no guts, until we remove those ideas we won't get anywhere with him. (Reston 1991, 290)

British Prime Minister Harold Macmillan, meeting Kennedy afterward in London, thought him completely overwhelmed. Harriman described the president as "shattered." Lyndon Johnson, Kennedy's erstwhile rival and now vice president, told friends, "Khrushchev scared the poor little fellow dead" (Taubman 2003, 495).

Despite Kennedy's unsteady hand during his first year in office, it is still difficult to understand why Khrushchev was so reckless as to install nuclear missiles in Cuba. He and other Soviet sources would later explain that it was to deter another American invasion of the island, a prospect made vivid by the attempt at the Bay of Pigs and continuing plots by the CIA to assassinate Castro (Hersh 1997). An additional reason may have been to redress the overwhelming advantage the United States held in intercontinental missiles by countering them with medium-range missiles stationed nearby. And there was a matter of equity: Since the United States had Jupiter missiles in Turkey and elsewhere near the Soviet Union, why shouldn't the Soviet Union have similar weapons near the border of the United States?

The plan was to install the missiles secretly and then notify the Americans once they were in place. Khrushchev thought that Kennedy, faced with the accomplished fact, would accept their presence calmly. He presented the plan to his Kremlin colleagues, and though some doubted that an American president could acquiesce to the placement of hostile nuclear weapons only ninety miles away, they obediently approved the project.

Weapons were headed to the Caribbean by September 4, 1962, when Kennedy announced—more for U.S. than Soviet consumption—that ground-to-ground missiles in Cuba would raise the "gravest issues." National Security Advisor McGeorge Bundy later commented, "We [issued that warning] because of the requirement of domestic politics, not because we seriously believed that the Soviets would do anything as crazy from our standpoint as placement of Soviet nuclear weapons in Cuba" (Beschloss 1997, 420). If Kennedy had made this explicit warning earlier, he might have deterred Khrushchev from his adventure. If the president knew Soviet missiles were already en route, he might not have drawn so clear a line in the sand. Kennedy later regretted his statement of September 4 because it compelled him to either forcefully oppose the weapons or again knuckle under to Khrushchev.

The morning of October 16, Kennedy learned from McGeorge Bundy that a CIA U-2 spy plane had taken photographs over Cuba showing crated missiles and launch sites under construction. The president regarded the news as a personal affront: "He can't do that to *me!*" (R. Neustadt and G. Allison in R. Kennedy 1971, 122). Robert Kennedy, the president's brother and closest personal adviser, later wrote that this "was the beginning of the Cuban missile crisis—a confrontation between the two giant atomic nations, the U.S. and the USSR, which brought the world to the abyss of nuclear destruction and the end of mankind" (1971, 1).

This was an overstatement of potential consequences. A decade later the United States and USSR each held roughly ten thousand nuclear warheads, enough to obliterate the Northern Hemisphere, but there were far fewer atomic weapons during the Cuban crisis, and the United States held more than a ten-to-one advantage in warheads and missile launchers. At most a Soviet nuclear attack on the United States could have used some dozens of Cuban missiles, a few intercontinental missiles, and several long-range bombers based in the USSR, and missile-carrying submarines off our East Coast. Some of these platforms would have been taken out by U.S. warplanes before they could release their weapons. Most of the United States would have escaped direct blasts, although New York City, Washington, and other cities might have been hit.

Very quickly President Kennedy formed an advisory group that met almost continuously (and initially secretly) in the White House Cabinet Room during the thirteen days of the crisis. Called the "Ex Comm" (the Executive Committee of the National Security Council), it was made up of about fourteen relevant officials and area experts. Like any small group, it had a dominance hierarchy. At the top were the president's closest advisers: Bobby Kennedy, Mac Bundy, and Secretary of Defense Robert McNamara. Chaired by Bobby during the president's frequent absences, the Ex Comm was a useful sounding board for various policy options, but the president's actions did not always follow its collective recommendations.[2]

From the moment the Ex Comm first met on October 16, there was agreement that the missiles must leave Cuba, but there was no agreement on the reasons for this. The position of the Joint Chiefs was that the weapons posed a new and unacceptable military threat to the American mainland. Secretary of Defense McNamara disagreed:

> BUNDY: What is the strategic impact on the position of the United States of [missiles] in Cuba? How gravely does this change the strategic balance?
>
> MCNAMARA: I asked the Chiefs that this afternoon, in effect. And they said, "Substantially." My own personal view is: Not at all. . . .
>
> PRESIDENT KENNEDY: You may say it doesn't make any difference if you get blown up by an ICBM flying from the Soviet Union or one that was 90 miles away. Geography doesn't mean that much. (May and Zelikow 1997, 89–91)

For the president and his core advisers, the ultimate reason was not military but political. If Khrushchev got away with this, he might try other adventures, perhaps applying pressure to the American presence in Berlin. With a congressional election the next month, domestic politics seemed even more on Kennedy's mind. How would Democrats fare with the American electorate if he let Khrushchev push him around? It was no time to look weak.

Kennedy had to decide on a course of action to eliminate the missiles without precipitating a nuclear war. One option stressed diplomacy, bringing American and international pressure to bear on Khrushchev and forcing his retreat. A stronger approach was a naval blockade, preventing the importation into Cuba of any more weapons or support equipment. Also there were attack options, ranging from a limited strike on the missile sites to a full-scale invasion of the island, assuming these could be accomplished before the missiles became operational.

The ultimate hawk was General Curtis LeMay, the cigar-chomping Air Force Chief of Staff and probable model for General Buck Turgidson in Stanley Kubrick's *Dr. Strangelove*. During World War II, LeMay commanded the bombing of Japan, not only the nuclear attacks on Hiroshima and Nagasaki but the firebombing of Tokyo that incinerated one hundred thousand residents in a single night. (McNamara then worked for LeMay.) Now he wanted to thoroughly bomb Cuba, opining that a blockade and political action were as bad as Neville Chamberlain's appeasement of Hitler at Munich (May and Zelikow 1997, 178).

President Kennedy himself favored a "quarantine," the word chosen in preference to "blockade," which constituted an act of war. Robert McNamara also felt that a violent military strike was too risky and inappropriate a solution. He emphasized repeatedly, "I don't believe it's primarily a military problem. It's primarily a domestic political problem" (May and Zelikow 1997, 114).

The evening of October 22, President Kennedy addressed the nation, revealing the presence of the missiles in Cuba and telling his initial course of action. Beforehand, a copy of his speech and a personal letter were delivered to the Kremlin, accusing Khrushchev of deliberate deception, announcing the quarantine, and calling upon the Soviet leader to eliminate this "reckless and provocative threat to world peace." Khrushchev had just returned from a walk with his son Sergei when he was given a brief version, before the full translation. Sergei recalled his father saying, "They've probably discovered our rockets. . . . The missiles aren't operational yet. They're defenseless; they can be wiped out from the air in one swipe" (Taubman 2003, 560).

Calling all Politburo members to meet at the Kremlin in an hour, a red-faced Khrushchev told the group, "We were not going to unleash war. We just wanted to intimidate them, to deter the anti-Cuban forces. . . . This may end up in a big war." General Pliyev, the Soviet commander in Cuba, was instructed to repel any invasion, short of using nuclear weapons. One participant recalled that when they finally heard a Russian translation of Kennedy's full text,

> Khrushchev's first reaction was "relief rather than anxiety. . . ." The blockade "seemed like something intangible. . . . It did not look like an ultimatum or a direct threat of an attack on Cuba." Instantaneously Khrushchev's mood swung from alarm to elation. "We've saved Cuba!" he exclaimed. Then he began composing a hot reply to a president who seemed to have blinked . . . , labeling Kennedy's actions . . . "naked interference in the domestic affairs of Cuba and the USSR." (Taubman 2003, 562)

Radio Moscow announced heightened combat readiness over the face-off in Cuba and a cancellation of military leaves. Some of the missiles on the island were nearly operational. His confidence restored, Khrushchev went to the opera and "could now sit back and hope that the fear of war would force Kennedy to back down" (Fursenko and Naftali 1997, 256).

Bobby Kennedy called on Soviet ambassador Anatoly Dobrynin the next evening, October 23. Dobrynin remembered the president's brother as agitated, repeating himself, going off on tangents. Asked how Soviet ship captains would respond to the quarantine, Dobrynin answered that they would not obey anyone's unlawful order to stop. Bobby emphasized, "We are determined to stop your ships." Dobrynin countered, "But that would be an act of war" (Taubman 2003, 564).

The next morning, October 24, the U.S. Strategic Air Command moved to condition DEFCON 2, the level below actual war. All American long-range missiles were on alert. Planes loaded with atomic bombs were aloft and awaiting the signal to proceed to targets in Cuba and the Soviet Union. Soviet submarines approached the quarantine line, poised to attack any American warship that interfered with a Soviet transport. The Americans dropped depth charges near the subs, forcing some to the surface. Bobby thought this the time of greatest tension for his brother as the president waited to see if Soviet ship captains would cross the quarantine line.

His face seemed drawn, his eyes pained, almost gray. We stared at each other across the table. . . . I felt we were on the edge of a precipice with no way off. . . . The minutes in the Cabinet Room ticked slowly by. What could we say now—what could we do?

Then it was 10:25 [a.m.]—a messenger brought in a note. . . . "Mr. President, we have a preliminary report which seems to indicate that some of the Russian ships have stopped dead in the water." (Kennedy 1969, 49)

Secretary of State Dean Rusk famously commented to Mac Bundy, "We're eyeball to eyeball, and I think the other fellow just blinked." When the Politburo met the next day, Khrushchev rejected any more barbed exchanges with Kennedy and wanted to resolve the crisis, proposing to ask for an American pledge not to invade Cuba in return for his removing the missiles. But in Cuba, construction of sites was proceeding rapidly, as was the assembly of bombers. In the meantime, U.S. forces were readying an attack on the island. More than one hundred thousand infantrymen were deployed to East Coast ports. A huge navy fleet with forty thousand marines was pointed toward Cuba.

On October 26 Khrushchev dictated a long and emotional letter to Kennedy, offering a settlement:

I propose we, for our part, will declare that our ships bound for Cuba are not carrying any armaments. You will declare that the United States will not invade Cuba with its troops and will not support any other forces which might intend to invade Cuba. Then the necessity for the presence of our military specialists in Cuba will be obviated. . . .

Mr. President, you and I should not now pull on the ends of the rope in which you have tied a knot of war, because the harder you and I pull, the tighter this knot will become. And a time may come when this knot is tied so tight that the person who tied it is no longer capable of untying it, and then the knot will have to be cut. What that would mean I need not explain to you, because you yourself understand perfectly what dread forces our two countries possess. (Dept. of State, LS No. 46118)

But Khrushchev's posture hardened overnight. On October 27 he proposed to the Politburo a new letter, demanding that the Americans withdraw their Jupiter missiles from Turkey in exchange for his withdrawal of the Cuban missiles. He would pledge not to invade Turkey while asking for a similar pledge from the Americans toward Cuba.

Kennedy and his men were stunned when the second letter reached Washington, essentially ignoring the deal offered in the first letter. To accept this new condition would have looked like the president was surrendering. Actually, the Turkish missiles were not important strategically, and Kennedy had earlier considered removing them as a cost-saving measure, but he didn't want to appear forced to do it. Following Mac Bundy's suggestion,

Kennedy ignored the second letter and answered the first one positively: If the Soviets removed all offensive weapons from Cuba, he would end the quarantine and assure that there would be no future invasion of the island.

But the crisis was not over. On October 27, Captain Antonyets, commanding a Soviet SAM battery, shot down a U-2 over Cuba, killing the pilot. I described this episode of local autonomy in chapter 2. Without intending to, Antonyets contravened Khrushchev's explicit desire to avoid provoking the Americans. This "error" nearly brought retaliation, which Kennedy vetoed for the time being. The incident made McNamara fear the Soviets would attack the Jupiter missiles in Turkey, requiring a military response from NATO. It seemed that events were spiraling out of control. Castro was no help, apparently encouraging Khrushchev to preemptively strike the United States.

Desperately seeking a solution, the president again sent his brother to Ambassador Dobrynin, this time carrying a secret carrot as well as a stick. Extremely agitated, Bobby threatened military action against Cuba if the missiles were not withdrawn. But, he assured Dobrynin, if they were removed, then the Jupiter missiles in Turkey would be dismantled—a pledge that would not be revealed for twenty-seven years because it would embarrass the president in front of the U.S. electorate and the Turks. "Time is running out," said Bobby. "We mustn't miss our chance" (Hersh 1997; Taubman 2003, 573).

The next day, October 28, Khrushchev met with the Politburo and accepted the Kennedy brothers' offer. An irate Castro, neither consulted nor informed until the deal was concluded, complained that Khrushchev had no *cojones*.

Since it was not generally known that the president acquiesced to Khrushchev's demand that Turkish missiles be removed, the ending of the crisis was treated in the United States as a victory for Kennedy. The president himself bragged about Khrushchev, "I cut his balls off"—perhaps the only time JFK shared a sentiment with Castro. On the other side, Khrushchev declared himself the winner for securing Cuba from invasion *plus* having the Jupiters removed from Turkey, but it is doubtful that he truly believed it. Many in the Soviet Union, including Sergei Khrushchev, regarded the crisis a humiliation for his father. (Too bad we cannot test this with testosterone measurements from the two leaders.)

In retrospect, it was foolish of Khrushchev to believe that any U.S. president would accept atomic weapons near the American mainland, and needlessly frightening. Khrushchev admitted to *Saturday Review* editor Norman Cousins, "Of course I was scared. It would have been insane not to be scared" (Taubman 2003, 583). When Khrushchev was removed from power in a coup two years later, one of the complaints raised against him was excessive risk taking in Cuba.

President Kennedy faced few charges of recklessness, despite so cavalierly placing Americans in jeopardy. Journalist Seymour Hersh, one of a smattering of revisionist commentators, later wrote, "Kennedy brought the world to the edge of nuclear war to gain a political victory: to humble an adversary who had humbled him before" (1997, 345). The crisis was more hair triggered than the president or his advisers realized at the time. They did not know until years later that Soviet troops in Cuba were equipped with short-range tactical atomic weapons. If avid Soviet defenders, acting like Captain Antonyets on their own initiative, had launched these against American forces landing on the beaches, they could have initiated an escalation of nuclear exchanges and an unprecedented disaster, killing millions of Cubans, Americans, and Soviets.

What if Kennedy and Khrushchev had not been so strongly motivated to personally dominate one another? They might have cut the same deal without risking so many lives. When Kennedy's ambassador to the United Nations, Adlai Stevenson, had earlier urged a peaceful exchange of Jupiter missiles in Turkey and Italy for Cuban missiles, he was dismissed in the Ex Comm as a weakling. The final settlement was not very different from Stevenson's proposal. Both leaders knew the risks they were taking. At the height of the crisis, when President Kennedy briefed congressional leaders on his intentions in Cuba, he told them it would be "one hell of a gamble." It surely was.

NOTES

1. Many biological factors have been suggested as causes of violent behavior, for example, chromosomal abnormalities, birth complications, or neurological or emotional deficits (e.g., Raine, Brennan, and Mednick 1994; Raine et al. 1996; Davidson, Putnam, and Larson 2000), but lacking corroboration, I do not pursue them here.

2. Ex Comm members, excepting Bobby, were unaware that the president tape-recorded their deliberations, which were later edited and published by May and Zelikow (1997).

11

Take a Chimp, Add Language, Melt the Glaciers . . .

Conventional social scientists treat humans as sui generis, a species apart from the rest of the animal kingdom. Ignoring evolution, sociologists explain our behavior and institutions as if we were created afresh by God, without roots in our simian ancestry. At the other extreme are evolutionary sociobiologists who ignore fundamental differences between humans and colony insects, invoking common genetic mechanisms to explain all social behavior. Two camps so far apart will never find common ground.

My aim in this closing chapter is to present a middle position, placing humankind firmly among the anthropoids—specifically as a modified chimpanzee—while eschewing any analog to arthropods. The reader should not take literally all I say here because I have stretched a few points and do not take it all literally myself. As a rhetorical flourish, hyperbole in the service of moderation is not so perverse as it may at first seem.[1]

THE HUMAN GENOME

With thirty thousand genes, only two or three times more than in a fruit fly, the human genome is far smaller than had been suspected. A surprising number of our genes are commonplace, about 10 percent clearly related to particular genes in the fly and the worm. Identities between humans and other animals will become more striking as additional genomes are sequenced. With the human blueprint serving as a template, we may expect a quick decoding of the complete chimpanzee genome, which almost certainly will look nearly identical to our own (Paabo 2001; Ruvolo 2004).

Do small genetic differences between humans and chimps suffice to explain their large behavioral differences? In a tautological sense they must. But in an intuitive sense it is unsatisfying to place so great a burden on so few genes. The runaway tendency of some theorists to explain multitudinous subtleties of human behavior with equally multitudinous genetic variations seems headed for a brick wall.

Faced with so obvious a dilemma, there has been a rush to explain how a few genes can produce many effects. Until recently, a central notion of genetics was that one gene codes for one protein, and these diverse proteins then combine to produce structures and functions of the organism. Now the focus of study is moving from genomics to "proteomics," the analysis of proteins, including not only their identification but also their localization, modifications, interactions, and so on.

> Unlike the decoratively challenged DNA, proteins get phosphorylated, glycosylated, acetylated, ubiquitinated, farnesylated, sulphated, linked to glycophosphatidylinositol anchors, and embellished in numerous other ways. A single gene can encode multiple different proteins—they can be produced by alternative splicing of the mRNA transcript, by varying translation start or stop sites, or by frameshifting during which a different set of triplet codons in the mRNA is translated. All of these possibilities result in a proteome estimated to be an order of magnitude more complex than the genome. . . . What is more proteins respond to altered conditions by changing their location within the cell, getting cleaved into pieces, and adjusting their stability as well as changing what they bind to. (Fields 2001, 1221)

Theorists inclined toward such anthropomorphisms as "selfish genes" might better focus on selfish proteins, which have a more direct effect on the phenotype and would therefore be under stronger selection pressure than genes. One might say an organism, or a gene, is simply a protein's way of reproducing itself.

A second implication of the near genetic identity of chimp and human is that, as behaving organisms, they are not so different. This flies in the face of any zoo-goer who compares those imprisoned with those visiting for the day, though comparisons would have been more appropriate before zoos—or civilizations—were invented. The difference between feral chimp and feral human behavior resides primarily in language (and secondarily in intelligence and peripheral modifications). If the few genes differentiating chimps from humans were mostly responsible for language, then nearly all behavioral differences would eventually follow. This thinking is a turn away from the genetic determinism of sociobiology, and is more in line with the cultural and structural determinism of traditional sociology.

SOCIOLOGY'S DISCONTENTS

Sociobiology introduced two problems that seriously annoyed traditional sociologists. First is its focus on *ultimate* causes of human nature, ignoring those *proximate* mechanisms through which behavior actually operates. A well-known example is the selectionist theory of sex differences in mating strategy. Males produce offspring with an ejaculation; females must invest a prolonged period of pregnancy and nursing. Therefore males maximize fitness by indiscriminately spreading their seed among many females, whereas females are selective, devoting their limited pregnancies to the finest sires and, if feasible, withholding sexual favors until they receive from the male a commitment for child support. (This reasoning seems to many sociologists a justification for the double standard, though Darwinians deny that implication.) The theory speaks of evolution long ago, ignoring those proximate influences—our psychology and culture—that are the explanatory currency of the social sciences. Thus it cannot explain or even query why one culture is polygamous, another monogamous; why marriages in some societies are arranged by parents and in others by romantic attraction; why divorce and birth rates are sometimes high, sometimes low.

Another annoyance is that some of classical sociobiology's claims defy common observation. Most sociologists do not maximize their inclusive fitness, instead limiting their children to two or fewer, even having themselves sterilized, and some "waste" resources by adopting unrelated infants. A well-known claim of classical sociobiology is that parents break away from children (to raise others) before children want to break away from parents (Trivers 1974). My own children, now in their thirties, have been trying to break the bonds of dependency for two decades while I've resisted the whole time. E. O. Wilson (1975) likens human homosexuals to sterile ant workers that maximize inclusive fitness not by raising their own offspring but by nurturing the fitness of siblings. This implies that homosexuals devote twice the resources to nieces and nephews that heterosexuals devote to their own children, an implausible assertion to anyone who has put children through college.

Evolutionary psychology eliminated some of these annoyances. Its leaders are scholars of human rather than animal behavior, hence their interest in a reformulation that avoids implausible statements about humans. Their most important innovation has been to reintroduce proximate causes, now in the form of a thinking, talking brain. When sociologists of the 1950s spoke of brains, which was not often, they thought of John Locke's blank slate, upon which a particular culture and language were written during a period of socialization. Evolutionary psychology has an entirely different concept, the "adapted mind," with specialized mechanisms for parenting, emotional communication, kinship, mate choice, sex, aggression, danger avoidance, mate guarding, child care, and so on (Barkow, Cosmides, and Tooby 1992, 99). Most notable is the Chomskyan mechanism for language, prewired though requiring a period of learning to accommodate any particular language.

Evolutionary psychologists tell the same "just so" stories as sociobiologists but emphasize that it is our minds that have evolved, not our disembodied behaviors: Evolution produced the mind, and the mind produces behavior. This is an ingenious corrective to sociobiology's exclusive focus on ultimate causes. With a language-speaking mind as a proximate mechanism, it is easy to incorporate learning, socialization, and cultural differences—all notions that are important to social science but excluded from insect-level sociobiology.

The adapted mind eliminates the untenable tenet that we maximize inclusive fitness. Instead our actions are explained by the calculations of these minds, which balance, say, a diabetic's primitive urge to eat sweets with her physician's advice to abstain. Married couples, whom sociobiologists required to have as many children as possible, are allowed by evolutionary psychologists to weigh their reproductive urges against the costs of a college education or the demands of a two-career family. The male mind still desires sex with many women, but the penis may be held in check by moral strictures or caution about venereal disease or fear of discovery by a wife. The female brain still seeks long-term commitment from a dominant male, but actual behavior may depend as well on availability of birth control pills and an active bar scene.

Having solved some of sociobiology's problems, evolutionary psychology introduces some of its own. Our minds, it says, were shaped by natural selection to a human environment of evolutionary adaptedness (EEA)—that is, the Pleistocene environment in which the overwhelming majority of human evolution occurred (Symons 1992). Often this is envisioned as an African savannah, in any case very different from Chicago or New York. Humans left the EEA only ten thousand years ago, when agriculture and settled communities began, so there has been too little time for our minds to readapt to these newer conditions. As a result, we cope with industrial society using Stone Age brains. Behaviors that were adaptive in the EEA may not be adaptive—may even be maladaptive—in Chicago. For example, we possess a taste mechanism that favors sweetness, an adaptation that improved our ancestors' reproductive fitness because sugar-producing fruit is most nutritious when its sugar content is highest, but which now leads us into unhealthy eating habits.

The EEA is reminiscent of the EOS (environment of original sin), the Garden of Eden where simpler creatures were transformed into fully human beings. As scientific concepts they have similar credibility. There is little reason to assume that human capabilities developed as an integrated package during a discrete time period beginning when the human lineage split from apes, and ending with the Pleistocene. Brain evolution is highly conservative, with newer structures added upon or modifying ancient structures. Our preference for sweets evolved long before there were humans, as did unequal investment by the sexes in progeny. Even human speech has important features that emerged before apes split from monkeys (Werker and Vouloumanos 2000; Hauser, Chomsky, and Fitch 2002). Almost certainly the human mind developed piecemeal, a mixture of some mental mechanisms that are ancient, others that are new. The EEA is more defensible if we take it to mean simply the time period when language capacity matured, but then it hardly seems a novel or useful concept.

Also problematic is the elaborated adapted human mind, far overreaching what is known from research on the brain (which is not the same as the mind in any case). And as asked at the outset, is there enough genetic difference between chimps and humans to construct complexly different minds?

Also, evolutionary psychology often focuses too narrowly on humans, usually ignoring our cousins, the nonhuman primates, which offer instructive models of behavior. Consider, for example, the theory of male and female mating strategies, which should apply to apes as well as humans. Male gorillas and orangutans seek multiple mates, while females are usually limited to a single male, consistent with the theory (Muller and Wrangham 2001). But gibbons and siamangs are monogamous. Among chimpanzees, both sexes mate with multiple partners (Goodall 1986). Among bonobos, females freely seek sexual relations with males and other females (de Waal 1995). Thus the hypothesized sex difference is not apparent in most apes nor in those most closely related to humans, the chimpanzees, casting doubt on the theory's underlying reasoning.

Despite its shortcomings, evolutionary psychology—by introducing a sophisticated concept of the mind—has taken a long step toward reconciling natural selection with sociology. This version accommodates psychology, socialization, and culture, and it eliminates implausible assertions from sociobiology's description of contemporary human behavior. But the ideological divide between sociology and natural selection remains wide. Social Darwinism in its various incarnations has too long a history of justifying why some people are inferior to others, or why some groups oppress others. This cauldron was stirred anew by the evolutionary theory of rape promoted by Thornhill and Palmer (2000; also see Shields and Shields 1983), who claim that forced intercourse is a successful reproductive strategy for males, and that all men are potential rapists. (There is an analogous argument for the evolution of cuckolding in women.) Thornhill and Palmer condemn rape as an immoral action but at the same time suggest a behavioral apology for the rapist: We (men) are all sinners; there but for God go I. Such theoretical rationalizations for oppression blow away any appeal that evolutionary psychology might have held for traditional sociologists.

Rape theory, by the way, suffers from the fallacy of misplaced specificity, drawing too narrow a conclusion from a broad argument. Hunger is as natural a motive for eating as libido is for coitus. Both appetites increase with the duration of time since the last consummation and both are stimulated by the presence of attractive objects of consumption. Normally, both appetites are satisfied without coercion, but either may be satisfied forcibly, by rape or by robbery of food (or of money to buy food). If one accepts the Thornhill-Palmer argument that men have psychological traits designed for the specific purpose of rape, one might as well accept that men have psychological traits designed specifically for food robbery. Indeed, the argument can be made for robbing any specific food, my favorite being cheese Danish, which I have stolen on numerous occasions (Mazur 1992).

ADD LANGUAGE

If the few genes separating humans from chimpanzees provided a language capability but little more, we might account for nearly the whole suite of uniquely human behaviors in cultural terms without invoking any special genetic tendency toward rape, another for cheese Danish, and so on. Language and culture are intertwined. The presence of culture—beyond an elementary level—almost certainly implies that language is present too.

We may assume the most recent common ancestor of chimpanzees and humans had capabilities found minimally in both lines of descent: elemental culture, a rich repertoire of facial expressions and body gestures, and the level of symbol manipulation demonstrated in ape "language" studies. How language evolved from there to here is a mystery. Chomsky, font of modern linguistics, eschews evolutionary speculation as pointless, while his popularizer, Steven Pinker (1994), insists the evolution of language, during the five or so million years since chimp and human lines split, presents no special problem for Darwinian theory. To envision an intermediate protolanguage, more advanced than chimpanzee signing, from which true language could have evolved, it is tempting to resurrect Haeckel's discredited principle that ontogeny recapitulates phylogeny. Perhaps the two- or three-word "sentences" of a two-year-old, sufficient to link an object to an action, or to relate two objects—re-create the lost utterances of an early hominid (Bickerton 1990). Even so, some theorists regard the further step to full grammar as too great to explain by Darwinian selection. Psychologist David Premack (1985), for example, "challenges" someone to reconstruct the scenario that would confer selective fitness on recursion, the ability of phrases to occur inside other phrases, producing indefinitely long sentences. (Actually, the scenario is not difficult; see Mazur 1996.)

The earliest accepted hominid tools, dated 2.5 million years ago, are sharp-edged flakes and lumps of stone called Oldowan tools. One attempt to teach a bonobo to make these tools suggests the task is not beyond an ape's mental capacity but requires better manual dexterity. In any case, there is little change in Oldowan technique for a million years. After the appearance of larger-brained *Homo erectus*, the more sophisticated Acheulean toolkit (and use of fire) is observed by about 1.5 mya, with its famous two-faced hand ax. Acheulean technique, like the Oldowan, is little modified for a million years, but by 200,000 years ago tool making had begun to change rapidly with regional differences in style. These changes are associated with the appearance of Neanderthals, late archaic humans, and modern-looking humans (Ambrose 2001). Such rapid development and diversification of cultures implies some improvement in language ability by 200,000 years ago.

Language empowers the group to create a collective culture that can be passed down, modified, or enhanced, from one generation to another. Without culture, life in one millennium is pretty much like life in the last or next one. Language-using humans are capable of constructing new environments, of building igloos on ice, planting and irrigating fields, assembling stations in space. Material habitats aside, cultures incorporating language and rules (norms) are our most influential surroundings, the hallmark of human society. At least since we have had the capability of language, humans have actively selected their material and cultural environments, perhaps more than environments have selected humans.

In virtually all sexually dimorphic species, males are the stronger sex and can physically coerce females. Physical size and strength are important contributors to dominant position, allowing maturing males to move upward in the hierarchy. Political alliances are well developed in monkeys and apes, with top positions in a group often held by a coalition of mutually supportive males (de Waal 1989). For these reasons, leading males have inordinate power in primate societies.

As language and culture developed, leading men realized that they could make rules for their group, including rules to prolong their own privilege as they aged, and to protect the privileges of their children and friends. The most obvious prerogatives to be maintained were material wealth, authority, and sexual access to attractive women. The realization that these perquisites could be preserved better by cultural rules than brute strength is as inevitable as the discovery that cooked meat is better than raw, or the recognition of a spirit world in dreams of acquaintances recently dead. These simple ideas occur nearly universally in language-using groups and are passed down the generations, attaining the authority of tradition.

One of the earliest insights of anthropology is that alliances are maintained by the exchange of food, gifts, or favors (Mauss 1925). As primitive cultures developed lore on the collection or manufacture of material items, these must have become currencies for exchange to establish solidarity among leading men. Captives would serve the same purpose, with females more valued than males as slaves because they could more easily be physically controlled, and attractive women would be particularly desired for sexual pleasure. Perhaps women indigenous to the group, especially younger or lower-status women, also were seen as a medium for exchange among leading men.

In any case, early human groups must have regularly incorporated rules that reinforced the privileges of leading males, ensuring them wealth, authority, and sexual access to women, and extending these privileges to their male children. Captive women or those of low status often became chattel. If not literally property, women still must have held an inferior position to men, serving at their pleasure. Thus, the selection by dominating males of an environment enforcing sexual inequality was perhaps an inevitable consequence of the emergence of language-based culture, requiring no new mating strategy beyond that common to the higher primates.

In this version of human evolution, the oppression of women derives from the superior physical power men could wield to influence primitive cultures, not in behavioral genes or the biologically adapted mind. Sexist traditions, once formed, passed from generation to generation, at least until the present time, when in some societies they are changing, if not yet completely.

MELT THE GLACIERS

As recently as ten thousand years ago the world's people lived in small societies as scavengers and hunters. Then, within a few thousand years, life in several places was transformed into an agrarian mode, settled in permanent communities supported by nearby fields of grain and by animal husbandry (Richerson, Boyd, and Bettinger 2001). The animals became sources of power and transport as well as of food. Populations of growing towns became differentiated into separate classes, one better off than another, with some form of king holding control, partly through hereditary right and partly through the strength of military alliances. Cultures grew, merged, diffused, and diversified. Never had there been such a profound change in the human condition.

We cannot know with certainty why these changes occurred, but their coincidence in time with the end of the last Ice Age ten thousand years ago is so striking it is likely that climate warming was an important spur. Large glaciers covering parts of Eurasia and North America melted, increasing atmospheric humidity and therefore rainfall. The tropics, which had been dry while global water was frozen into ice sheets, became moist again. The sea level rose, flooding shorelines, but the receding ice also opened land to habitation. These changes affected local growing conditions and must have influenced the growth and movement of human and animal populations. As a result of climate change, certain plants became more widely available, including the large-seeded annual grasses ancestral to wheat and barley, providing convenient seed stocks for early planters.

This new agrarian life was the base upon which civilization would emerge within another five thousand years. By "civilization" I mean an advanced form of society usually with writing, calendars, astronomical observation, mathematics, monumental architecture, planned ceremonial and religious centers, specialization in arts and crafts, metallurgy, and intensive irrigation projects. The transformation of hunter-gatherer society into civilization occurred not once but in at least six places, more or less independently: Mesopotamia, Egypt, India, China, Mexico, and Peru.

These were not all alike. The pristine states in Asia occur in major river valleys, but not all those in America do. Egypt was much less urbanized than Mesopotamia. The appearance of any one cultural element is variable—for example, the use of animals and the wheel for transportation was important in the Old World civilizations but not in America; metallurgy has appeared in some precivilized cultures but not in all civilized ones; writing was not a part of Peruvian civilization. Thus, the transformation did not take exactly the same form in all places. Nonetheless, one can hardly fail to be impressed by the degree of similarity and simultaneity that did occur or to wonder why it happened that way.

Different societies, facing similar environmental contingencies, respond in similar ways. For example, different peoples seeing the same sky produce consistent astronomies. Every culture between the Arctic and Antarctic Circles has something like our twenty-four-hour day as a unit of time. People usually see changing phases of the moon as another natural time period, calculating it at about 30 days (actually 29 1/2), the approximate length of the menstrual cycle. The cycle of seasons, whether wet-dry near the equator, or summer-winter in temperate latitudes, is a longer, virtually universal time period.

Winter days are shorter than summer days because the earth's orbit around the sun is tilted at an angle of 23 1/2 degrees from the plane of the equator. The shortest day of the year (December 21 in the Northern Hemisphere) occurs when the earth reaches the "top" its orbit, the longest day (about June 21) when earth reaches "bottom." These winter and summer solstices are generally recognized and often mark special festivals.

As far as we can tell, all civilizations knew that the year, the cycle of seasons, was about 365 days. Some calendars used for ritual purposes are based on other counts, such as the 260-day year of the Aztecs or the 354-day Moslem year, but astronomers of each civilization were aware of the 365-day cycle correlated with the seasons. The calculation follows simply from observation of sunrises or sunsets. The sun rises (and sets) at a slightly different point on the horizon every day, moving northward as the date approaches the summer solstice, then southward as the date approaches the winter solstice. To calculate the length of a year, one counts the days it takes for the rising sun to return to one of these extreme points, which is about 365 (Aveni 1989). Any civilization supporting specialized astronomers would be carried further along this path, perhaps recognizing the year is actually a bit longer than 365 days (365 1/4) and confronting the problem that 30-day months do not divide evenly into 365.

There is a danger of becoming too fanciful in explaining how environmental conditions pushed agrarian societies one way rather than another. As in Rudyard Kipling's *Just So Stories*, imaginary accounts can be conjured for any development. With no serious way to test speculations about events in the distant past, such claims are impervious to empirical refutation. Jared Diamond's *Guns, Germs, and Steel* (1997) is a recent example, explaining that white Europeans came to dominate the world largely because Eurasia, but not Africa or the Americas, has a predominately east-west axis. (Probably if he had been writing in the year 1500, Diamond could equally well have explained why China had the most glorious civilization on earth.) It is enough to speculate in broad overview, even if details are elusive, that melting glaciers ten thousand years ago initiated a string of contingencies converting human society from hunting and scavenging to agrarianism and most recently to industrialism. This has been a long-standing view in traditional sociology.

CONCLUSIONS

If the difference between the human and chimpanzee genomes is very small, as seems likely, then we should invoke a minimum of biology to explain their behavioral differences. The advanced language capability of humans, developed within the past two hundred thousand years or so, is the critical proximate mechanism allowing elaborate culture and cultural rules to exist, thus setting the feral human increasingly apart from the feral ape. There were other modifications, but language was the critical one. If humans have a few language-producing genes lacking in chimps, that could explain much of the behavioral difference that existed before the agrarian revolution.

The transformation of human society ten thousand years ago, from a hunter-gatherer to an agrarian mode, was likely caused by the warming climate and melting glaciers at the end of the last Ice Age. Language-using humans were affected more profoundly than other species. Whereas human cultures had been relatively static for the prior two million years, their subsequent history has been one of accelerating change. Most important among these changes were new ways humans came to rank themselves with respect to one another, in formal organizations, and in the social stratification of large societies, opening opportunities for inequality not known during the Paleolithic era.

NOTE

1. This chapter draws heavily from Mazur (2002).

Appendix:
Stress-Induced Coalitions

Humans experience stress as both a feeling of discomfort and a syndrome of bodily responses activated by the hypothalamic-pituitary-adrenal axis (Axelrod and Reisine 1984). Cortisol is a central element of stress physiology, entering the bloodstream from the adrenal cortex and flowing to the brain and other organs, where it mobilizes the body's physical resources in preparation for fight or flight.

I propose that the physiology of stress also mobilizes a *social* response—the joining of protective coalitions. Faced with danger, parents reliably shield their children, while children cling to their parents. This intensification of family (or community) cohesion when confronting an outside threat is adaptive and has analogs in all social vertebrates. The tendency to form defensive alliances is evolutionarily ancient and must operate through a limbic or emotional mechanism, without requiring language-based cognition. These presumptions and hypotheses apply to interpersonal coalitions, and not to tactical combinations formed by nations or other large social units.

The stress response is multilayered, and any one (or more) of its components might conceivably induce the formation of protective coalitions. It is known that hormones can affect social relationships, as in the case of oxytocin, which encourages mother-infant bonding (Insel 1993; Winslow et al. 2003). Therefore it is reasonable to cast cortisol, the primary stress hormone, as the central actor in stress-induced coalition formation. This is consistent with Henry and Wang's suggestion that children lacking normal cortisol responsiveness also lack normal attachment behavior (1998). However, this a priori choice is somewhat arbitrary and may be overruled by future empirical investigation. Therefore I take the physiological response to stress in toto as the motivator of hypothesized coalition behavior.

161

Hypothesis #1. Elevated stress motivates Ego to affiliate with allies and to polarize against adversaries.

Under stressful conditions, isolated individuals seek companions. Alliances can be soothing. The coming together of parent and child, or neighbors, or colleagues at work, often produces relief from physiological distress and a diminution of elevated cortisol (Sachser, Dürschlag, and Hirzel 1998). Thus there is a negative feedback: A stressor elevates the physiological response, which encourages coalescence with allies, which reduces the stress response, which (in the absence of danger) loosens the coalition.

The link between stress physiology and coalition formation has not been a subject of much prior investigation; however, Wagner, Flinn, and England (2000), studying rural domino players in the Caribbean, show that cortisol reaches higher levels when two-man domino teams compete with teams from another village than when competing with teams from their own village.

My intent is to present a coherent model of stress-induced coalitions, laying a foundation for empirical study in humans. Two additional hypotheses govern the selection of coalition partners.

Hypothesis #2. When Ego chooses sides in a conflict, elevated stress induces him to join those whom he most closely identifies with.

Hypothesis #3. When Ego chooses sides in a conflict, elevated stress induces him to ally with his enemy's enemies.

STRESS-INDUCED AFFILIATION

Stress reinforces affiliation. According to Hypothesis #1, this is because stress produces a physiological motivation to coalesce. The solidarity of comrades at arms who have survived battle is mythic. A safer stressor, the horror film, is one of the most popular destinations for teenage dates because shared fright generates emotional rapport, facilitating later sexual activity (Weaver 1996). The stress-affiliation connection may explain to people who do not like baseball why anyone watches the first eight innings. At an engrossing game, the stress response heightens inning by inning, gradually intensifying the bond between a team and its fans. Victory is much sweeter to spectators who have received this physiological priming than to someone watching only the last inning.

Playwrights and filmmakers exploit the same effect to produce stories about a hero's ultimate revenge or triumph. The formulaic plot introduces a sympathetic protagonist as underdog or victim, then shows stressful scenes that build audience support for this person, and then climaxes with his or her victory. Successful instances produce a cathartic release of tension in the audience and can elicit cheering and applause even when there are no actors present in the motion picture theater.

Hypothesis #1 contains an important cognitive component: the recognition of allies and adversaries. Normally, Ego's allies are members of his group, easily recognized as specific personalities. Enemies are often strangers, or at least not intimate acquaintances. Furthermore, friends and foes present themselves differently. Allies display gestures and postures of affiliation, while enemies communicate threat or wariness. Nonetheless, distinguishing friend from foe is not always certain, and on rare occasions, Ego confuses the two. Then the stress response has the bizarre effect of increasing Ego's affiliation with enemies. The most famous incident of this kind occurred in 1974 when newspaper heiress Patty Hearst was kidnapped and held for ransom by activists of the Symbionese Liberation Army. During her stressful confinement, Hearst was unable or unwilling to differentiate enemies from allies. As a result, she affiliated with members of the SLA and eventually joined them voluntarily in an armed robbery. This outcome is called the "Stockholm Syndrome," after a similar case in Sweden (Hearst and Moscow 1988).

More typically, Ego's selection of allies is intuitively understandable. We turn now to two criteria for choosing sides, described in Hypotheses #2 and #3.

IDENTITY ALLIANCES

Group identity is the tendency to sympathize more with members of one's own collectivity (whether a family, a community, a formal organization, an ethnic group, or a nation) than with individuals outside that collectivity. Spectator sports demonstrate the ease with which we can identify with "our" team, being joyful at its victories and sorrowful at its defeats. In a more serious arena, citizens "rally round the flag" to support their nation and its leader against hostile foreign powers.

Normally, Ego identifies more closely with a nuclear family member or dear friend than with an unrelated member of the community, and more closely with a member of the community than with a foreigner. Members of minority ethnic groups often share a sense of identification, vis-à-vis the majority, even when they are personally unacquainted. In formal terms, if there are three people, A, B, and C; and if A and B identify more with each other than they do with C; then we will say that "A and B are *close* with respect to C." By Hypothesis #2, if A's stress is elevated, he or she will more likely seek a coalition with B than with C.

When stress is at moderate levels, as during playful contests, group identity is often irrelevant to the choosing of sides. Brothers or friends may play on opposing teams in schoolyard games. But if a serious fight breaks out, brothers and friends usually line up on the same side.

The Six Day War between Israel and six Arab nations, in June 1967, allowed an unusual study of identity alliance under stress. Earlier that year, prior to any hint of war, I interviewed nearly all identifiably Jewish (male) professors of sociology, psychology, political science, and anthropology at Harvard, Brandeis, and Boston Universities for a study of ethnic self-concept (Mazur 1973b). As a group, these professors were more assimilated than American Jews generally, but they showed considerable variation. I asked two questions about ethnic identity that are relevant here:

1. "How strong an interest or feeling would you say you have for Israel?" I coded these responses *high* or *low*.

2. "Roughly 15 percent of Nobel Prize laureates since 1907 have been Jewish. Also several of the major intellects of the last one hundred years were Jewish. Do you feel pride in this intellectual achievement of Jews?" I also coded these responses *high* or *low*.

During the tense days leading up to the war, and the combat itself, the concern of American Jews had an extraordinary fervor. Many Jewish professors participated in pro-Israel activities and showed high emotional involvement in ongoing events. Given the intense expressions of alarm at that time, it is reasonable to presume some activation of stress physiology, except in subjects who reported no Jewish identification.

After the war, I sent a letter to all subjects, asking if they were surprised at the extent of their emotional involvement in the fighting. Forty-seven out of sixty-three subjects answered. Of these, 23 percent reported that yes, they were surprised at their own emotional response.

The typology shown in Table A.1 divides mail respondents into four categories, determined by their *prewar* feelings about Israel and Jewish intellectual achievement. Those who reported high interest in Israel *and* pride in Jewish intellect—consistent Jewish identity—are in the upper left cell. Those who reported low interest in both—the least identified Jews—are in the lower right cell. Those giving one high and one low response are in the upper right and lower left cells.

Table A.1. Percentage of Respondents Who Were Surprised at the Extent of Their Emotional Involvement in the Six Day War, as a Function of Pride in Jewish Intellect and Interest in Israel

	Pride in Jewish Intellect	
Interest in Israel	*High*	*Low*
High	11%	0%
	(n = 9)	(n = 4)
Low	53%	6%
	(n = 17)	(n = 17)

Each cell shows the percentage of subjects in that category who were surprised by their strong emotions during the war. Nearly all of the surprised professors were ethnically identified before the war, as indicated by their pride in Jewish intellect, but they had little or no nationalistic feeling for Israel. The stress of the June crisis thrust them into alignment with the Jewish nation, inducing intense affiliations that were wholly unexpected.

MY ENEMY'S ENEMY

Stress-induced coalitions form in a predictable way even in the absence of identity alliances. A second enlistment principle is found in Heider's (1958) classic formulation of "structural balance." For present purposes, the balance principle is adequately encapsulated in folk wisdom: *My enemy's enemy is my friend.* During the calm of everyday life, balance is not an important principle of interpersonal relationships, and its prescriptions are frequently violated (Taylor 1970). But, according to Hypothesis #3, elevated stress implements this slogan.

An important consequence of Hypothesis #3 is that *in stressful situations, there is no more than one focal conflict at a time.* Secondary conflicts are submerged as individuals polarize into no more than two mutually exclusive camps. This is because three (or more) mutually opposing camps would violate the principle that an enemy's enemy is an ally.

Hypotheses #2 and #3, acting together, produce shifting coalitions when the locus of conflict changes. For example, two brothers, engaged in a serious argument, will abandon their quarrel to coalesce against a neighbor who tries to intervene. If a hostile stranger appears on the scene, the brothers may join their neighbor in repelling that intruder. With the stranger disposed of, the brothers resume their face-off against the neighbor. With the neighbor disposed of, the brothers return to their original quarrel.

Among police, intervention in a domestic dispute is known to be especially dangerous because of abruptly shifting coalitions. An officer coming to the aid of a battered wife may find the warring spouses suddenly combining to attack the peacemaker.

Police use coalition shifting to their advantage in the "good cop/bad cop" technique of questioning. The "bad cop" is an antagonistic and dislikable interrogator, ensuring that the suspect is highly stressed and desirous of an ally. The "good cop," objecting to the bad cop's callous treatment of the suspect, feigns a break in the police coalition, portraying his erstwhile partner as the common enemy. The suspect's best option for an ally (assuming no attorney is present) is the good cop. Often this is sufficient to establish rapport between the suspect and the good cop, producing a confession.

Pairs of swindlers pull the same scam. One swindler picks a fight with the mark. The second swindler, pretending to be a Good Samaritan, rushes to the mark's rescue, driving off the first swindler. The mark now has an "ally" and is set for plucking.

PUBLIC OPINION

If stress rises throughout the population in times of national crisis and falls during eras of good feeling, these aggregate hormonal changes may be reflected in collective behavior and in opinions surveys. In most years from 1974 through 1994, interviewers for the General Social Surveys asked random samples of Americans whether they liked or disliked "Russia" (http://sda.berkeley.edu:7502/cgi-bin/hsda?harcsda+gss02). Dislike was especially high during the early 1980s (Figure A.1). There was no proximate threat of war at the time, but there was a well-noted increase in the fear of nuclear holocaust when the U.S. Senate failed to ratify the SALT II arms control agreement with the Soviet Union, and President Ronald Reagan advocated a strong stance against the Soviets. These were the years of the Nuclear Freeze Movement, culminating in 1982 with perhaps the largest political rally in the nation's history, bringing a million people to Central Park (Adams 2002; Wittner 2003). The beginning of the Gorbachev era in 1985 brought a rapid relaxation in Soviet-American tensions.

Apart from year-to-year variations, stress levels (as measured by cortisol) are inversely related to social class (Mazur 1995). That is, the stress response is generally higher among Americans with low education and income than among those well educated and with high incomes. Therefore, other things equal, we should expect stronger polarization among lower-class Americans than among those of higher social class. Consistent with this expectation, the General Social Surveys show that college-educated respondents were less negative toward Russia than respondents with only a grammar school education (Figure A.1).

DISCUSSION

The model presented here may be contrasted with theories of coalition formation that emphasize rational choice or economic considerations as major desiderata (e.g., Luce and Raiffa 1957). In that view, actors join or reject a coalition, depending on their rational calculations of the consequences for payoffs. Out-group prejudices represent rationalizations rather than root causes (Silverman and Case 1998, 2001). Obviously there are situations encountered in business and elsewhere when deliberate calculations of profit

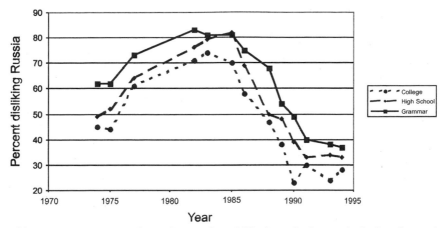

Table A.1.   Percentages of Americans Who Disliked Russia, by Level of Education and Year (General Social Surveys).

do dictate decisions to join one coalition or another. Rational-choice theory works well when actors share expectations for rational behavior, and when stress levels are sufficiently low that strong emotions are not incited. However, these scope conditions are not met when stress-induced emotions overwhelm rational calculation.

Under stressful conditions, we affiliate with those whom we identify with, and with our enemies' enemies. These behaviors are neatly explained by the supposition that elevated stress physiologically motivates affiliation with allies and polarization against adversaries. The present conjectures are novel and have not been tested empirically.

References

Abbott, D., E. Keverne, F. Bercovitch, C. Shively, S. Mendoza, W. Saltzman, C. Snowdon, et al. 2003. Are subordinates always stressed? A comparative analysis of rank differences in cortisol levels among primates. *Hormones and Behavior* 43:67–82.

Ackerman, J. 1998. Dinosaurs taking wing. *National Geographic* 194 (July): 74–99.

Adams, D. 2002. *The American peace movement.* New Haven, CT: Advocate Press.

Albert, D., M. Walsh, and R. Jonik. 1994. Aggression in humans: What is its biological foundation? *Neuroscience & Biobehavioral Reviews* 17:405–425.

Allee, W., N. Collias, and C. Lutherman. 1939. Modification of the social order in flocks of hens by the injection of testosterone propionate. *Physiological Zoology* 12:412–440.

Allison, G. 1971. *Essence of decision.* Boston: Little Brown.

Allman, J. 1999. *Evolving brains.* New York: Scientific American Library.

Ambrose, S. 2001. Paleolithic technology and human evolution. *Science* 291:1748–1753.

Anderson, E. 1978. *A place of honor.* Chicago: University of Chicago Press.

———. 1991. *Streetwise.* Chicago: University of Chicago Press.

———. 1994. The code of the streets. *The Atlantic Monthly* 5:81–94.

Anderson, F., and F. Willis. 1976. Glancing at others in preschool children in relation to dominance. *Psychological Record* 26:467–472.

Anderson, R., J. Bancroft, and F. Wu. 1992. The effects of exogenous testosterone on sexuality and mood of normal men. *Journal of Clinical Endocrinology and Metabolism* 75:1503–1507.

Archer, J. 1991. The influence of testosterone on human aggression. *British Journal of Psychology* 82:1–28.

———. 1994. *Male violence.* London: Routledge.

Argyle, M., and M. Cook. 1976. *Gaze and mutual gaze.* Cambridge, UK: Cambridge University Press.

Atkinson, R. 1989. *The long gray line.* Boston: Houghton, Mifflin.

Attenborough, D. 1998. *The life of birds*. London: BBC Books.

Aveni, A. 1989. *Empires of time*. New York: Basic Books.

Axelrod, J., and T. Reisine. 1984. Stress hormones. *Science* 224:452–459.

Bagatell, C., J. Heiman, J. Rivier, and W. Bremner. 1994. Effects of endogenous testosterone and estradiol on sexual behavior in normal young men. *Journal of Clinical Endocrinology and Metabolism* 78:711–716.

Bain, J., R. Langevin, R. Dickey, and M. Ben-Aron. 1987. Sex hormones in murderers and assaulters. *Behavioral Science and the Law* 5:95–101.

Baldwin, J., and J. Baldwin, 1981. The squirrel monkeys, genus *Saimiri*. In *Ecology and behavior of neotropical primates*, ed. A. Coimbra-Filho and R. Mittermeier, 277–330. Rio de Janeiro: Academia Brasileira de Ciencias.

Bales, R. 1953. The equilibrium problem in small groups. Chapter 4 in *Working papers in the theory of action*, ed. T. Parsons, R. Bales, and E. Shils. New York: Free Press.

Bambach, C. 2003. *Leonardo da Vinci, master draftsman*. New York: Metropolitan Museum of Art.

Banks, T., and J. Dabbs Jr. 1996. Salivary testosterone and cortisol in a delinquent and violent urban subculture. *The Journal of Social Psychology* 136:49–56.

Barkow, J, L. Cosmides, and J. Tooby, eds. 1992. *The adapted mind*. New York: Oxford University Press.

Barrett, G., K. Shimizu, M. Bardi, S. Asaba, and A. Mori. 2002. Endocrine correlates of rank, reproduction, and female-directed aggression in male Japanese macaques (*Macaca fuscata*). *Hormones and Behavior* 42:85–96.

Bartlett, D., and G. Meier. 1971. Dominance status and certain operants in a communal colony of rhesus macaques. *Primates* 12 (December): 209–219.

Barton, J., D. Press, J. Keenan, and M. O'Connor. 2002. Lesions of the fusiform face area impair perception of facial configuration in prosopagnosia. *Neurology* 58:71–78.

Bateup, H., A. Booth, E. Shirtcliff, and D. Granger. 2002. Testosterone, cortisone, and women's competition. *Evolution and Human Behavior* 23:181–192.

Benson, P., and D. Perrett. 1994. Visual processing of facial distinctiveness. *Perception* 23:75–93.

Berdecio, S., and L. Nash. 1981. Chimpanzee visual communication. Anthropological Research Papers No. 26. Tempe, AZ: Arizona State University.

Berger, J., B. Cohen, and M. Zelditch Jr. 1972. Status characteristics and social interaction. *American Sociological Review* 37:209–219.

Bergman, T., J. Beehner, D. Cheney, and R. Seyfarth. 2003. Hierarchical classification by rank and kinship in baboons. *Science* 302:1234–1236.

Bernstein, H. 1918. *The Willy-Nicky correspondence, being the secret and intimate telegrams exchanged between the kaiser and the tsar*. New York: A. A. Knopf.

Bernstein, I. 1981. Dominance: The baby and the bathwater. *Behavioral and Brain Sciences* 4 (3):419–429.

Berscheid, E., and E. Walster. 1974. Physical attractiveness. In *Advances in experimental social psychology*, ed. L. Berkowitz, 157–215. New York: Academic Press.

Beschloss, M. 1997. *Reaching for glory: Lyndon Johnson's secret White House tapes, 1964–1965*. New York: Simon and Schuster.

Bhasin, D., T. Storer, N. Berman, C. Callegari, D. Clevenger, J. Phillips, T. Bunnell, R. Tricker, A. Shirazi, and R. Casaburi. 1996. The effects of supraphysiologic doses of testosterone on muscle size and strength of normal men. *The New England Journal of Medicine* 335:1–7.

Bickerton, D. 1990. *Language and species.* Chicago: University of Chicago Press.

Björkqvist, K. 2001. Social defeat as a stressor in humans. *Physiology & Behavior* 73:435–442.

Blair, R., J. Morris, C. Frith, D. Perrett, and R. Dolan. 1999. Dissociable neural responses to facial expressions of sadness and anger. *Brain* 122 (Pt. 5): 883–893.

Blomberg, S., and T. Garland Jr. 2002. Tempo and mode in evolution: Phylogenetic inertia, adaptation and comparative methods. *Journal of Evolutionary Biology* 15:899–910.

Blomberg, S., T. Garland Jr., and A. Ives. 2003. Testing for phylogenetic signal in comparative data: behavioral traits are more labile. *Evolution: International Journal of Organic Evolution* 57:717–745.

Booth, A., and P. Amato. 1991. Divorce and psychological stress. *Journal of Health and Social Behavior* 32:396–407.

Booth, A., and J. Dabbs Jr. 1993. Testosterone and men's marriages. *Social Forces* 72:463–477.

———. 1995. Cortisol, testosterone, and competition among women. Sociology Department Report. University Park: Pennsylvania State University.

Booth, A., D. Johnson, D. Granger, A. Crouter, and S. McHale. 2003. Testosterone and child and adolescent adjustment: The moderating role of parent-child relationships. *Developmental Psychology* 39:85–98

Booth, A., A. Mazur, and J. Dabbs Jr. 1993. Endogenous testosterone and competition: The effects of fasting. *Steroids* 58:348–350.

Booth, A., and D. Osgood. 1993. The influence of testosterone on deviance in adulthood. *Criminology* 31:93–117.

Booth, A., D. Johnson, L. White, and J. Edwards. 1985. Predicting divorce and permanent separation. *Journal of Family Issues* 6:331–346.

Booth, A., G. Shelley, A. Mazur, G. Tharp, and R. Kittok. 1989. Testosterone, and winning and losing in human competition. *Hormones and Behavior* 23:556–571.

Brain, P. 1994. Hormonal aspects of aggression and violence. In *Understanding and preventing violence*, Vol. 2., ed. A. Reiss Jr., K. Miczek, and J. Roth, 173–244. Washington DC: National Academy Press.

Breedlove, S. 1992. Sexual differentiation of the brain and behavior. In *Behavioral endocrinology*, ed. J. Becker, S. Breedlove, and D. Crews, 39–68. Cambridge, MA: MIT Press.

Brinkerhoff, D., and A. Booth. 1984. Gender, dominance, and stress. *Journal of Social and Biological Structures* 7:159–177.

Brodal, P. 1998. *The central nervous system*, 2nd ed. New York: Oxford University Press.

Brown, D. 1991. *Human universals.* Philadelphia: Temple University Press.

Brown, E., and D. Perrett. 1993. What gives a face its gender? *Perception* 22:829–840.

Brugioni, D. 1990. *Eyeball to Eyeball.* New York: Random House.

Bryant, H., and A. Russell. 1992. The role of phylogenetic analysis in the inference of unpreserved attributes of extinct taxa. *Philosophical Transactions of the Royal Society of London* 337:405–418.

Burnham T., J. Flynn, P. Gray, M. McIntyre, S. Lipson, and P. Ellison. 2003. Men in committed, romantic relationships have lower testosterone. *Hormones and Behavior* 44:119–22.

Byrne, R. 2001. Social and technical forms of primate intelligence. In *Tree of origin*, ed. F. de Waal, 145–172. Cambridge, MA: Harvard University Press.

Calhoun, J. 1962. *The ecology and sociology of the Norway rat.* Bethesda, MD: U.S. Department of Health, Education, and Welfare.

Cameron, A., O. John, D. Keltner, and A. Kring. 2001. Who attains social status? Effects of personality and physical attractiveness in social groups. *Journal of Personality and Social Psychology* 81:116–132.

Campbell, A., and J. Gibbs. 1986. *Violent transactions.* Oxford: Blackwell.

Campbell, B., M. O'Rourke, and M. Rabow. 1988. Pulsatile response of salivary testosterone and cortisol to aggressive competition in young males. Paper presented at Annual Meeting of the American Assn. of Physical Anthropologists, Kansas City.

Canli, T., H. Sivers, S. Whitfield, I. Gotlib, and J. Gabrieli. 2002. Amygdala response to happy faces as a function of extraversion. *Science* 296:2191.

Carter, C. 1992. Hormonal influences on human sexual behavior. In *Behavioral endocrinology*, ed. J. Becker, S. Breedlove, and D. Crews, 131–142. Cambridge, MA: MIT Press.

Cashdan, E. 1995. Hormones, sex, and status in women. *Hormones and Behavior* 29:354–366.

Chapple, E. 1970. *Culture and biological man.* New York: Holt, Rinehart and Winston.

Chevalier-Skolnikoff, S. 1973. Facial expression of emotion in nonhuman primates. In *Darwin and facial expression*, ed. P. Ekman, 11–89. New York: Academic Press.

Chomsky, N. 1957. *Syntactic structures.* The Hague: Mouton.

Clark, D., P. Mitra, and S. Wang. 2001. Scalable architecture in mammalian brains. *Nature* 411:189–193.

Clarke, L. 1999. *Mission impossible: Using fantasy documents to tame disaster.* Chicago: University of Chicago Press.

Coe, C., A. Savage, and L. Bromley. 1992. Phylogenetic influences on hormone levels across the Primate order. *American Journal of Primatology* 28:81–100.

Cohen, J., and F. Tong. 2001. The face of controversy. *Science* 293:2405–2407.

Collaer, M., and M. Hines. 1995. Human behavioral sex differences: A role for gonadal hormones during early development? *Psychological Bulletin* 118:55–107.

Collins, M., and L. Zebrowitz. 1995. The contributions of appearance to occupational outcomes in civilian and military settings. *Journal of Applied Social Psychology* 25:29–163.

Constantino, J., D. Grosz, P. Saenger, D. Chandler, R. Nandi, and F. Earls. 1993. Testosterone and aggression in children. *Journal of the American Academy of Child & Adolescent Psychiatry* 32:1217–1222.

Conway Morris, S. 1998. *The crucible of creation.* New York: Oxford University Press.

Corballis, M. 1999. The gestural origins of language. *American Scientist* 87 (March–April): 138–145.

Cox, D., E. Meyers, and P. Sinha. 2004. Contextually evoked object-specific responses in human visual cortex. *Science* 304:115–117.

Dabbs, J., Jr. 1990. Salivary testosterone measurements: Reliability across hours, days, and weeks. *Physiology & Behavior* 48:83–86.

———. 1991. Saliva testosterone measurements: Collecting, storing, and mailing saliva samples. *Physiology & Behavior* 49.

———. 1992. Testosterone and occupational achievement. *Social Forces* 70:813–824.

———. 2000. *Heroes, rogues and lovers: Testosterone and behavior.* New York: McGraw-Hill.

Dabbs, J., Jr., B. Campbell, B. Gladue, A. Midgley, M. Navarro, G. Read, E. Susman, L. Swinkels, and C. Worthman. 1995. Reliability of salivary testosterone measurements. *Enzymes and Protein Markers* 41:1581–1584.

Dabbs, J., Jr., and M. Hargrove. 1997. Age, testosterone, and behavior among female prison inmates. *Psychosomatic Medicine* 59:477–80.

Dabbs, J., Jr., and R. Morris. 1990. Testosterone, social class, and antisocial behavior in a sample of 4,462 men. *Psychological Science* 1:209–211.

Dabbs, J., Jr., R. Ruback, R. Frady, C. Hopper, and D. Sgoutas. 1988. Saliva testosterone and criminal violence among women. *Personality and Individual Differences* 9:269–275.

Daitzman, R., and M. Zuckerman. 1980. Disinhibitory sensation seeking, personality and gonadal hormones. *Personality and Individual Differences* 1:103–110.

Daly, M., and M. Wilson. 1988. *Homicide.* New York: Aldine de Gruyter.

Darrow, C. 1987. Clarence Darrow's cross-examination of William Jennings Bryan. *Classics of the courtroom*, Vol. III. Minnetonka, MN: Professional Education Group.

Davidson, J., J. Chen, L. Crapo, G. Gray, W. Greenleaf, and J. Catania. 1983. Hormonal changes and sexual functioning in aging men. *Journal of Clinical Endocrinology and Metabolism* 57:71–77.

Davidson, R., K. Putnam, and C. Larson. 2000. Dysfunction in the neural circuitry of emotion regulation—A possible prelude to violence. *Science* 289:591–594.

Davies, N. 1992. *Dunnock behaviour and social evolution.* New York: Oxford University Press.

———. 1996. *Europe: A history.* New York: Oxford University Press.

Davis, J., T. Smith, and P. Marsden. 2003. *General social surveys, 1972–2002.* Ann Arbor, MI: Inter-University Consortium for Political and Social Research, University of Michigan.

de Kruif, P. 1945. *The male hormone.* New York: Harcourt, Brace.

Derber, C. 1979. *The pursuit of attention.* Boston: G. K. Hall.

DeVore, I. 1965. *Primate behavior: Field studies of monkeys and apes.* New York: Holt, Rinehart and Winston.

de Waal, F. 1989. *Chimpanzee politics.* Baltimore: Johns Hopkins University Press.

———. 1995. Bonobo sex and society. *Scientific American* (March): 82–88.

———. 2000. Primates: A natural heritage of conflict resolution. *Science* 289:586–590.

———. 2001. *Tree of origin.* Cambridge, MA: Harvard University Press.

de Waal, F., and F. Lanting. 1997. *Bonobo: The forgotten ape.* Berkeley: University of California Press.

Dewar, H., and D. Milbank. 2004. Cheney says he "felt better" after uttering expletive. *Syracuse Post-Standard* (June 26): A7.

Diamond, J. 1997. *Guns, germs, and steel.* New York: W. W. Norton.

DiFiore, A., and D. Rendall. 1994. Evolution of social organization. *Proceedings of the National Academy of Sciences* 91:9941–9945.

Dolan, R. 2002. Emotion, cognition, and behavior. *Science* 298:1191–1194.

Drigotas, S., and J. Udry. 1993. Biosocial models of adolescent problem behavior: Extension to panel design. *Social Biology* 40:1–7.

Duncan, S., Jr., and D. Fiske. 1977. *Face-to-face interaction.* New York: Wiley.

Dynes, R., and K. Tierney, eds. 1994. *Disasters, collective behavior, and social organization.* Newark: University of Delaware Press.

Ehlers, C., K. Rickler, and J. Hovey. 1980. A possible relationship between plasma testosterone and aggressive behavior in a female outpatient population. In *Limbic epilepsy and the dyscontrol syndrome,* ed. M. Girgis and L. Kiloh, 183–194. New York: Elsevier.

Ehrenkranz, J., E. Bliss, and M. Sheard. 1974. Plasma testosterone: Correlation with aggressive behavior and social dominance in men. *Psychosomatic Medicine* 36:469–475.

Ekman, P., and W. Friesen. 1971. Constants across culture in the face and emotion. *Journal of Personality and Social Psychology* 17:124–129.

Ekman, P., R. Levenson, and W. Friesen. 1983. Autonomic nervous system activity distinguishes among emotions. *Science* 221:1208–1210.

Eldredge, N. 1991. *Fossils.* New York: Harry N. Abrams.

Elias, M. 1981. Serum cortisol, testosterone, and testosterone-binding globulin responses to competitive fighting in human males. *Aggressive Behavior* 7:215–224.

Ellis, L. 1995. Dominance and reproductive success among nonhuman animals: a cross-species comparison. *Ethology and Sociobiology* 16:257–333.

Ellis, L., and J. Nyborg. 1992. Racial/ethnic variations in male testosterone levels. *Steroids* 57:72–75.

Ellyson, S., J. Dovidio, and B. Fehr. 1981. Visual behavior and dominance in men and women. In *Gender and Nonverbal Behavior,* ed. C. Mayo and N. Henley. Heidelberg, Germany: Springer.

Exline, R. 1972. Visual interaction. In *Nebraska Symposium on Motivation,* ed. J. Cole. Omaha: Nebraska University Press.

Federal Bureau of Investigation. 2004. *Crime in the United States 2003.* Washington DC: Department of Justice.

Feldstein, S., and J. Welkowitz. 1978. A chrongraphy of conversation. In *Nonverbal behavior and communication,* ed. A. Seligman and S. Feldstein. New York: Wiley.

Fielden, J., C. Lutter, and J. Dabbs. 1994. *Basking in glory: Testosterone changes in World Cup soccer fans.* Psychology Department. Georgia State University.

Fields, S. 2001. Proteomics in Genomeland. *Science* 291:1221–1224.

Filley, C. 1995. *Neurobehavioral anatomy.* Niwot: University of Colorado Press.

Finkelstein, J., E. Susman, V. Chinchilli, S. Kunselman, M. D'Arcangelo, J. Schwab, L. Demers, L. Liben, G. Lookingbill, and H. Kulin. 1997. Estrogen or testosterone increases self-reported aggressive behaviors in hypogonadal adolescents. *Journal of Clinical Endocrinology and Metabolism* 82:2433–2438.

Fisek, M., and R. Ofshe. 1970. The process of status evolution. *Sociometry* 33:327–346.

Fleagle, J. 1999. *Primate adaptation and evolution.* San Diego: Academic Press.

Fouts, R. 1997. *Next of Kin.* New York: William Morrow.

Fursenko, A., and T. Naftali. 1997. *One hell of a gamble.* New York: W. W. Norton.

Fussell, P. 1983. *Class.* New York: Ballantine Books.

Gardner, B., and R. Gardner. 1969. Teaching sign language to a chimpanzee. *Science* 165: 664–672.

Gerth, H., and C. W. Mills, eds. 1948. *From Max Weber: Essays in Sociology.* London: Routledge & Kegan Paul.

Gimbel, C., and A. Booth. 1996. Who fought in Vietnam? *Social Forces* 74:1137–1157.

Gladue, B. 1991. Aggressive behavior characteristics, hormones, and sexual orientation in men and women. *Aggressive Behavior* 17:313–326.

Gladue, B., M. Boechler, and K. McCaul. 1989. Hormonal response to competition in human males. *Aggressive Behavior* 15:409–422.

Glassner, B. 1988. *Bodies.* New York: G. P. Putnam's Sons.

Goffman, E. 1963. *Stigma: Notes on the management of spoiled identity.* Philadelphia: University of Pennsylvania Press.

Goffman, E. 1967. *Interaction ritual.* Garden City, NY: Doubleday.

Goldenthal, P., R. Johnston, and R. Kraut. 1981. Smiling, appeasement, and the silent bare-teeth display. *Ethology and Sociobiology* 2:127–133.

Gonzalez-Bono, E., A. Salvador, M. Serrano, and J. Ricarte. 1999. Testosterone, cortisol, and mood in a sports team competition. *Hormones and Behavior* 35:55–62.

Goodall, J. 1986. *The Chimpanzees of Gombe.* Cambridge, MA: Harvard University Press.

Goodman, S., and J. Benstead, eds. 2003. *The natural history of Madagascar.* Chicago: University of Chicago Press.

Goodwin, C. 1980. Restarts, pauses and the achievement of a state of mutual gaze at turntaking. *Sociological Inquiry* 50:272–302.

Gould, S. 1977. *Ontogeny and phylogeny.* Cambridge, MA: Harvard University Press.

Goy, R., F. Bercovitch, and M. McBriar. 1988. Behavior masculinization is independent of genital masculinization in prenatally androgenized female rhesus macaques. *Hormones and Behavior* 22:552–571.

Grant, V., and J. France. 2001. Dominance and testosterone in women. *Biological Psychology* 58:41–47.

Gregory, S., Jr. 1983. A qualitative analysis of temporal symmetry in microsocial relations. *American Sociological Review* 48:129–135.

Guthrie, J. 1973. The evolution of menace. *Saturday Review* (May): 22–28.

Guthrie, R. 1976. *Body hot spots.* New York: Van Nostrand Reinhold.

Halpern, C., J. Udry, B. Campbell, and C. Suchindran. 1993. Testosterone and pubertal development as predictors of sexual activity. *Psychosomatic Medicine* 55:436–447.

Harris, J., J. Rushton, E. Hampson, and D. Jackson. 1996. Salivary testosterone and self-report aggressive and pro-social personality characteristics in men and women. *Aggressive Behavior* 22:321–331.

Hatfield, E., and S. Sprecher. 1986. *Mirror, mirror....* Albany: State University of New York Press.

Hauser, M., N. Chomsky, and W. Fitch. 2002. The faculty of language: What is it, who has it, and how did it evolve? *Science* 298:1569–1579.

Hayes, C. 1970. A chimpanzee learns to talk. In *Psychological studies of human development,* ed. R. Kuhlen and G. Thompson, 331–399. New York: Appleton-Century-Crofts.

Hearst, P., and A. Moscow. 1988. *Patricia Hearst: Her own story.* New York: Avon.

Heider, F. 1958. *Psychology of interpersonal relations*. New York: Wiley.

Heller, J. 1963, *Catch-22*, New York: Dell.

Henry, J. 1992. Biological basis of the stress response. *Integrative Physiological and Behavioral Science* 27:66–83.

Henry, J., and S. Wang. 1998. Effects of early stress on adult affiliative behavior. *Psychoneuroendocrinology* 23:863–875.

Hersh, S. 1997. *The dark side of Camelot*. Boston: Little, Brown and Company.

Hess, E. 1975. The role of pupil size in communication. *Scientific American* 233:110–119.

Hey, J. 2001. *Genes, categories, and species*. New York: Oxford University Press.

Hirata, S., K. Watanabe, and M. Kawai. 2001. Sweet-potato washing revisited. In *Primate origins of human cognition and behavior*, ed. T. Matsuzawa, 487–508. New York: Springer.

Hof, P., E. Nimchinsky, D. Perl, and J. Erwin. 2001. An unusual population of pyramidal neurons in the anterior cingulated cortex of hominids contains the calcium-binding protein calretinin. *Neuroscience Letters* 307:139–142.

Homans, G. 1961. *Social behavior: Its elementary forms*. New York: Harcourt, Brace and World.

Horn, G., A. Nicol, and W. Brown. 2001. Tracking memory's trace. *Proceedings of the National Academy of Sciences* 98:5282–5287.

Horowitz, R. 1983. *Honor and the American dream*. New Brunswick, NJ: Rutgers University Press.

Inoff-Germain, G., G. Arnold, E. Nottelmann, E. Susman, G. Cutler Jr., and G. Chrousos. 1988. Relations between hormone levels and observational measures of aggressive behavior of young adolescents in family interactions. *Developmental Psychology* 24:129–139.

Inoue-Nakamura, N. 2001. Mirror self-recognition in primates: An ontogenetic and phylogenetic approach. In *Primate origins of human cognition and behavior*, ed. T. Matsuzawa, 297–312. New York: Springer-Verlag.

Insel, T. 1993. Oxytocin and the neuroendocrine basis of affiliation. In *Hormonal induced change in mind and brain*, ed. J. Schulki. San Diego: Academic Press.

IS/OOP Group. *Online Magazine.* http://www.online-magazine.com/mast.htm.

Jackendoff, R. 1994. *Patterns in the mind*. New York: Basic Books.

Jay, P. 1968. *Primates: Studies in adaptation and variability*. New York: Holt, Rinehart and Winston.

Johnson, Paul. 1983. *Modern times*. New York: Harper & Row.

———. 1991. *The birth of the modern*. HarperCollins.

Jolly, A. 1966. *Lemur behavior*. Chicago: University of Chicago Press.

———. 1972. *The evolution of primate behavior*. New York: Macmillan.

Jordan, P. 1999. *Neanderthal*. Phoenix Mill, UK: Sutton.

Julian, T., and P. McKenry. 1989. Relationship of testosterone to men's family at midlife. *Aggressive Behavior* 15:281–289.

Kagan, J., J. Reznick, and N. Snidman. 1988. Biological bases of childhood shyness. *Science* 240:167–171.

Kalma, A. 1991. Hierarchisation and dominance assessment at first glance. *European Journal of Social Psychology* 21:165–181.

———. 1992. Gazing in triads: A powerful signal in floor apportionment. *British Journal of Social Psychology* 31:21–39.

Kappeler, P. 1998. Nests, tree holes, and the evolution of primate life histories. *American Journal of Primatology* 46:7–33.

Kappeler, P., and C. van Schaik. 2002. Evolution of primate social systems. *International Journal of Primatology* 23:707–740.

Katz, J. 1988. *Seductions of crime.* New York: Basic Books.

Keating, C., A. Mazur, and M. Segall. 1977. Facial gestures which influence the perception of status. *Sociometry* 40:374–378.

———. 1981. A cross-cultural exploration of physiognomic traits of dominance and happiness. *Ethology and Sociobiology* 2:41–48.

Keating, C., A. Mazur, M. Segall, P. Cysneiros, W. Divale, J. Kilbride, S. Komin, R. Leahy, B. Thurman, and R. Wirsing. 1981. Culture and the perception of social dominance from facial expression. *Journal of Personality and Social Psychology* 40:615–626.

Kemper, T. 1990. *Social structure and testosterone.* New Brunswick, NJ: Rutgers University Press.

Kendon, A. 1967. Some functions of gaze direction in social interaction. *Acta Psychologica* 26:22–63.

Kennedy, R. 1971. *Thirteen days.* New York. W. W. Norton.

Khrushchev, N. 1970. *Khrushchev remembers.* Boston: Little, Brown and Company.

Kivlighan, K., D. Granger, and A. Booth. 2005. Gender differences in testosterone and cortisol response to competition. *Psychoneuroendocrinology* 30:58–71

Kochakian, C. 1993. Anabolic-androgenic steroids. In *Anabolic steroids in sport and exercise,* ed. C. Yesalis, 3–33. Champaign, IL: Human Kinetics.

Koubi, M. Psychology and sometimes a slap: The man who made prisoners talk. *New York Times,* December 12, 2004.

Kouri, E., S. Lukas, H. Pope, and P. Oliva. 1995. Increased aggressive responding in male volunteers following the administration of gradually increasing doses of testosterone cypionate. *Drug and Alcohol Dependence* 40:73–79.

Kreuz, L., R. Rose, and J. Jennings. 1972. Suppression of plasma testosterone levels and psychological stress. *Archives of General Psychiatry* 26:479–482.

Kummer, H. 1968. *The social organization of hamadryas baboons.* Chicago: University of Chicago Press.

Laumann, E., J. Gagnon, R. Michael, and S. Michaels. 1994. *The social organization of sexuality.* Chicago: University of Chicago Press.

LeDoux, J. 2002. *Synaptic self.* New York: Viking.

Lee, M., and R. Ofshe. 1981. The impact of behavioral style and status characteristics on social influence. *Social Psychology Quarterly* 44:73–82.

Lenneberg, E. 1967. *Biological foundations of language.* New York: John Wiley.

Loftus, E., and J. Doyle. 1997. *Eyewitness testimony.* Charlottesville, VA: Lexis Law Publications.

Luce, R., and J. Raiffa. 1957. *Games and decisions.* New York: Wiley.

MacLean, P. 1990. *The triune brain in evolution.* New York: Plenum Press.

Maris, R. 2000. *Comprehensive textbook of suicidology.* New York: Guilford Press.

Martin, R. D. 1990. *Primate origins and evolution.* Princeton, NJ: Princeton University Press.

Masters, R., and B. Way. 1996. Experimental methods and attitudes toward leaders. In *Research in biopolitics*, Vol. 4, ed. A. Somit and S. Peterson. Greenwich, CT: JAI Press.

Matsuzawa, T. 2001. *Primate origins of human cognition and behavior.* New York: Springer-Verlag.

Mattsson, A., D. Schalling, D. Olweus, H. Low, and J. Svensson. 1980. Plasma testosterone, aggressive behavior, and personality dimensions in young male delinquents. *Journal of the American Academy of Child Psychiatry*: 476–490.

Mauss, M. 1925 (1967). *The gift: Forms and functions of exchange in archaic societies.* New York: W. W. Norton.

May, E., and P. Zelikow, eds. 1997. *The Kennedy tapes.* Cambridge, MA: Harvard University Press.

Mazur, A. 1973a. A cross-species comparison of status in small established groups. *American Sociological Review* 38:513–530.

———. 1973b. Increased tendency toward balance during stressful conflict. *Sociometry* 36:279–283.

———. 1976. Effects of testosterone on status in primate groups, *Folia Primatologica* 26:214–26.

———. 1985. A biosocial model of status in face-to-face primate groups. *Social Forces* 64:377–402.

———. 1992. The evolutionary psychology of rape and food robbery. *Behavioral and Brain Sciences* 12:397.

———. 1994. Do cortisol and thyroxin correlate with nervousness and depression among male army veterans? *Biological Psychology* 37:259–263.

———. 1995. Biosocial models of deviant behavior among army veterans. *Biological Psychology* 41:271–293.

———. 1996. Evolution in humans of macro-level social stratification and language. In *Social science microsimulation*, ed. K. Troitzsch, U. Mueller, G. Gilbert, and J. Doren, 171–178. Berlin: Springer.

———. 1998. Aging and testosterone. *Science* 279:305–306.

———. 2001. Darwin and sociology: Oil and water. In *Evolutionary approaches in behavioral sciences*, ed. S. Peterson and A. Somit, 235-245. Greenwich, CT: JAI Press.

———. 2002. Take a chimp, add language, melt the glaciers . . . *Journal for the Theory of Social Behavior* 32:29–63.

Mazur, A., and A. Booth. 1998. Testosterone and dominance in men. *Behavioral and Brain Sciences* 21:353–363.

Mazur, A., A. Booth, and J. Dabbs Jr. 1992. Testosterone and chess competition. *Social Psychology Quarterly* 55:70–77.

———. 1993. Endogenous testosterone and competition: The effect of fasting. *Steroids* 58:348–350.

Mazur, A., and M. Cataldo. 1989. Dominance and deference in conversation. *Journal of Social and Biological Structures* 12:87–99.

Mazur, A., C. Halpern, and J. Udry. 1994. Dominant looking male teenagers copulate earlier. *Ethology and Sociobiology* 15:87–94.

Mazur, A., and T. Lamb. 1980. Testosterone, status, and mood in human males. *Hormones and Behavior* 14:236–246.

Mazur, A., J. Mazur, and C. Keating. 1984. Military rank attainment of a West Point class: Effects of cadets' physical features. *American Journal of Sociology* 90:125–150.

Mazur, A., and J. Michalek. 1998. Marriage, divorce, and male testosterone. *Social Forces* 77:315–330.

Mazur, A. and U. Mueller. 1996a. Channel modeling: From West Point cadet to general. *Public Administration Review* 56 (March/April): 191–198.

———. 1996b. Facial dominance. *Research in Biopolitics* 4:99–111.

Mazur, A., U. Mueller, and W. Krause. 2002. Causes of sexual decline in aging married men: Germany and America. *International Journal of Impotence Research* 14:101–106.

Mazur, A., E. Rosa, M. Faupel, J. Heller, R. Leen, and B. Thurman. 1980. Physiological aspects of communication via mutual gaze. *American Journal of Sociology* 90:125–150.

Mazur, A., E. Susman, and S. Edelbrock. 1997. Sex difference in testosterone response to a video game competition. *Evolution and Human Behavior* 18:317–326.

McBurnett, K., B. Lahey, P. Rathouz, and R. Loeber. 2000. Low salivary cortisol and persistent aggression in boys referred for disruptive behavior. *Archives of General Psychiatry* 57:38–43.

McCaul, K., B. Gladue, and M. Joppa. 1992. Winning, losing, mood, and testosterone. *Hormones and Behavior* 26:486–506.

McEwen, B. 1981. Endocrine effects on the brain and their relationship to behavior. In *Basic neurochemistry*, 3rd ed., ed. G. Siegel, R. Albers, B. Agranoff, and R. Katzman, 775–799. Boston: Little Brown.

McGrew, W. 1992. *Chimpanzee material culture*. Cambridge: Cambridge University Press.

McNeill, D. 1998. *The face: A natural history*. Boston: Little, Brown.

Milgram, S. 1974. *Obedience to authority*. New York: Harper and Row.

Mithen, S. 1996. *The prehistory of the mind*. London: Thames and Hudson.

Monaghan, F., and S. Glickman. 1992. Hormones and aggressive behavior. In *Behavioral endocrinology*, ed. J. Becker, S. Breedlove, and D. Crews, 261–285. Cambridge, MA: MIT Press.

Moore, D., and B. Trout. 1978. Military achievement: The visibility theory and promotions. *American Political Science Review* 72:452–468.

Morris, J., C. Firth, D. Perrett, D. Rowland, A. Young, A. Calder, and R. Dolan. 1996. A differential neural response in the human amygdala to fearful and happy facial expressions. *Nature* 383:812–815.

Moura, A., and P. Lee. 2004. Capuchin stone tool use in Caatinga dry forest. *Science* 306:1909.

Mueller, U., and A. Mazur. 1996. Facial dominance of West Point cadets as a predictor of later military rank. *Social Forces* 74:823–850.

———. 1997. Facial dominance in *Homo sapiens* as honest signaling of male quality. *Behavioral Ecology* 8:569–579.

Muller, M., and R. Wrangham. 2001. The reproductive ecology of male hominids. In *Reproductive ecology and human evolution*, ed. P. Ellison. New York: Aldine.

———. 2004. Dominance, cortisol and stress in wild chimpanzees (*Pan troglodytes schweinfurthii*). *Behavioral and Ecological Sociobiology* 55:332–340.

Muller-Schwarze, D., and L. Sun. 2003. *The beaver as ecosystem engineer: Natural history, behavior, and ecology*. Ithaca, NY: Cornell University Press.

Nakamichi, M. 2001. Mother-offspring relationship in macaques. In *Primate origins of human cognition and behavior*, ed. T. Matsuzawa, 418–440. New York: Springer-Verlag.

Napier, J., and P. Napier, 1985. *The natural history of the primates*. London: Museum.

Neave, N., and S. Wolfson. 2003. Testosterone, territoriality, and the "home advantage." *Physiology & Behavior* 78:269–275.

Nieschlag, E., and E. Wickings. 1981. The role of testosterone in the evaluation of testicular function. In *Radioassay systems in clinical endocrinology*, ed. G. Abraham, 169–196. New York: Marcel Dekker.

Nisbett, R. 1993. Violence and U.S. regional culture. *American Psychologist* 48:441–449.

Nisbett, R., and D. Cohen. 1996. *Culture of honor*. Boulder, CO: Westview Press.

Nishida, T. 1970. Social behavior and relationships among wild chimpanzees of the Mahali Mountains. *Primates* 11:47–87.

Nowak, R. 1995. *Walker's mammals of the world*, 6th ed. Baltimore: Johns Hopkins University Press.

———. 1999. *Primates of the world*. Baltimore: Johns Hopkins Press.

O'Connor, D., J. Archer, W. Hair, and F. Wu. 2002. Exogenous testosterone, aggression, and mood in eugonadal and hypogonadal men. *Physiology & Behavior* 75:557–566.

O'Connor, D., J. Archer, and F. Wu. 2004. Effects of testosterone on mood, aggression, and sexual behavior in young men: A double-blind, placebo-controlled, cross-over study. *Journal of Clinical Endocrinology and Metabolism* 89:2837–2845.

Olweus, D., A. Mattsson, D. Schalling, and H. Low. 1980. Testosterone, aggression, physical, and personality dimensions in normal adolescent males. *Psychosomatic Medicine* 42:253.

———. 1988. Circulating testosterone levels and aggression in adolescent males. *Psychosomatic Medicine* 50:261.

Oren, M. 2002. *Six days of war*. New York: Oxford University Press.

Paabo, S. 2001. The human genome and our view of ourselves. *Science* 291:1219–1220.

Patzer, G. 1985. *The physical attractiveness phenomenon*. New York: Plenum.

Peretti, P., and B. Lewis. 1969. Effects of alcoholic consumption on the activity patterns of individual rhesus monkeys and their behavior in a social group. *Primates* (June): 181–188.

Pfeiffer, J. 1982. *The creative explosion*. New York: Harper & Row.

Phillips, M., A. Young, C. Senior, M. Brammer, C. Andrew, A. Calder, E. Bullmore, et al. 1997. A specific neural substrate for perceiving facial expressions of disgust. *Nature* 389:495–498.

Pinker, S. 1994. *The language instinct*. New York: HarperCollins.

Pope, J., Jr., and D. Katz. 1990. Homicide and near-homicide by anabolic steroid users. *Journal of Clinical Psychiatry* 51:28–31.

———. 1994. Psychiatric and medical effects of anabolic-androgenic steroid use. *Archives of General Psychiatry* 51:375–382.

Pope, H., E. Kouri, and J. Hudson. 2000. Effects of supraphysiologic doses of testosterone on mood and aggression in normal men: A randomized control trial. *Archives of General Psychiatry* 57:133–140.

Potter, S. n.d. *The theory and practice of gamesmanship*, or *The art of winning games without actually cheating*. New York: Holt, Rinehart and Winston.

Premack, D. 1985. "Gavagai!" or the future history of the animal language controversy. *Cognition* 19:207–296.

Purifoy, F., and L. Koopmans. 1979. Androstenedione, testosterone, and free testosterone concentration in women of various occupations. *Social Biology* 26:179–188.

Rada, R., D. Laws, R. Kellner, L. Stivastava, and G. Peake. 1983. Plasma androgens in violent and nonviolent sex offenders. *Bulletin of the American Academy of Psychiatric Law* 11:149–158.

Rahe, R., S. Karson, N. Howard, R. Rubin, and R. Poland. 1990. Psychological and physiological assessments on American hostages freed from captivity in Iran. *Psychosomatic Medicine* 52:1–16.

Raine, A., P. Venables, and M. Williams. 1990. Relationships between central and autonomic measures of arousal at age 15 years and criminality at age 24 years. *Archives of General Psychiatry* 47:1003–1007.

———. 1995. High autonomic arousal and electrodermal orienting at age 15 years as protective factors against criminal behavior at age 29 years. *American Journal of Psychiatry* 152:1595–1600.

Raine, A., P. Brennan, B. Mednick, and S. Mednick. 1996. High rates of violence, crime, academic problems, and behavioral problems in males with both early neuromotor deficits and unstable family environments. *Archives of General Psychiatry* 53:544–549.

Raine, A., P. Brennan, and S. Mednick. 1994. Birth complications combined with early maternal rejection at age 1 year predispose to violent crime at age 18 years. *Archives of General Psychiatry* 51:984–988.

Rejeski, W., M. Gagne, P. Parker, and D. Koritnik. 1989. Dominant and submissive males physiologic/endocrine reactivity to contested dominance. *Behavioral Medicine* 15:118–124.

Rejeski, W., P. Parker, M. Gagne, and D. Koritnik. 1990. Cardiovascular and testosterone responses to contested dominance in women. *Health Psychology* 9:35–47.

Reston, J. 1991. *Deadline: A memoir.* New York: Random House.

Riad-Fahmy, D., G. Read, R. Walker, and K. Griffiths. 1982. Steroids in saliva for assessing endocrine function. *Endocrine Review* 3:367–395.

Richards, R., F. Svec, W. Bao, S. Srinivasan, and G. Berenson. 1992. Steroid hormones during puberty. *Journal of Clinical and Endocrinological Metabolism* 75:624–631.

Richerson, P., R. Boyd, and R. Bettinger. 2001. Was agriculture impossible during the Pleistocene but mandatory during the Holocene? A climate change hypothesis. *American Antiquity* 66:387.

Romano, E., R. Baillargeon, H. Wu, M. Zoccolillo, F. Vitaro, and R. Tremblay. 2004. A new look at inter-informant agreement on conduct disorder using a latent class approach. *Psychiatry Research* 129:75–89.

Roosevelt, T. 1926. A colonial survival. In *Literary essays.* 300–316. New York: Scribner's.

Rosa, E., and A. Mazur. 1979. Incipient status in small groups. *Social Forces* 58:18–37.

Rose, R., I. Bernstein, and T. Gordon. 1975. Consequences of social conflict on plasma testosterone levels in rhesus monkeys. *Psychosomatic Medicine* 37:50–61.

Ross, R., L. Bernstein, H. Judd, R. Hanisch, M. Pike, and B. Henderson. 1986. Serum testosterone levels in healthy young black and white men. *Journal of the National Cancer Institute* 76:45–48.

Rouse, W., trans. 1938. *Homer: The Iliad.* New York: New American Library.

Rowe, R., B. Maughan, C. Worthman, E. Costello, and A. Angold. 2004. Testosterone, antisocial behavior, and social dominance in boys: Pubertal development and biosocial interaction. *Biological Psychiatry* 55:546–552.

Rubin, C., and E. Newton, eds. 2000. *The Pulitzer Prize photographs.* Arlington, VA: Newseum.

Rubin, R., J. Reinisch, and R. Haskett. 1981. Postnatal gonadal steroid effects on human behavior. *Science* 211:1318–1324.

Rudwick, M. 1985. *The great Devonian controversy.* Chicago: University of Chicago Press.

Rutter, M., H. Giller, and A. Hagell. 1998. *Antisocial behavior by young people.* New York: Cambridge University Press.

Ruvolo, M. 1997. Molecular phylogeny of the hominoids: Inferences from multiple independent DNA sequence data sets. *Molecular Biology and Evolution* 14:248.

———. 2004. Comparative primate genomics: The year of the chimpanzee. *Current Opinion in Genetics & Development* 14:650–656.

Sachser, N., M. Dürschlag, and D. Hirzel. 1998. Social relationships and the management of stress. *Psychoneuroendocrinology* 23:891–904.

Sacks, H., E. Schegloff, and G. Jefferson. 1974. A simplist systematics for the organization of turn-taking for conversation. *Language* 50:696–735.

Sadowsky, M., H. Antonovsky, R. Sobel, and B. Maoz. 1993. Sexual activity and sex hormone levels in aging men. *International Psychogeriatrics* 5:181–186.

Salvador, A., V. Simon, F. Suay, and L. Llorens. 1987. Testosterone and cortisol responses to competitive fighting in human males. *Aggressive Behavior* 13:9–13.

Salvador, A., F. Suay, E. Gonzalez-Bono, and M. Serrano. 2003. Anticipatory cortisol, testosterone and phychological responses to judo competition in young men. *Psychoneuroendocrinology* 28:364–375.

Salvador, A., F. Suay, S. Martinez-Sanchis, V. Simon, and P. Brain. 1999. Correlating testosterone and fighting in male participants in judo contests. *Physiology & Behavior* 68:205–209.

Sampson, S. 1997. Dinosaur combat and courtship. In *The complete dinosaur,* ed. J. Farlow and M. Brett-Surman, 383–393. Bloomington: Indiana University Press.

Sanchez-Jankowsky, M. 1991. *Islands in the street.* Berkeley: University of California Press.

Savage-Rumbaugh, S., S. Shanker, and T. Taylor. 1998. *Ape, language, and the human mind.* New York: Oxford University Press.

Schaal, B., R. Tremblay, R. Soussignan, and E. Susman. 1996. Male testosterone linked to high social dominance but low physical aggression in early adolescence. *Journal of the American Academy of Child and Adolescent Psychiatry* 35:1322–1330.

Schaller, G. 1993. *The year of the gorilla.* Chicago: University of Chicago Press.

Schubert, J., M. Curran, and C. Strungaru. 1997. *Physical appearance and candidate viability.* Political Science Department, Northern Illinois University.

Schultheiss, O., K. Campbell, and D. McClelland. 1999. Implicit power motivation moderates men's testosterone responses to imagined and real dominance success. *Hormones and Behavior* 36:234–241.

Schultheiss, O., and W. Rohde. 2002. Implicit power motivation predicts men's testosterone changes and implicit learning in a contest situation. *Hormones and Behavior* 41:195–202.

Schwartz, H., and J. Jacobs. 1979. *Qualitative sociology.* New York: Free Press.

Scott, W. 1962 printing, *Ivanhoe.* New York: Collier Books.

Senghas, A., S. Kita, and A. Özyürek. 2004. Children creating core properties of language: Evidence from an emerging sign language in Nicaragua. *Science* 305:1779–1782.

Shea, B. 1985. Ontogenetic allometry and scaling: A discussion based on the growth and form of the skull of African apes. In *Size and scaling in primate biology,* ed. W. Jungers, 175–205. New York: Plenum.

Shields, W., and L. Shields. 1983. Forcible rape: An evolutionary perspective. *Ethology and Sociobiology* 4:115–136.

Shils, E., and M. Janowitz. 1948. Cohesion and disintegration in the Wehrmacht in World War II. *Public Opinion Quarterly* 12: 280–315.

Siegel, A., T. Roeling, T. Greeg, and M. Kruk. 1999. Neuropharmacology of brain-stimulation-evoked aggression. *Neuroscience and Biobehavioral Reviews* 23:359–389.

Silk, J. 2002. Practice random acts of aggression and senseless acts of intimidation: The logic of status contests in social groups. *Evolutionary Anthropology* 11:221–225.

Silverman, I., and D. Case. 1998. Ethnocentrism vs. pragmatism in the conduct of human affairs. In *Indoctrinability, ideology, and warfare,* ed. I. E. Eibesfeldt and F. Salter. New York: Berghahn Books.

———. 2001. The role of ethnic nepotism vs. economic pragmatism in inter-group conflict: Data on the Yugoslavian civil war. *Journal of Bioeconomics* 3:91–98.

Smith, N., and D. Wilson. 1979. *Modern linguistics: The results of Chomsky's revolution.* Bloomington: Indiana University Press.

Smuts, B., D. Cheney, R. Seyfarth, R. Wrangham, and T. Struhsaker. eds. 1987. *Primate societies.* Chicago: University of Chicago Press.

Somit, A., and S. Peterson, eds. 1989. *The dynamics of evolution.* Ithaca, NY: Cornell University Press.

Southwick, C. A., ed. 1963. *Primate Social Behavior.* Toronto: Van Nostrand.

Southwick, C. H. 1967. An experimental study of intragroup agonistic behavior in rhesus monkeys (*Macaca mulatta*). *Behavior* 28: 182–209.

Stemmler, G., M. Heldmann, C. Pauls, and T. Scherer. 2001. Constraints for emotion specificity in fear and anger: The context counts. *Psychophysiology* 38:275–291.

Stouffer, S., A. Lumsdaine, M. Lumsdaine, R. Williams Jr., M. Smith, I. Janis, S. Star, and L. Cottrell. 1949. *The American soldier: Combat and its aftermath.* Princeton NJ: Princeton University Press.

Strauss, R., R. Lanese, and W. Malarkey. 1985. Weight loss in amateur wrestlers and its effect on serum testosterone levels. *Journal of the American Medical Association* 254:3337–3338.

Strodtbeck, F., R. James, and C. Hawkins. 1957. Social status in jury deliberations. *American Sociological Review* 22:713–719.

Strongman, K., and B. Champness. 1968. Dominance hierarchies and conflict in eye contact. *Acta Psychologica* 28:376–386.

Suarez, E., C. Kuhn, S. Schanberg, R. Williams Jr., and E. Zimmermann. 1998. Neuroendocrine, cardiovascular, and emotional responses of hostile men: The role of interpersonal challenge. *Psychosomatic Medicine* 60:78–88.

Suay, F., A. Salvador, E. Gonzalez-Bono, C. Sanchis, M. Martinez, S. Martinez-Sanchis, V. Simon, and J. Montoro. 1999. Effects of competition and its outcome on serum testosterone, cortisol, and prolactin. *Psychoneuroendocrinology* 21:551–566.

Susman, E., G. Inoff-Germain, E. Nottelmann, D. Loriaux, G. Cutler Jr., and G. Chrousos. 1987. Hormones, emotional dispositions, and aggressive attributes of young adolescents. *Child Development* 58:1114–1134.

Svare, B., ed. 1983. *Hormones and aggressive behavior.* New York: Plenum Press.

Symons, D. 1992. On the use and misuse of Darwinism in the study of human behavior. In *The adapted mind,* ed. J. Barkow, L. Cosmides, and J. Tooby, 137–159. New York: Oxford University Press.

Takeshita, H., and J. van Hooff. 2001. Tool use by chimpanzees (*Pan troglodytes*) of the Arnhem Zoo Community. In *Primate origins of human cognition and behavior,* ed. T. Matsuzawa, 519–536. New York: Springer.

Tattersall, I. 1995. *The fossil trail.* New York: Oxford University Press.

Taubman, W. 2003. *Khrushchev: The man and his era.* New York: W. W. Norton.

Tavare, S., C. Marshall, O. Will, C. Soligo, and R. Martin. 2002. Using the fossil record to estimate the age of the last common ancestor of extant primates. *Nature* 416 (18 April): 726–729.

Taylor, H. 1970. *Balance in small groups.* New York: Von Nostrand Reinhold.

Taylor, W. 1991. *Macho medicine.* London: McFarland.

Teleki, G. 1973. *The Predatory Behavior of Wild Chimpanzees.* Lewisburg, PA: Bucknell University Press.

Terrace, H. 1979. *Nim.* New York: Knopf.

Thompson, W., J. Dabbs Jr., and R. Frady. 1990. Changes in saliva testosterone levels during a 90-day shock incarceration program. *Criminal Justice and Behavior* 17:246–252.

Thornhill, R., and C. Palmer. 2000. *A natural history of rape: The biological basis of sexual coercion.* Cambridge, MA: MIT Press.

Thrasher, F. 1963. *The gang.* Chicago: University of Chicago Press.

Tinniswood, A. 1998. *Visions of power.* New York: Stewart, Tabori & Chang.

Townsend, J. 1998. *What women want—what men want.* New York: Oxford University Press.

———. 1993. Gender differences in mate preferences among law students. *Journal of Psychology* 127:507–528.

Trainor, B., I. Bird, and C. Marler. 2004. Opposing hormonal mechanisms of aggression revealed through short-lived testosterone manipulations and multiple winning experiences. *Hormones and Behavior* 45:115–121.

Tremblay, R. 2000. The development of aggressive behaviour during childhood: What have we learned in the past century? *International Journal of Behavior and Development* 24:129–141.

Tremblay, R., B. Schaal, B. Boulerice, L. Arseneault, R. Soussignan, D. Paquette, and D. Laurant. 1998. Testosterone, physical aggression, dominance, and physical development in adolescence. *International Journal of Behavior and Development* 22:753–777.

Tricker, R., R. Casaburi, T. Storer, B. Clevenger, N. Berman, A. Shirazi, and S. Bhasin. 1996. The effect of supraphysiological doses of testosterone on angry behavior in healthy eugonadal men. *Journal of Clinical Endocrinology and Metabolism* 81:3754–3758.

Trivers, R. 1974. Parent-offspring conflict. *American Zoologist* 14:249–264.

Truax, R., and M. B. Carpenter. 1964. *Strong and Elwyn's human neuroanatomy.* Baltimore: Williams & Wilkins.

Truscott, L., IV, 1978. *Dress grey.* New York: Fawcett Crest.

Trut, L. 1999. Early canid domestication: The farm-fox experiment. *American Scientist* 87:160–169.

Tsitouras, P., C. Martin, and S. Harman. 1982. Relationship of serum testosterone to sexual activity in healthy elderly men. *Journal of Gerontology* 37:288–293.

Udry, J. 1988. Biological predispositions and social control in adolescent sexual behavior. *American Sociological Review* 53:709–722.

———. 1990. Biosocial models of adolescent problem behaviors. *Social Biology* 37:1–10.

Udry, J., J. Billy, N. Morris, T. Groff, and M. Raj. 1985. Serum androgenic hormones motivate sexual behavior in adolescent boys. *Fertility and Sterility* 43:90–94.

Uris, L. 1961. *Mila 18.* Garden City, NY: Doubleday.

Van Lawick-Goodall, J. 1968. A preliminary report on expressive movements and communications in the Gombe Stream chimpanzees. In *Primates: Studies in adaptation and variability,* P. Jay, 313–374. New York: Holt, Rinehart and Winston.

van Schaik, C., M. Ancrenaz, G. Borgen, B. Galdikas, C. Knott, I. Singleton, A. Suzuki, S. Utami, and M. Merrill. 2003. Orangutan cultures and the evolution of material culture. *Science* 299:102–105.

Veblen, T. 1902. *The theory of the leisure class: An economic study of institutions.* New York: Macmillan.

Wagner, J., M. Flinn, and B. England. 2002. Hormonal response to competition among male coalitions. *Evolution and Human Behavior* 23:437–442.

Walzer, M. 1977. *Just and unjust wars.* New York: Basic Books.

Wang, C., S. Plymate, E. Nieschlag, and C. Paulsen. 1981. Salivary testosterone in men: Further evidence of a direct correlation with free serum testosterone. *Journal of Clinical Endocrinology and Metabolism* 53:1021–1024.

Watson, D. 1970. *Proxemic behavior: A cross-cultural study.* The Hague: Mouton.

Weaver, J. 1996. *Horror films: Current research on audience preferences and reactions.* Mahwah, NJ: Lawrence Erlbaum.

Weisfeld, G. 1994. Aggression and dominance in the social world of boys. In *Male violence,* ed. J. Archer, 42–69. London: Routledge.

———. 1997. Research on emotions and future developments in human ethology. In *New aspects of human ethology,* ed. A. Schmitt, K. Atzwanger, K. Grammer, and K. Schafer, 25–46. New York: Plenum Press.

———. 2002. Neural and functional aspects of pride and shame. In *The neuroethology of Paul MacLean: Convergences and frontiers,* ed. R. Gardner Jr. and G. Cory. Westport CT: Greenwood Praeger Group.

Weisfeld, G., and J. Beresford. 1982. Erectness of posture as an indicator of dominance or success in humans. *Motivation and Emotion* 6:113–131.

Weisfeld, G., and J. Linkey. 1985. Dominance displays as indicators of a social success motive. In *Power, dominance, and nonverbal behavior,* ed. J. Dovidio and S. Ellyson, 109–128. New York: Springer-Verlag.

Werker, J., and A. Vouloumanos. 2000. Who's got rhythm? *Science* 288:280–281.

Wilson, E. 1975. *Sociobiology: The new synthesis.* Cambridge, MA: Harvard University Press.

Wilson, J., and R. Herrnstein. 1985. *Crime and human nature.* New York: Simon and Schuster.

Wilson, M., and M. Daly. 1993. Spousal homicide risk and estrangement. *Violence and Victims* 8:3–16.

Wilsson, Lars. 1971. Observations and experiments on the ethology of the European beaver (*Castor fiber L.*). *Viltrevy Swedish Wildlife* 8:117–266.

Wingfield, J., R. Hegner, A. Dufty Jr., and G. Ball. 1990. The "challenge hypothesis": Theoretical implications for patterns of testosterone secretion, mating systems, and breeding strategies. *American Naturalist* 136:829–846.

Winslow, J., P. Bovle, C. Lyons, S. Sterk, and T. Insel. 2003. Rearing effects on cerebrospinal fluid oxytocin concentration and social buffering in rhesus monkeys. *Neuropsychopharmacology* 28:910–918.

Winter, J., I. Hughes, F. Reyes, and C. Faiman. 1976. Pituitary-gonadal relatins in infancy. *Journal of Clinical Endocrinology & Metabolism* 42:679–686.

Witmer, L. 1995. The extant phylogenetic bracket and the importance of reconstructing soft tissues in fossils. In *Functional morphology in vertebrate paleontology*, ed. J. Thomason, 19–33. New York: Cambridge University Press.

Wittner, L. 2003. *The struggle against the bomb*, Vol. 3. Stanford, CA: Stanford University Press.

Wolfe, W., et al. 1990. Health status of air force veterans occupationally exposed to herbicides in Vietnam. *Journal of the American Medical Association* 264(Oct. 10): 1824–31.

Wolfgang, M. 1958. *Patterns of criminal homicide.* Philadelphia: University of Pennsylvania.

Yates, W., P. Perry, J. MacIndoe, T. Holman, and V. Ellingrod. 1999. Psychosexual effects of three doses of testosterone cycling in normal man. *Biological Psychiatry* 45:254–260.

Yeager, C., and L. Janos. 1985. *Yeager.* New York: Bantam Books.

Zebrowitz, L., K. Olson, and K. Hoffman. 1993. Stability of babyfaceness and attractiveness across the life span. *Journal of Personality and Social Psychology* 64:453–466.

Zimmerman, D., and C. West. 1975. Sex roles, interruptions and silences in conversation. In *Language and Sex*, ed. B. Thorne and N. Henley. Rowley, MA: Newbury House.

Zug, G. 1993. *Herpetology: An introductory biology of amphibians and reptiles.* San Diego: Academic Press.

Index

Abbott, D., 89
Achulean style, tools of, 50, 157
adaptation: evolution as parallel, 24, 27; of owl monkey, 52, 57; of primate, 52, 57
adrenaline, 88
affiliation impulse, 2–3
Africa, hominid in, 50
aggression: alpha behavior and, 2, 37, 60; in defense of territory, 2; within dominance hierarchy, 2; in human, 109; status and, 63; testosterone and, 109, 113–14; without domination, 110
Alexandra of Russia, 140
Alice in Wonderland (Lewis), 100
Allee, W., 112
alligator, 36–37
allocortex, 34–35, 36. *See also* brain; limbic system
alpha, behavior of, 2, 37, 60
Alyeska consortium, 9–10, 11
Amer, Defense Minister, 137–38
American dream, 15
American Sign Language (ASL), 97–98
amino acids, 26
amniote, 22, 24, 34
amphioxus, 34. *See also* chordate

amygdala, 36, 88. *See also* brain; emotion
ancestry: as common, 26, 29; DNA and, 25; as evolving, 22, 23, 24; mutation from, 26
Anderson, Elijah, 122
androsterone, 112
animals: behavior of, 2, 29–31, 37, 60, 113; dominance hierarchies of, 1–2, 7–8, 8–9, 18, 42, 58–63; experiments on, 109; as extinct, 26, 29; food supply for, 2
anterior commissur, 36. *See also* brain
anthropology, 157
anxiety, 36
apes: characteristics of, 46, 47–48, 53; culture of, 56; dominance hierarchy in, 62; dominant/deferent behavior of, 90; hominid split from, 52; language for, 98; phylogeny of, 46, 49, 64n2; rank allotment by, 79; reproduction by, 53, 155; self-awareness in, 56; sign language/symbol system for, 56, 93
apes, great. *See* bonobo; chimpanzee
apes, lesser. *See* gibbon; siamang
arboreal lifestyle, 53
Archaeopteryx, 22

About the Author

Allan Mazur, a sociologist and an engineer, is professor of public affairs in the Maxwell School of Syracuse University. Earlier he was on the social science faculties of MIT and Stanford University and worked some years in the aerospace industry. His degrees are a BS in physics from IIT in 1961, an MS in engineering from UCLA in 1964, and a PhD in sociology from Johns Hopkins University in 1969. A fellow of the American Association for the Advancement of Science, he is author or coauthor of seven books and more than one hundred and fifty academic articles. Most of his research falls into two areas: biosociology and the sociology of science and technology. His biosocial work focuses on hormones and behavior, comparative primate behavior, and physiognomy (in its modern sense).